Climbing Higher
Answering Big Questions

Robert Wheeler, PhD

Copyright 2019 Robert Wheeler, PhD

All rights reserved. No part of this book may be reproduced or transmitted in any form or by any means, electronic or mechanical, including photocopying, recording or by any information storage and retrieval system, without permission in writing from the publisher.

The information in this book is not meant to supplement or replace proper training for mountain climbing. Like any sport involving equipment, balance, and environmental factors, mountain climbing imposes some inherent risks. The author and publisher advises readers to take full responsibility for their safety and know their limits. Be sure your equipment is well maintained and do not take risks beyond your level of experience, aptitude, training, and comfort level.

OntosScience Press—St. Louis, Missouri, USA
ISBN: 978-0-578-50856-6
Library of Congress Control Number: 2019905339
Title: Climbing Higher: Answering Big Questions
Author: Robert Wheeler, PhD
Printed in the United States
Distribution: Ingram

www.ontosscience.com
Robert Wheeler, PhD.: *wheelerrj@juno.com*

Contents

Preface vii
Introduction xi
Chapters:
  1. First Climb: Mount Fuji 1
  2. Born to Strive: Stimulation Challenge 9
  3. High Points: Taum Sauk Mountain & Mount Whitney 12
  4. Goal Orientation: Sense of Purpose & Life Esteem 19
  5. Higher Point: Mount Aconcagua 26
  6. Awe: Emotions & Mysticism 49
  7. Mystical Points: Mount Heipori & Machu Picchu 57
  8. Personal reality: Consciousness 76
  9. Sacred Points: Blanca Peak & Humphreys Peak 89
10. Ultimate Reality: Beyond Ourselves 102
11. Most Sacred: Mount Moriah 128
12. Existential Reality: Conflict, Dilemma, & Paradox 138
13. Traditional Climb: Mount Fuji 156
14. Pragmatic Reality: Coherence & Conciliation 167
15. Uncertain Climb: Mount Kilimanjaro 182
16. Living with Paradox 194
Epilogue 199
Endnotes 206
References 211
Appendices:
    A. Sense of Purpose & Life Esteem 225
    B. Life Esteem Survey 261
    C. General Well-Being Evaluation 263
    D. Relative Effects of Stressors on Mountain Climbers 269
    E. Plaza de Mulas 283
    F. Five Factor Evaluation 291
About the Author 293
Index 295

"Kilimanjaro is a snow covered-mountain 19,710 feet high, and it is said to be the highest mountain in Africa. Its western summit is called by the Masai, "Ngaje Ngai," the House of God. Close to the western summit is the dried and frozen carcass of a leopard. No one has explained what the leopard was seeking at that altitude." (Hemingway, 1927, p 3)

PREFACE

In Earnest Hemmingway's *The Snows of Kilimanjaro*, the famous riddle asks why a leopard would climb to such a high elevation that it froze to death. This was popularized by Gregory Peck who played the movie role of a writer who wasted his talents. The frozen leopard has come to symbolize the urge to seek something "higher" than currently experienced in life; to constructively use one's talents. This book is written for those people that seek something "higher"; those who have looked up into the sky on a clear night and wondered what was beyond the limit of their vision and why they experienced a feeling of mystery; people who wonder about meaning, purpose, and value of their lives with questions of the why of their existence and efforts; those who want information about mysteries of the world and beyond; and those who feel a pull to something more or higher than they currently have. It attempts to use a scholarly approach building on objective information reasonably free of assumptions, beliefs, and speculation. But also, it attempts to use the subjective appeal of adventure and to avoid intimidation by technical language. This book is the result of one person's lifetime of pursuing these fundamental goals with a feeling of adventure, and of that person's desire to share the resulting benefits.

My experiences and study of history and psychology indicate that we all harbor these fundamental goals, but it is amazing how differently they affect people. Some live in the "here and now" without concern for "whys and wherefores." Some reject the idea that there is anything beyond observable material phenomena. Some suppress such considerations because of demands of daily life. However, like other established personality traits, we all have within us a need to provide for questions about where we came from, where we are going, and why we are here. Like many people, I became aware of it when I was about twelve years old, and although dormant during much of my life, it surfaced more as adult years progressed.

I remember irritating Aunt Bess by demanding to know why the sun did not explode. I had just read the first book that made an impression on me: *The New Background of Science* by Sir James Jeans. My father had bought this book in 1933 just before he died from pneumonia. It was about seven years further that I had the fortitude to wade through some of the books he had left. World War II with the atomic bomb came on at that time, and I was fascinated with the extension of the "new scientific world" to nuclear energy and quantum theory. I was aiming to be a physicist, but the role of a military professional impressed me more because of its impact on society at that time. Education at West Point oriented me not only to the military but also to the physical sciences. Military duties did not leave much time for philosophizing about fundamental questions, and it was not until the Army assigned me to a university for graduate education in engineering that I was able to reflect on what I was doing. The feeling of acquiring academic knowledge and social experience was so liberating that I began a quest for knowledge beyond the physical sciences. I looked in many places. Religion and theology were too narrow, philosophy was too general, and mentalism or parapsychology was too nebulous. After many years, it was psychology that seemed to be the middle ground for bringing things together logically with science, history, and religion.

As I learned more about human nature, I realized that the answers to the fundamental questions were not as important as the view that people had (or did not have) of the questions and their degree of awareness or concern about them. My studies also caused me to realize that my concerns were not so unique—every human seems to have these concerns lurking somewhere within themselves. Some call it philosophy of life, for some it is belief or religion, and some call it nature. For all, though, it provides existence with coherence, meaning, purpose, and manageability when formulated into a personally acceptable concept.

There are many benefits of being aware of these fundamental questions and the quest for answers. Through this book, I hope to share the benefits of that adventure.

INTRODUCTION

A mountain is formally defined as a land mass that projects conspicuously above the surrounding terrain. Informally though, a mountain is usually considered to be a rugged land mass that is so tall it is a challenge to surmount and is a formidable barrier. Each year hundreds of people die or get injured climbing mountains for little reason other than to reach the summit—not for contributing to society, productivity, or earning money. When asked why one climbs a mountain, the traditional answer is "because it's there." However, there may be reasons that are more fundamental.

More direct answers to why people climb mountains are challenge, excitement, thrill, awe, physical exercise, or even symbolism. As a rugged obstacle to surmount physically, not everyone attempts to climb a mountain; however, as a symbol of an obstacle along life's path, everyone must make an attempt because none of us can navigate our lives without overcoming obstacles. When we think about these obstacles, questions arise about why they occur, the value of surmounting them, why they are on our path, and where the path leads—questions that can only be answered by personal speculation and intuition or acceptance of answers provided by other people, organizations, or institutions. We all seem to be on some kind of path that involves wonders of why and faith that the journey is worthwhile. Despite the tremendous advances for comfort, health, and well-being provided by physical science, science has not been able to answer these fundamental questions, so culture has filled in with metaphysical, supernatural, or speculative provisions. It is these latter provisions that lead to the significance of mountains. As the most impressive features of the environment, mountains have been associated with the most impressive features of those questions: mystery, mysticism, and even sacredness. Throughout known human history, sacredness has been attributed to special mountains. They may be sacred because of stories about associated transcendent and divine phenomena, or because of powerfully symbolizing the mysteries and challenges of life.

This book attempts to relate the innate needs people have for answers to fundamental questions about their existence, the activities they pursue, the beliefs to which they subscribe, and their general well-being. Where these needs came from and their purpose is not as important as recognition of their existence and impact on belief systems, culture, and society. The resulting belief systems not only affect personal well-being directly but also indirectly through clashes of belief systems incorporated into social organizations.

However, this book does not start with search for answers to fundamental questions. Chapter 1 gives an example of a mountain climbing experience that came close to tragedy, posing the question of why people do such things. Subsequent chapters indicate that such activity may not be as foolish as they appear and alternate between actual climbing experiences and scientifically based explanations. The experiences progress from natural to symbolic and the explanations progress from well-established reasons to those considered esoteric. So, this book is about more than mountain climbing. It is about basic human motivation—what moves people to pursue difficult activities and to persist in the struggles of existence. Most information about motivation focuses on rewards, reinforcements, productivity, and efficiency, but the focus here is more basic—why people are motivated to strive for those things.

As reasons for motivation are explored, the support builds for the role of an innate need people have to provide for the unknown that is so strong and elusive that logic many times is subjugated to emotions, social influences, and pressures of daily life. This need I call the "ontological imperative." Ontology is the branch of philosophy that studies reality at its most basic level, involving the meaning of existence and purpose of life. An imperative is a necessity, something that cannot be avoided. The major purpose of this book is to support the ontological imperative as a personality trait innate to all thinking humans. However, many people are not aware of this innate need because the press of daily life and the need for material resources that push this less demanding need into subconscious recesses of the mind—that is, until some crisis or experience increases its importance. Or, it might lie dormant creating a nebulous yearning for an abstract goal that could be sensed as a call to something larger, better, or higher than these daily struggles—a call of the unknown, a call of the mountain. Mountains can be seen here as metaphors representing this call to something higher, a call to use one's talents constructively, and maybe even for a nebulous transcendent goal.

The chapter following each mountain climbing experience is the result of my psychology research and study that strived for reliable information about particular aspects of human motivation, building from needs for challenge and stimulation through goal seeking and positive emotions to both natural and supernatural explanations of ultimate reality and cause in order to meet the ontological imperative: what is the meaning of existence? A bottom-up inductive approach attempts to build objectively to resulting philosophical concepts. This approach is objective because it attempts to draw conclusions and inferences from objective information rather than starting with an assumption, theory, or belief and then selecting supporting information. It must be recognized, though, that we cannot be completely objective. Even the bottom-up approach cannot avoid subjective selection of information and its interpretation. I have attempted to comprehensively sift through all available information (although probably missed much) and present that which I think is most pertinent to the topic.

Chapter 14 ties together this information with a view toward summarizing what is important about the human need to seek knowledge and experience that supports a coherent provision for the unknown—what is generally referred to as ultimate reality. This leads through considerations of science, spirituality, personal religion, and institutional religion to concepts that make personal life meaningful and manageable. True, it is the story of one personal path, but I am convinced that it is a path everyone should navigate. What a difference our world would be if these considerations were universally recognized, or at least emphasized by media, educators, and politicians rather than the current emphasis on sensation, gratification, and violence. It would reduce aggression and the need for conflict, and improve both personal and social well-being.

If, as you read, you become impatient about what it is leading to or become irritated about the scientific explanations and textbook atmosphere, skip to Chapter 14 where conclusions and impacts are presented. Then you may want to go back and pick up the antecedent information. Many scientific findings are introduced without detailed explanation in order to support later concepts while avoiding pedantic distraction. For additional explanation, the reader is referred to sources cited.

This is not a comprehensive treatment of ontological philosophy or human motivation, but rather it is an attempt to apply useful objective information pertaining to these topics.

Nor is this a comprehensive treatment of mountain climbing or of the world's sacred mountains, but rather it tells about some of the mountains climbed by the author that had special significance. For a comprehensive view of mountains, the reader is referred to Edwin Bernbaum's *Sacred Mountains of the World* (1977) or for specific mountains, to such books as *Seven Summits* by Bass, Wells, and Ridgeway (1986) and *Circling the Sacred Mountain* by Thurman and Wise (1999). Much information is also available on the Internet about specific mountains. This book uses mountains as vehicles to explore the underlying fundamental motivations for the behaviors of human individuals and their societies.

The mountain climbing stories describe adventures that were challenging, but not requiring technical skill in the use of pitons, ropes, or special climbing equipment. They are the kind of activity average people desiring outdoor adventure can pursue. They require only a moderate level of fitness, courage, and an appreciation of nature. The last story in Chapter 15 is appropriately about Kilimanjaro made famous by Ernest Hemmingway (1927) and Gregory Peck. In *The Snows of Kilimanjaro*, the riddle of the "frozen leopard" was used to symbolize the search for success and enlightenment through symbolically climbing to higher elevations. As a last climb, the author set a new Guinness World Record (2015) as the oldest man to summit that mountain without becoming a "frozen carcass." Hopefully the descriptions of these adventures will encourage more participation in activities providing enjoyment of nature, physical and mental stimulation, and manageable challenge.

Chapters 10 and 12 deal with conflicts between the scientific and religious views of ultimate reality, but please keep in mind that this is not a diatribe about science or religion. Both start with the ontological imperative. Most religions fill the imperative with faith in beliefs about some form of metaphysical realm that provides explanations. Because science investigates only objectively observable phenomena, it has been unable to deal with the metaphysical realm, but it has uncovered explanations (such as evolution) that are contrary to some religious explanations. The result is a conflict between religious dogma and scientific information that sows seeds of doubt about religious beliefs. This conflict varies both between and within different religions, however in most there is a fundamental faction that stimulates the issue. Many philosophers and religious thinkers have wrestled with this issue, so it is not new, and the information presented here produces interpretations and conclusions that the author thinks follow logically. A basic theme here is that both religion and science are needed despite conflict between religious dogma and scientific research findings, so this book is an attempt to explore a solution—if and how we should believe in a transcendent causative realm and at the same time doubt its actual validity.

Please keep in mind that a mass of information is available about topics addressed, and each could, and maybe should, be treated in more detail. Presented here are only what the author thinks are most important. A major problem in assembling this book was deciding what to include and what to omit. Much of the information was originally published by the author in *Mountains and Minds* (2010), but many new research results have been incorporated here.

Endnotes are used to show sources of specific information presented where a text citation is not complete (source name and date). They are designated by superscript numbers in the text that can be located in the endnotes section designated by chapter number and sequence number in the chapter. Full citations are in a consolidated bibliography arranged alphabetically by source name.

Chapter 1
First Climb: Mount Fuji

One of the most impressive and beautiful scenes on our planet is Mount Fuji in Japan (on a clear day). Most mountains are in ranges nestled in with others, but Fuji is all by itself—a symmetrical cone projecting skyward from sea level to 12,389 feet. Furthermore, it dominates one of the most densely populated areas even though its view is normally obscured by clouds. At about seventy miles southwest of Tokyo, an estimated 12.5 million people live near it with some trepidation because its rumblings are treated with great respect. It is a volcano that last erupted in 1707 and may now be overdue. It is little wonder that this mountain has become a national symbol invested with sacred features and deeply ingrained in Japanese culture. For many people it is associated with ultimate reality and reason for existence.

The name "Fuji" has been traced back to the Ainu word "Fuchi" associated with a fire goddess. Lineage of the Japanese people is still somewhat hazy; however, it is thought that the original settlers migrated in prehistoric times from Central Asia and had Caucasoid characteristics. Around 500 BCE, Orientals from South Asia started moving into the southern Japanese islands from Korea. After several generations of intermingling, these people pushed the non-mingled original settlers, who became known as Ainu, north similar to the way American colonists pushed American Indians west. As in most prehistoric cultures, the people were very dependent on forces of nature that seemed divine. Supplicating to and worshiping these forces seemed beneficial and resulted in animism as an early form of religion. Although most cultures started moving away from animism about four thousand years ago, it continues to be an underlying theme in many societies. In Japan, this is seen in Shintoism and Buddhism that are the dominant religions and philosophies. Shintoism combined animism with belief in an afterlife producing worship of dead ancestors and great respect for elders. After World War II, the impassioned loyalty of Shintoism was discouraged, but its mysticism and superstition continue along with those built up around Buddhism. Mount Fuji, referred to as Fuji-san, exemplifies this and accounts for the estimated two to four hundred thousand people that climb the mountain each year during the eight-week climbing season in July and August. Witnessing the sun rising from the summit (called *goraiko*) is a goal of most Japanese people. It elicits favor from the fire goddess and ancestors and thwarts any bad spirits or curses that may have been following.

For mountain climbers, Fuji-san is not a very challenging ascent. It is rocky and steep toward the top, requiring good physical condition and endurance, but not requiring special skill or equipment. There are other difficulties, though. During the climbing season in July and August, the slopes are crowded with people desiring not only a memorable and patriotic outing but also purification and redemption by arriving on the summit at sunrise. At other times, snow, ice, wind, and storms make the summit dangerous. The traditional way for getting to the summit is to start at the base on the north side and take several days stopping for rest at shelters or stations along the route.

Now though, most start the climb part way up the mountain at station 5 that is at the end of a road.

Aerial view of Fuji on a clear day

In 1959, I was a young captain in the US Army on duty in Korea with the Seventh Infantry Division guarding the Demilitarized Zone referred to then as Freedom's Frontier. A friend, Duane, and I arranged a leave of absence to visit Tokyo and to climb Mount Fuji, but the only time available was in November when weather made the mountain treacherous. However, we did not think that off-season time would pose much problem for us, because we were hardened soldiers, parachute and ranger qualified, and experienced in surviving harsh conditions. Having spent a year in Japan previously, I was acquainted with the respect of local people for the mountain and was likewise impressed by it. Closer examination was worth the risk of off-season climbing.

After sampling Japanese culture in the Ginza with appropriate relaxations, a four-hour bus ride got us to the village of Fujiyoshida at the base of Mount Fuji. The largest hotel had two floors and the greatest possibility of language compatibility. That worked out well because between broken English and broken Japanese, we understood that no one climbs the mountain now since it has ice, snow, and strong winds on the summit. However, aside from all that, we understood that we could leave our travel bags there and go by taxicab one quarter of the way up the mountain to a small hotel at station 5 where, if it was still open, we might find accommodations. Fortunately, a taxicab driver who could speak some English was located. He said, "Sure, I can take you to station 5, but you must first buy a walking stick to go up the mountain." OK, so we spent considerable time searching for a shop that was still open and still had walking sticks. Our patience was rewarded with two sticks mounting small Japanese flags. The shop owner warned us that the cost included getting stamps on the stick at the way stations, but none was open now; and since we could not get to the top anyway because of the weather, our efforts were silly.

The hotel at station 5 was a shack consisting of three rooms: a dining room, kitchen, and sleeping room that had one large platform covered with a straw mat. The only staff was a woman who must have been one hundred years old, with no teeth and no use of English. Since the monetary exchange rate then was 360 yen to a dollar, we were able to compensate the driver well for his negotiations with "mamasan." We were to sleep for five hours; she would wake us and provide rice and tea before we left at 1:00 a.m. to reach the summit for the 7:00 a.m. sunrise.

Station 5 Hotel in 1959

So far, so good. For four hours, we picked our way up the rocky slope with starlight helping to point out the semblance of a trail. The going was slow because we were not used to high altitude and the cold wind that came from the wrong direction. Breathing became a major problem; we could not move fast enough to keep body temperature comfortable. If we climbed slow or rested long enough to breathe comfortably, the cold wind was excruciating. It was about 6:00 a.m. when we could climb no further. Recognizing the dangers of hypothermia, we tried to build a small fire. We did have matches, toilet paper, candy and gum wrappers, but they went quickly. How about the walking sticks? No, the hard wood was uncooperative. The cloth flags were more obliging, and after getting proper recognition of their national role, they relinquished a few ounces of heat. None of this reduced the shivering that dominated our bodies, so we struggled up the slope a few more yards before collapsing from complete exhaustion.

I had been in tight situations before. Usually, though, I was too busy attempting to do something than to be scared; but with hypothermia, all that can be done is to be scared. Some previous tight situations started hazily emerging in my mind's eye. First, the parachute jump where after the turmoil of exiting the airplane and peacefully floating down toward the ground, I saw not the open field that was supposed to be the drop zone but instead, the dense foliage of a green forest—a rough way to make contact with the earth. However, I knew that medics would be close by and would evacuate my broken body for immediate repair. Then came the time when I was piloting a single-engine airplane under instrument conditions in the clouds and suddenly the engine became deathly quiet. While stumbling through emergency procedures, I thought about the flight plan and radar control and how quickly the crash rescue team would be on the scene. And the time in army ranger training when I was point man for a patrol crawling through the swamps of Florida at night, and came face-to-face with a wild boar that was protecting her young. A medic was right behind me to bandage my bruised head. This time the emergency was different in that there was no support or rescue immediately available; mamasan did not even know who we were. Death from hypothermia comes quickly and quietly without immediate attention, and it might be spring before our frozen bodies would be discovered.

After exchanging ideas about this situation, Duane and I decided that if we were going to die, we would not do it lying down. I thought of the Dylan Thomas poem (1957, p 128):

> Do not go gentle into that good night,
> Old age should burn and rage at close of day;
> Rage, rage against the dying of the light.

So, we struggled to upright positions as much as possible and began clutching rocks with numb hands and pushing with aching feet to inch our way toward the summit. We briefly tried descending, but the steep slope, loose rock, and darkness made that seem like sudden death. As a glow appeared in the sky and the stars dimmed, I thought, "This must be what a near-death experience is." Just then, a bright orange ember appeared in the distance, and as it grew larger, I had sufficient rationality to realize that it was not the tunnel to heaven—it was the rising sun. We were close to the summit—the first people to see the sunrise in the Eastern Hemisphere that day. We crawled to a stone bunker at the summit and watched the sun rise in the sky. And as the sun's warmth fingered our bodies, and breathing became easier, we realized *we were alive*.

As feeling returned to hands and feet, we also realized we were cold and that we should descend as soon as possible. It was not very long until we could walk and pick our way down using the same route as before. There was a big difference now—we could see. Before, all we could see were stars overhead and rocks encountered by our hands and feet. Now there was a vast panorama of fluffy cloud tops stretching to infinity. It was like the cartoon pictures of heaven, and it would not have been surprising for St. Peter to appear. Despite the peaceful beauty of this scene, though, more practical issues dominated. And they were scary because the rocky path down looked incredibly steep, and leading with feet instead of hands was awkward and unsettling. Going down was more difficult than climbing. A stumble or slip could cause an uncontrolled tumble down the steep slope. As the slope became less steep, we noticed about fifty yards to the left, a gray river of fine gravel scree flowing down through the clouds. Could we get on that flow and in a controlled manner slide down as on a sandy chute?

It was shaky at first, but only a few minutes were required to master the footwork and balance to capitalize on gravity's power to propel us down the gravel slide at amazing speed. At the end of the chute was the welcome sight of a road. In about twenty minutes, we had descended farther than we had climbed and were below the station 5 elevation. Roads have to lead somewhere, and it was only about a mile when a small building came into view. It turned out to be a restaurant, but like the hotel at station 5, it was closed for the season and contained a single occupant, this time an old man who could barely speak English. Through a combination of sign language and quasi-verbal communication, it was arranged that if we were patient, he would drive us to Fujiyoshida.

It was dusk when we arrived at our hotel. After checking in, washing hurriedly, enjoying a delicious meal of odd-looking fish and rice (anything would have been delicious), we relaxed in a Jacuzzi-like hot bath without turbulence (water was hot, so don't make waves) with flasks of hot sake to review the recent experience. With the help of the sake, we agreed on now being wiser and more appreciative of being alive and free of frostbite, broken bones, or other infirmity.

Why do people do such foolish things?

Chapter 2
Born to Strive: Stimulation and Challenge

Each year we hear and see from the news media about injury and death of mountain climbers. Although total statistics are not available, such reported accidents increase each year. Most of these were recreational; that is, they resulted from activities not required because of a profession or line of work. In most cases, the individuals had spent a considerable amount of money, time, and energy and had endured hardship and discomfort to get to the site of their demise. That is not all. Many more are killed or seriously injured in other recreational activities such as skydiving, motorcycling, mountain biking, spelunking, skiing, and various forms of racing. Why do people expend such time, effort, and expense in activities with such great risks and little productive benefit?

A well-established theory that has been extensively researched is that humans have an innate need for stimulation. Comfort follows an n-shaped curve starting at a low point of discomfort in a boring situation and, after increasing with more stimulation, drops to another low point of overload. This is called the Yerkes-Dodson law after researchers that first demonstrated the effect.[1] People vary in the amount of stimulation with which they are most comfortable, but many will take such great steps to avoid boredom that they accept high levels of stress and risk that have many unhealthy impacts.

Another theory popularized and supported by psychologist Marvin Zuckerman[2] and others is built on the need for arousal that forms the type T personality—the thrill seeker. These are people with a high threshold for stimulation and seek out activities mainly for the feeling of thrill. Related to this is a long line of research about the importance of physiological activities in the brain called excitation level and reactivity.[3] Quiet, shy introverts tend to be more reactive and thus experience a higher level of excitation (lower threshold) than outgoing extraverts for the same challenging activities. They are less comfortable with higher levels of sensory stimulation and therefore avoid the stimulating activities that are enjoyed by aggressive extraverts with type T personalities. Also related is the hard-driving type A personality who tends to be an extravert seeking excitement, wanting to do bigger things and exceed the accomplishments of other people. They think fast, react fast, talk fast and loud, and make good leaders and executive officers, but they have a high risk of heart attack or other impacts of cardiovascular disease.[4]

The human need for achievement is another phenomenon that explains why some people strive with difficult tasks. In this case the drive comes from need for accomplishment and has been related to the vast human ability for sophisticated cognitive processes that seek meaning and social identity.[5] Those with high need for achievement will seek challenges others may avoid, but they are careful and do not normally take unusual risks. In other words, they would be more inclined to climb Mount Fuji than Mount Everest.

Thrill seeking and high need for achievement are two components of the type A personality that has been associated with heart problems and other stress-related health conditions. These personality characteristics are valued in our competitive society; however, such people tend to take risks that can cause injury, reduce body immune functions, as well as increase cardiovascular problems. Before those difficulties occur, though, these people accomplish much and are hardworking, highly energized goal seekers. We all seem to have within us some of this characteristic: an urge to pursue activities that will produce success, recognition, and stimulation. Many people, though, already have a high level of stimulation. They are not high thrill seekers or ambitious executives. They are the bulk of the people who encounter sufficient stress in their daily activities to want to avoid unnecessary excitement. This applies particularly to those in high-performance jobs such as police, fire and rescue, and combat military. For infantry soldiers, daily activities provide so much challenge and stimulation that it would seem unlikely they would voluntarily plan and undertake in their recreation time a project like climbing a difficult mountain. There must be more than the need for challenge and stimulation.

Chapter 3
High Points

Taum Sauk Mountain

It was the work started by the famous English psychologist, Hans Eysenck, introduced in Chapter 2 that showed the importance of a person's predisposition for reactivity and excitation thresholds to the activities that person is comfortable with. Those with a high threshold for excitation and low reactivity are usually hard-driving, thrill-seeking type A people while those that are easily excited and highly reactive are usually the conservative type B people. These latter people do not normally go out of their way seeking challenging or thrilling activities — the pace of today's daily events is usually enough.

I must fall into the latter group because many years passed before I attempted any further mountain climbing. During that time, my activities went from being a small unit combat leader to an instructor in the US Army Ranger School where I was the leading expert in how to kill people using ambush, then to an airborne company commander getting into battle by jumping out of airplanes. Since that did not seem like a good way of getting into battle, I became an Army aviator hoping to improve air mobility of soldiers. That resulted in interesting experiences flying and managing airplanes and helicopters that included working with Koreans, Chinese, and Vietnamese in addition to Europeans and Americans. Particularly challenging was assignment to a civilian graduate school for studying engineering in preparation for work with aircraft research and development. Student life was stressful because during that time, in addition to competing with young brilliant university minds, I got married and started a family. Vietnam then took priority, and it was five more years before I was finally settled with my family in St. Louis, assigned to a relatively stable job in research and development. Then I thought once more about mountain climbing, the main stimulus being my three children who were learning about the fascinating world around them.

I told my children that to have a good view of the fascinating things going on around them, they should climb to the highest spot in the local area. For people in Missouri that means Taum Sauk Mountain, the highest spot in the state, about one hundred miles south of St. Louis rising from the Mississippi Valley at 500 feet to an elevation of 1,772 feet—not high by mountaineering standards but impressive for flatlanders. My daughter, as an emerging teenager, was a little beyond this, but my two young boys were eager to undertake the project. So borrowing a friend's truck, loading it with camping and mountain climbing gear, we set out with the goal of conquering this formidable mountain. Our plan was to set up base camp at a nearby campground and reconnoiter the area the first day and then climb to the top and return to the base camp the next day.

During the reconnoiter, we were surprised to find a road on which we drove all the way to the top of the mountain where there was a fire watchtower and camp facilities. This seemed to be a much more efficient way to get to the top of the highest mountain in Missouri than struggling up on foot. We enjoyed an awesome view from the watchtower and felt like seasoned mountain climbers as we drove back to base camp. After a delicious supper of warmed beans, burned franks, charred marshmallows, and melted chocolate, we decided that since we had already accomplished our goal of conquering the mountain, it might be good to sleep in the next day and explore the nearby river instead of climbing the mountain we had already topped. Therefore, the next day, we hiked along the river, splashed in the swimming hole, and plunged between the rocks through the water rapids. Another night of rustic sleep and smoke-flavored food allowed us to arrive home in St. Louis with heroic tales of how the mountain summit goal was so efficiently met.

Mount Whitney

Having conquered the tallest mountain in the state, climbing was subjugated to other pressing activities such as scouting, Indian guide outings, baseball, and my own retirement from the military and retread into the work of a research psychologist. It was a number of years later that my son Jack, who was then a navy pilot flying out of San Francisco, said, "Dad, remember when you said it was important to have a goal to climb the tallest mountain in the area? Well, the tallest mountain in mainland United States is just down the road from here, so come out and climb it with me." That was my next climbing experience: getting to the top of Mount Whitney.

We waited until August when the weather was supposed to be best and all snow was melted, but two complications occurred. The weather was warm enough to energize extremely healthy mosquitoes, but not warm enough to eliminate snow and ice from the higher elevations. Furthermore, our vehicle could not get us very far up the mountain because the road stopped at a parking lot just a few miles off the main highway. Fortunately, we stopped at the nearby town of Lone Pine, registered with the Forest Service, learned about the snow and ice, and rented crampons and ice axes before leaving civilization. From Lone Pine we drove about thirteen miles to the parking area at the Whitney Portal. The climb from there was not difficult going from an elevation of 8,360 feet to our camp for the night at 11,000 feet. During the night, our main concern was about the bears that were supposed to inhabit the area waiting for campers to exploit; however, it were the mosquitoes that did most harm. Netting kept them out of the tent pretty well, but they detracted from the joy of dinner at a camp fire and appreciation of a sunset.

Approach to Mount Whitney

Climbing the next day was challenging. A steep traverse to the ridge leading to the summit was covered with snow and ice and required judicious footwork. Except for breathing difficulty (typical for flatlanders), going was easier on the ridge because wind and sun had eliminated the snow. From there to the summit at an elevation of 14,491 feet, footwork was still important because of loose rock and distraction by the impressive view of the vast drop-off below. At the summit, though, the impressive view reached awesome magnitude. To the west was the rolling terrain leading to the Pacific Ocean and to the east was the descending terrain with Death Valley visible in the distance. How unique it was to be standing on the highest spot in the country looking at the lowest spot—a thrilling thought.

In descending, we took a shortcut that did not seem fair but sure saved a lot of energy and time. Just before getting to the beginning of the traverse off the ridge, we met some other climbers that were preparing to slide down a snow bank about 1,500 feet to the base of the steep ridge approach. It was scary, but if they could do it, so could we. After carefully observing what happened to them, each of us, one at a time, wearing a poncho like a diaper, descended in a sitting position, controlling speed somewhat with the ice ax. Despite some bruises, ice scrapes, and covered with snow, arriving at the snow slide base was exhilarating. How much easier and faster than descending the traverse traditionally by foot.

Death Valley view from Mount Whitney summit

Having arrived at the campsite sooner than expected, we decided to pack up and descend to the park rather than endure another battle with mosquitoes. Because of approaching darkness, we moved fast, which was a mistake because after arriving at the parking lot and resting during the drive to a motel, I could hardly walk. In some ways, coming down a mountain is harder than going up. Rarely used muscles become strained, but more important is the jamming of toes into the front of the boot that does not hurt at the time, but causes excruciating pain after the skin starts repairing itself.

So be it; we had achieved the significant goal of climbing to the top of the tallest point in our contiguous country, from which could be seen the lowest point. The sense of accomplishment was impressive. In addition to filling the need for stimulation, mountain climbing seems to fill another important need: to successfully manage a difficult goal.

Chapter 4
Goal Orientation: Sense of Purpose and Life Esteem

Inherent in all living organisms is purposeful goal striving based on continued existence and reproduction. For a petunia plant turning toward light, the goal is to nourish its chlorophyll process. For a single-celled amoeba, it may be nothing more than getting nourishment to enable cell division. For humans, though, a sophisticated set of goals are added that interact with thoughts and feelings providing complicated motivations for activities. This system is further complicated by subconscious goals hidden from normal awareness that frequently conflict with conscious rational goals and are difficult to fill. Did you ever ask yourself, "why did I do that?" While mountain climbing can fill a rational conscious need to achieve a difficult goal and provide stimulation, it might also fill less obvious needs that may be subconscious such as to move higher in life, to overcome obstacles, to transcend daily activities, or to reach into novel territory. However, let us start with the immediate aspect of goal orientation.

Although many of our actions may be automatic without conscious contemplation, most seem to us to be associated with conscious thought, and all result from some form of goal or intention. Psychology researchers agree that our intentions and goals are of major importance in explaining why we do things and have proposed many ways to study them. The term "personal projects" refers to goals people set on a daily basis, such as get to work on time so my boss sees me as a reliable and punctual person.[1] At a more generalized level are "life task strategies," such as meet timely schedules as a way of being an efficient person.[2] The term "propriate striving" was coined by the famous psychologist Gordon Allport to emphasize the dynamic drive that people have to develop a coherent self-concept and to set goals accordingly.[3] Abraham Maslow showed goals forming a hierarchy that at the most basic level meet physiological needs such as food and warmth. Then come security needs, followed by belongingness, self-esteem, and actualization at the highest level.[4] Although all can exert a force on a person's activities, successfully filling the lower needs facilitates meeting the higher ones. Actualization at the highest level involves one's striving for "metaneeds" such as justice, beauty, and harmony.

Goals that dominate one's conscious activities have been termed "personal strivings,"[5] and longer-range goals that provide a general orientation to activities are called "life commitments."[6]

Many notable psychologists and psychiatrists have emphasized long-range goals similar to actualization and life commitments. "Fictional finalism" describes a goal that is so big and elusive it seems fictional and so important that it is final.[7] William Menninger, who established the Menninger Clinic, stated that the longer the range and the more difficult to achieve a goal is, the better it is for psychological health.[8] The famous Swiss psychiatrist Carl Jung took the long-range aspect further by saying that we all have a "transcendent function" that causes us to reach out for something beyond our personal selves.[9] The Austrian psychiatrist Viktor Frankl, who used the term "will to meaning," emphasized the process of finding and pursuing a life goal. The central task here is to find a major goal that provided meaning and purpose for life. In his book *Man's Search For Ultimate Meaning*, Frankl (1977) explained the term "noogenic neurosis" as a condition of two-thirds of his psychiatric patients caused by lack of a sense of major purpose. In Austria, he developed logotherapy to treat this. James Crumbaugh, who developed the Purpose in Life questionnaire to measure the degree to which a person had such an orientation, applied it to therapeutic settings in the United States.[10] Another self-report type of measuring instrument is the Life Regard Index developed and used to assess two components of a person's sense of purpose: framework which is the conceptualized content and fulfillment that is one's perspective about fulfilling a framework.[11] Research continues and other methods have been recently developed to measure an individual's view of meaning and purpose in life.

Sense of purpose, purpose in life, and meaning in life are sometimes used interchangeably when referring to this long-range or highest level of human goals; however, there are subtle differences. Purpose in life is an objective statement of this ultimate goal, sense of purpose is a person's view of ultimate purpose, and meaning in life is a more general term reflecting the significance and value of life or life's purpose. As with sense of purpose, meaning in life has been related to many factors of personal health and well-being, and has been shown to be a major function of religion.[12] The Meaning in Life Questionnaire includes purpose in life and sense of purpose, and has been used in recent research to validate importance of these concepts.[13] A mass of research and theory about the human need for meaning has been summarized by psychologists Phillip Shaver and Mario Mikilincer (2012) in *Meaning, Mortality, and Choice* supporting meaning as an inherent human need that drives science and social organizations, particularly religion. Examples of topics they relate to this need are attachment theory, death anxiety, and terror and uncertainty management.

My own experiences in working with people from many different cultures in many different capacities provided me a great interest in the view that people had about their overall sense of purpose in life and its relation to their performance and well-being. This interest was so strong that after twenty years of military service with eligibility to retire, I enrolled in university courses to find out what was known about this topic, and to organize and develop information that could be used to enhance performance and sense of well-being. In trying to use Crumbaugh's Purpose In Life questionnaire and Battista's Life Regard Index to collect data, I found that neither fully captured useful aspects of a person's personal view of purpose in life. So, as a good researcher, I developed a questionnaire entitled Life Esteem Survey that measured framework (is there a purpose in my life?), perspective (how am I doing?), commitment (am I involved?), and quality (what is the nature of my purpose?).

"Life esteem" is the view that a person has of purpose in life and particularly purpose in their own life. Most researchers that dealt with this topic excluded the nature and content of the framework. Dr. Viktor Frankl claimed the nature of one's purpose was not important as long as there was one. My theory was that the view people have of their purpose in life included the quality of the purpose and the degree to which they pursued it or thought it was important for their general well-being—not just feeling good, but also physical, mental, and emotional health.

To investigate this, I had to also measure general well-being. It was a surprise to find that although there were measures of subjective well-being (i.e. happiness, contentment, satisfaction, etc.), there was no adequate measure at that time to include physical, mental, emotional, social, and performance factors. Therefore, once again as a dedicated researcher, I developed a measure of general well-being that took me into the field of health promotion and health risk assessment diverting me from the study of life esteem. However, during my work with health promotion, I was able to collect data about life goal orientation and its relationship with health, performance, and well-being.

Analysis of one major project involving 304 public school employees, out of 22 possible life goals, teachers chose most often belonging (to have companionship, love, and affection). A sample of 86 young adults working in various commercial fields chose most often individualization (to find and develop one's own potential). A sample of 205 university students chose understanding (to acquire wisdom and knowledge), and a sample of 30 theology students at the same university chose religion (to live in accordance with belief in a supreme being). A number of studies confirmed a positive relationship between life esteem, general well-being,[14] and performance.[15] These studies are summarized in Appendix A along with information about the background, structure, definitions, and measures of both life esteem and general well-being. A shortened self-scoring version of the Life Esteem Survey is Appendix B, and a self-scoring version of the General Well-Being Questionnaire is Appendix C. You might be interested in seeing how you stand on these measures and how you compare with other people.

Since the time when I started trying to measure general well-being and how it improves in health promotion programs, major advances have been made in its definition, importance, and enhancement. Martin Seligman, a past president of the American Psychological Association was instrumental in developing "positive psychology" that emphasized health promotion and disease prevention as opposed to disease diagnosis and treatment.[16] In his 2011 book *Flourishing*, Dr. Seligman proposed as the gold standard for measuring well-being the term "flourishing" that consisted of positive emotions, engagement, positive relationships, meaning, purpose, and sense of accomplishment. He reported successful programs aimed at increasing flourishing that reduced post-traumatic stress disorder and medical problems. Although this seems like something new, it can be traced back in time to Aristotle who used the ancient Greek term "eudaimonia" to emphasize a goal of effective living in additional to a goal of happiness.[17] In the book *The Best Within Us*, psychologist Alan Waterman (2013) brought together theory and research information showing the importance of "eudaimonic well-being" that includes flourishing, self-realization, self-concordance (sense of competence), and happiness. These factors are all included in my definition of general well-being.

The way people pursue goals varies considerably due to differences in temperament, experiences (learning), and present situation. For example, some people are more goal oriented where some are more process oriented. The latter tend to focus on the circumstances of pursuing the goal rather than the final accomplishment. They emphasize the experience and want to "stop to smell the roses" while the more goal oriented want to push to the intended goal. Mountaineers likewise vary in their focus, but in either case, the draw of a physical activity associated with nature and height is strong for them.

The process of selecting a mountain, planning, financing, and preparing for the outing, and then completing the process fill a need for challenge, stimulation, and goal accomplishment. Once again, though, for most people daily activities require sufficient goal seeking and accomplishment to satisfy those needs. We all expend considerable energy each day pursuing goals at many different levels. There must still be more to support reasons for climbing difficult mountains and repeatedly surmounting challenging obstacles not necessary for immediate existence.

Chapter 5
Higher Point: Mount Aconcagua

Need for stimulation, challenge, and goal accomplishment only partially explained why JC and I set out to climb Aconcagua, the tallest mountain outside of the Himalayan Range—tallest in the Western Hemisphere. His family was from Argentina with relatives and friends living in Mendoza, a major city in western Argentina close to Mount Aconcagua. From him I heard fascinating stories of ancient civilizations that held the mountain in reverence and about mystical experiences of climbers. The summit at 22,841 feet above sea level was accessible without the requirement for technical skill in rock climbing. Furthermore, a base camp complete with sleeping accommodations was only a two-day hike from the nearest road. It did require a guide with special provisions, good physical conditioning, and about fifteen days during the limited summer climbing season in December and January. Even then, though, it would not be easy because of the likelihood of snowstorms, high winds, and subfreezing temperatures above the base camp.

Answering Big Questions

Mount Aconcagua from Horcones Lagoon

Statistics available for the 1995–96 season are rather typical. Of 1,956 who attempted to climb, fewer than half reached the summit, and three died.[1] Mount Aconcagua has become particularly popular for climbers due to its accessibility and nontechnical requirements. Situated about eighty miles northeast of Santiago, Chile, and about the same distance northwest of Mendoza, Argentina, the base camp at 13,879 feet can be reached after two days of hiking (usually with mule assistance) from the village of Puente del Inca (8,400 feet). The summit at 22,841 feet can be reached under ideal conditions by acclimated climbers with three days of climbing from the base camp. Even at the warmest period of the summer, though, the upper part of the mountain is subject to frequent snowstorms with winds up to 65 mi/hr and temperatures as low as -40°F, so that normally a summit attempt is a significant challenge both physically and psychologically for even experienced climbers. Usually this is done in five days making two trips to each of two temporary camps, with the summit attempt made from and back to the second temporary camp in one day. Out of those that attempted this summit in the 1995-96 season, 395 required medical attention and 27 were evacuated.[1]

JC and I had collaborated on research projects before, and this seemed like a great opportunity to use his experience with medical measures and my experience with psychological measures to investigate the relative effects of altitude, physical stress, and psychological stress. He was a psychiatrist interested in disease prevention, and I was a psychologist interested in health promotion. We planned to take measures from our expedition members of six moods, strength, and physical condition at five different times and determine effects using standard statistical methods. A report about this study is Appendix D.

It was cold and dreary that third day after Christmas when we left from St. Louis. We were well prepared with special sleeping bags, clothing, parkas, and double-insulated boots, but we may have done too much to get into physical shape. On the way to the airport, I stopped at a drugstore to get some cough drops because my throat was feeling scratchy. My youngest son had flown in from San Francisco, and we all met at the airport and, with keen anticipation, departed for Miami where we got on an international flight to Mendoza via Santiago, Chile. Mendoza was so warm and sunny when we arrived that we changed into summer clothes at the airport while waiting for JC's friend, Nicholas, to pick us up for the trip into town.

Downtown Mendoza was warm, comfortable, and quaint—a pleasant change from cold, snowy St. Louis. Streets were lined with trees with many activities taking place on the broad sidewalks. Nicholas settled us in to the International Hotel and then took us to lunch at a nearby restaurant. Since everything closes after lunch and siesta is observed until 4:00 p.m., he insisted we rest and he would pick us up again at 7:00 p.m. for dinner at his home. My voice was almost gone by then, so it was with great reluctance that I begged off the evening's activities and had a steak sandwich by myself at the small hotel restaurant before turning in early for a long sleep. The next morning, Gabriel, the leader of the group we were joining for an expedition to Aconcagua, met us. We also met his girlfriend, Andriana, also an experienced guide who would be with us. A female in the party made things a little less intimidating. We were to join another guide, Federico, and five other climbers in four days at the Argentine army camp in Puente del Inca where the expedition would get organized and gain entrance to the National Aconcagua Park. The climb would start at the end of a road in the park.

Nicholas was a gracious host and took us on a tour of the local area. He runs two major wineries that had been established by his father and now were showpieces of Argentine productivity. Each winery had museums with guides that showed us the relics of early days in the wine business as well as the modern facilities. At the second winery, Nicholas's family joined us for a sumptuous lunch. It seems that lunch is the main meal after a busy morning and before a restful afternoon. Activity picks up again in the evening with a late dinner. Schedules are flexible, and we soon learned that punctuality took second place to stress-free functioning. Therefore, it was in a comfortable relaxed state that we loaded up our gear on an undersized van and drove off to Puenta del Inca the next day.

Gabriel had arranged for provisions and accommodations so that we would have three days at the Puente del Inca army camp (Ejercito Argentino) to acclimate at an altitude of 8,400 feet. Moreover, it gave us the opportunity to explore the ancient village that was a luxury outpost for ancient travelers along the western side of the Andes Mountains. My scratchy throat had stabilized into laryngitis, and added to this was another adversity known commonly as Montezuma's revenge. How appropriate this was since I was encroaching on a territory similar to Montezuma's and needed such a humbling experience to subdue exuberance. That it did, but my body seemed to be under adequate control when the morning came for our departure—weak but controllable. An army medic had graciously provided me with an ample supply of medicines for diarrhea, constipation, and sore throat, so I felt somewhat reassured despite apprehension about my condition for the ensuing two-day hike and climb to the base camp.

In addition to the three of us from the United States, our group consisted of seven other males who had come from various parts of South America and two male and one female guide from Mendoza. Eight of us were attempting to reach the summit while the rest were going only to the base camp area. The summit group consisted of myself (aged sixty-eight), JC (fifty-five), Jack (twenty-seven), Cesar (twenty-nine-year-old lawyer and soccer player from Buenos Aires), Ganyi (forty-two-year-old real estate broker from Buenos Aires), and the three guides: Gabriel (forty, geologist), Federico (twenty-three, journalist), and

Andriana (thirty-nine, schoolteacher). Domingo, Corigliano, and his son Sebastian from Buenos Aires were the nonsummit trekkers. Ricardo and Daniel joined our party at the last minute because the party they were supposed to accompany rejected them. They were TV newsmen from La Plata, Argentina, on assignment to cover a group of girls that were attempting to establish a record of being the first all-girl party to reach the summit. Ricardo and Daniel had covered their preparation to this point but were now banned because they were not girls. The TV crew was now going to accompany us as far as they could carry their equipment.

The first day of the expedition started at the trailhead in the Horcones national park about five miles from Puente del Inca and consisted of hiking up the gravel floor of the Horcones River valley for about seven miles from an elevation of 8,400 feet to 11,400 feet. Even in my weakened and apprehensive condition, this leg was thoroughly enjoyable. Tents and provisions were going to the first campsite by mule, so we carried only light packs. The temperature was a balmy seventy degrees. The view ahead of snow-covered Aconcagua was impressive; the slope was gentle, and camaraderie was reassuring. JC, Jack, and I shared a four-man mountain tent; and after supper of hot tea, dried potato soup, wieners, cheese, and crackers, we all got a good night's sleep.

Most were up at six when daylight came the next morning. Breakfast consisted of hot tea, cheese, crackers, and cookies. On breaking camp, loads were assigned to each, and we started out with full packs at about nine. The slope was steeper, and we had to climb some ridges to avoid branches of the Horcones River swollen by melting snow. By noon, the going was getting rather strenuous;

and even after a lunch break (cold cuts, cheese, crackers, and juice) the outlook seemed grim to me and JC since this leg was supposed to be about fifteen miles. Although no one complained, Gabriel must have sensed the feeling because as a group of mules approached, he flagged down the muleteer (lead handler) and negotiated a lift to base camp for our provisions and tents. This left us with light packs again and renewed spirits. Six more hours of continually steeper ups and downs brought the welcome sight of what looked like a modern ski lodge. That was about 7:00 p.m., and even though the sun was still bright, temperature was down to about forty degrees.

After a steep climb up the side of a rocky ravine, we emerged on to a large meadow like area with Aconcagua towering up on the right, a high ridge of glacier in the front, and a drop-off into a valley on the left. The area is called Plaza de Mulas because this is as far as the mules can go. On a slight rise on the left before the drop-off was the ski lodge–type building called Hotel Refugio Plaza de Mulas.

The Hotel Refugio Plaza de Mulas has an interesting and disappointing history. Constructed between 1990 and 1991 with great fanfare as a magnet for tourists, it was inaugurated in December 1991 but never completed. Politics, funding, and accessibility halted completion after the basic structure was finished. Thirty-five rooms each have four bunk bed racks and a bathroom; however, lack of running water or central heat prevents them from being comfortable accommodations. Water was piped into a basement washroom from a glacier fed pond about two hundred feet away and provided hot showers (sometimes) for about an hour each evening. Two toilets were flushed by dipping water out of a drum by the stalls. A dining room is on the first floor with a kitchen to which water must be hand carried. Despite these rustic conditions, we enjoyed a delicious supper of shredded meat, carrots, cabbage, soup, and Jell-O with about twenty other guests, and bedded down for the night in our own sleeping bags.

The next day, Gabriel moved us to a small two-room hut that had been used by workers during the hotel construction. No running water was available there either, but there was a stove and sink to which we could bring water using jugs. It was cozy, and we quickly settled in as a congenial family. With only five sets of bunk beds, the guides slept on the floor. JC was not feeling good—said his legs hurt and were weak, so he got a lower bunk. I took an upper bunk because I thought it might be warmer. That was not necessary, though, because my Marmot negative-forty-degree sleeping bag was so warm I had to unzip it from the bottom to keep my feet from toasting. JC, being a medical doctor, had brought some medical supplies and offered to check blood pressures. This was a nice service but compounded his own problem because his was above 140/90. His heart rate was also extremely high. We all had been taking the altitude medicine Diamox which seemed to help some. Ganyi was also having difficulty with head ache and stomach upset that kept him in bed for two days. Andriana prepared a cheese and potato dish for supper so relaxing that the only other activity was getting a good night's sleep while wrestling with breathing difficulties and mild headaches.

The following day, Gabriel got everyone up with the announcement that we were going glacier climbing, and we knew he was not joking when he handed to each a pair of crampons (spiked devices attached to boot bottoms for gripping ice). So, after having hot tea and cookies for breakfast, we moved out (except for Ganyi) for our first real climbing experience. It was fascinating, but a little scary when going over or through ice crevices. On the way back, we went through a camping area about a mile from the hotel where a number of climbers and guides had pitched their tents. It was comforting to see that park rangers also had a tent well equipped as a headquarters. Even a doctor was there with emergency medical equipment.

Back at our camp, we had hot tea and cookies, relaxed, became better acquainted, and compared our feelings as optimistically as possible. All felt some discomfort from muscle fatigue and light-headedness. Jack had a full-blown headache, and JC was experiencing heart palpitations. Daniel was having breathing difficulty. Ganyi had been up but with diarrhea and a runny nose, felt bad enough to go back to bed. My concern was about diarrhea and sore throat, but as we visited and rested, symptoms improved for most of us. Only Gabriel and Frederico spoke English, so Jack and I had to rely on JC for communication with the others. As I had found in other foreign situations, communication was not solely by words. This was a jovial group of Argentineans whose body movements and sounds were quite expressive. We had already shared strenuous experiences, so camaraderie was strong. Everything seemed better after enjoying the steak and potatoes with hot vegetable soup that Andriana prepared for supper.

After supper when spirits were highest, JC and I took the first measurements for our proposed study of mountaineering effects. Gabriel had already consented to our project, and we had originally planned to take the first measures at Puenta del Inca before the first climb, but the hubbub of meeting and organizing made that impractical. Gabriel announced that the next day we would make a climb carrying a load to our first temporary camp at a saddle called Nido de Condores at 17,500 feet. We would return to base camp to spend the night before the second climb when we would pitch tents and camp for two nights. The plan was to spend five nights at the base camp for acclimatization with two trips to a temporary camp at Nido, from which two trips would be made to a second temporary camp at a 19,522 feet site called Berlin. That would be two nights at Nido and one night at Berlin from which the summit attempt would be made, and then a second night at Berlin before returning all the way to the base camp.

Aconcagua viewed from 14,000-foot base camp

On the third day at base camp, the first climb to Nido was made. The climb was strenuous, but not difficult. We followed a switchback trail over rocks and gravel on the way up. Coming down, we took what is called the Conway route, which was faster but more difficult because we went straight down the slope sliding on the gravel while dodging the rocks so that maintaining a steady pace and balance was a problem. Even though the plan was to start the climb about ten, it was noon before we left, and consequently, it was after dark when we got back to base camp. After some stew for supper, there was little discussion about going to bed. Everyone was tired.

The next morning, Daniel was having difficulty breathing and an irregular heartbeat, so he went to the doctor who advised him to leave immediately for Puenta del Inca by mule. Damian also left by mule, and Domingo, Corigliano, Sebastian, and Ricardo departed on foot. That left the summit party that seemed to be in fair shape except for JC who was concerned about his heart rhythm.

No one complained when Gabriel announced that we would not try the second climb to Nido for the next two days because the weather was deteriorating. He had a palmtop computer into which he maintained a plot of temperature and pressure data that indicated that bad weather was due. Sure enough, that afternoon, dark clouds started rolling in, and by night, snow was falling. Not only did this delay further climbing; it caused climbers already on the mountain to return to the base camp, and many abandoned summit attempts. We hunkered down for three more days until Gabriel thought it was safe to resume the climb. The delay caused anxiety about when the weather would improve and how schedules could be adjusted to accommodate airline commitments if a summit attempt became possible. Nevertheless, most of us enjoyed the delay since it gave us more time to acclimate to the altitude and rest our ailing bodies. All contributed stories that made the time pass quickly; however, Gabriel entertained us most with information about his experiences on Aconcagua. He worked for the Argentine government's National Institute of Geology in the Glacier and Snow Laboratory. This required field trips and expeditions to such places as Aconcagua and Patagonia. Two years ago, he had planted a temperature recorder in the Horcones Glacier, and he retrieved it during our glacier climb. On one of his climbs of Aconcagua, he discovered a child's mummy that he recovered and turned over to the University Nacional de Cuyo in Mendoza. This made him rather famous because the mummy turned out to be that of an Inca child that had been sacrificed about a thousand years ago in a ceremony to appease the forces of nature. It seems that the ancient Incas, who believed that gods inhabited the mountain making it a "stone sentinel," held Aconcagua in great reverence. Even today, local people report direct encounters with divine forces on the mountain and hold it in reverence.

On the morning of the seventh day, while having tea and crackers, Gabriel announced that the weather looked better now and that we would leave in one hour for Nido. JC was still having trouble with his heart rhythm and breathing and decided that he should not climb higher. It was arranged that he would stay at the hotel that night and return to Puenta del Inca the next day by mule. JC's explanation of why that trip off the mountain was an experience beyond all anticipations is Appendix E.

The rest of us scurried around getting ready for the climb, and we managed to get under way about noon. At 5:00 p.m., we were about one hundred yards from Nido when Gabriel stopped the climb and said that the weather was threatening again and that we should pitch tents below the saddle here where the wind would not be so strong. This was a wise decision because just as we finished pitching tents and securing provisions, snow started falling. Jack, Federico, and I were snug in our tent, heating snow in a pot to get water for our freeze-dried lasagna supper when the wind picked up. Fortunately, our tents were designed for this and were well anchored. When I went to the other tent to take the second set of measure for the mountaineering study, the wind was so strong I could not tell if the snow was coming from above or from the side of the mountain. The slope we were on prevented it from accumulating except around the tents and rocks. The next morning, the blowing snow obscured vision so that it seemed that we were engulfed within a huge snow cloud that was moving with a speed of about 60 mph. Ganyi was having difficulty breathing and seemed terribly depressed, so he joined a group that stopped at our tents on their way down to base camp. They had camped at Nido and, having survived the night, decided to abort their climb and descend.

Tents at Nido de Condores

Breathing and heart rhythm seemed to be the major altitude problems for our group. I, too, had difficulty breathing; however, it was most noticeable at night. I would frequently waken from sleep feeling "short of breath." I found, though, that this was alleviated by forcibly breathing deeply through pursed lips, so I did not feel concerned about it. Evidently, during normal waking activity, if my lungs needed more oxygen, my body would respond with deeper breaths without notice. We were watching for cerebral and pulmonary edema, which is the major danger, but there was no indication of that, except for headache that most experienced temporarily.

As the morning progressed, the wind slowed a little; however, it was necessary to stay in the tent and most of the time in the sleeping bag to stay warm. We kept busy melting snow for drinking water—a major activity that required care (don't use yellow snow, or confuse the drinking water bottles with those that allowed us to get through the night without having to leave the tent). We also drank hot tea, heated freeze-dried delights, and shared experiences. Federico gave horrible details about difficulties on previous climbs; Jack told about near crashes while flying MH53 helicopters, and I recounted some of the tight situations I had been in while flying in the Far East. After dark, the wind picked up again, and we were startled by four climbers that stumbled into our camp asking for help. They were trying to get off of the mountain when one had lost his balance in the wind, fell, and was badly mangled before coming to rest on rocks above our camp. Gabriel took the injured man and one other in his tent and radioed to base camp for help. The other two came in our tent. Base camp said it would be the next day before a rescue team could get up to our camp, so ten people spent the night in two four-man tents that are crowded with only three people each. The injured man's hands were frozen; his head had multiple gashes with loss of much blood, and he faded in and out of semi consciousness. It was doubtful that he would survive the descent to base camp, but the rescue team arrived about seven in the morning and placed him in a canvas bag for what was probably his last trip.

Since the sky had cleared, we were preparing to move our tents up the slope to Nido when two soldiers came into our camp and asked if they could rest in our tents. They had been on a military rescue mission but had to turn back because of altitude sickness. Therefore, we did not move to Nido and planned to leave early the next morning making a full-load one-time climb to a temporary camp at the site called Berlin. Time was running out, but if we could make it to Berlin and the weather cooperated, we might still be able to summit the next day, get back to base camp after a second night at Berlin, and meet our departure schedule.

As usual, we did not get a very early start the next morning. It was about noon when loads had been packed and the climb started. The wind had been so strong that most of the new snow was blown away, but this leg was difficult because of carrying full packs. Berlin was the floor of a saddle between two rock walls that provided protection from the wind. We arrived in time to set up camp before dark and were privileged to experience a sunset so brilliant the colors were breathtaking. It seemed like we were in a different world. Awe best describes my feeling when looking out over surrounding mountaintops to the distant Pacific Ocean. The wind had died down, and an eerie silence made the orange glow of our rocky campsite seem exquisitely peaceful. Contributing to this was a weightless feeling from struggling no longer under the heavy backpack and the thought of having gotten this far after so many delays. We were all tired, but also exhilarated by a sense of accomplishment and anticipation of being so close to the summit.

We had accomplished a lot. Many efforts had come together overcoming challenges, problems, and hardships; topped off now with inspiring sensations and expansive thoughts—awesome. It felt so good that I hoped that everyone had similar experiences. It reminded me of the time in Korea at the southern end of the Chorwon Valley in a rugged mountain area known as "Nightmare Range" where I had been directing air strikes that stopped because of approaching darkness. Even though this was a training exercise, the loud noises and explosions, danger of inaccuracies, and pressures of competence had created a vortex of intense stress. But now it was all over. I found myself sitting in the jeep with the radio operator in calm silence. Instead of thunderous aircraft, the sky was filled with brilliant colors as the sun set behind "Kimchi" Mountain. As we both sat in silence absorbing the serene situation, these words came to my mind, "God is now in His heaven, and all is right with the world."

View from second temporary camp

Our first task that evening was the melting of snow to fill water bottles. The plan was to get up at 4:00 a.m., have a light breakfast, and leave for the summit by five. Since we were all pretty tired and repulsed by the thought of eating anything, we turned in as soon as I had taken another set of measures for the mountaineering study and after forcing ourselves to drink hot tea. At this altitude, it is normal for the stomach to feel a little unsettled, but consuming liquid is extremely important for keeping the kidneys functioning. The body does not acclimate very well to altitudes above eighteen thousand feet and has a tendency to shut down nonessential functions, so it is important to keep vital organs operating.

One vital function is sleep, which explains why no one woke up until after six when the sun was shining brightly. Despite our haste in consuming hot coffee and cookies and getting organized, it was close to ten before we launched for the most important leg of our expedition. After about an hour of climbing, the ice and snow required the donning of crampons, which made progress slower but safer. Gabriel was pushing us hard because he said that it was doubtful that we could make the summit in time to return safely. There was not even enough time to be scared as we crossed an area called the traverse. This was an ascending trail with a rock face on the left and precipitous drop on the right—a dangerous part because a loss of balance, stumble, or slip could send a body down the steep slope until it was stopped by the jutting rocks. Everyone was occupied with the task of breathing and gaining solid footing in the fresh snow, so that as a less imposing rocky area appeared ahead, I was not prepared when Gabriel insisted we move faster. For me, it was physically impossible, and soon I was holding up the progress. Gasping for air was more difficult because moisture from my breath had formed ice around the opening in my balaclava (cloth head covering with openings for eyes and mouth), and my double-insulated boots that were keeping toes warm seemed to weigh one hundred pounds each. When we arrived at the base of a rocky slope that looked like about one hundred feet below the top, Gabriel said this is the Canaleta and that for me it was close enough to the summit. Clouds were moving in, temperature was dropping, and time was running out for us to get to the summit, back across the traverse, and far enough back to Berlin before dark. Federico and I were to start back immediately, and those that could still move strongly would try to climb the Canaleta to the summit.

Should I insist on continuing that last short distance or acquiesce and start back down? There was no in-between because hypothermia would occur quickly without adequate activity. I thought about JC who had planned this expedition with me so that we would reach the summit together; then I thought about the ancient Incas who believed that divine spirits inhabited this mountain and sometimes manifest themselves as clouds that punished undeserving mortals. Therefore, as a dark billowing cloud surrounded us and bit my face, I decided to go no further. I had brought an American flag that was to be placed at the summit, so I gave it to Jack and started back to the traverse with Federico. Going back was not easy, but definitely better than going up mainly because I could set the pace and not become exhausted. On the way down, Federico tried to make me feel good by saying that I was the oldest climber to get that far and had already exceeded predictions because the other guides at base camp were betting that I would not get that far.

Gabriel, Andriana, Cesar, and Jack made it to the summit and back across the traverse at dusk, arriving back at the tents around ten. The last part of their descent was in the dark, a tricky task. They were exhausted, and no one wanted to talk or eat, so we all bedded down for the night fortunate to be safe and relatively sound. I went to sleep thanking whatever spirits that be for us all to have gotten back to our tents without mishap despite the bad weather, fresh snow, and time constraint. This feeling was reinforced the next day when a climber came into our camp saying that a member of his party had fallen on the traverse and help was needed for his rescue. This was about noon, and we had broken camp and were starting to leave for the descent to base camp by way of Nido, where we had left some equipment. Gabriel said that Federico could lead us down and that he would go to help with the rescue, but that meant that we must divide and carry his load. This we did and made it to Nido at dusk safe but exhausted. As with the first climb to Nido, we descended on the Conway route, but this time there were two strikes against us. It was getting dark and difficult to see ahead for sound footing, and we were carrying heavy loads that interfered with balance and footing. Fortunately, some people at base camp knew of our situation and met us halfway with offers to help carry our loads. They also had word about Gabriel's rescue and were going up to assist him. We all got back to base camp about the same time and, despite a unanimous state of exhaustion, assembled in the hotel for wine, shredded meat, and cooked vegetables. Needless to say, it was one of the most delicious meals I ever had, and the wine was the most energizing. This was the first wine we had during the expedition, and I found it interesting that it was bottled in waxed cardboard cartons similar to milk cartons; however, that did not detract from its pleasant effects.

The hike from base camp to the trailhead at the park entrance normally takes about eight hours, so it was planned that we would leave the next morning at eleven. It was not surprising that the plan was delayed since most of us were slow in getting up and packing. The mules were waiting for us in front of the hotel where their handlers graciously accepted most of our loads so that we carried only light packs. It was about two when we finally got started, but since darkness did not come until about nine, we had daylight for most of the descent. The mules had beaten us to the trailhead, and it was a relief to find their cargo already loaded on a van that was waiting for us. After stopping at the Puenta del Inca army camp to pick up clothing that had been left there, the drive to Mendoza was drowsy and uneventful, except for a stop to get pizzas that we sleepily ate on the way to the International Hotel. A hot shower (first in fifteen days) and a comfortable bed signified the completion of the expedition and return to the "real world." The previous week now seemed like a dream, filled with feelings of awe and mystery.

The next day, JC, who had been staying with old friends, met us, and we all had supper together at a sidewalk café across the street from the hotel. Relaxing in the balmy summer afternoon breeze would have made the ice and snow of Aconcagua only part of a dream if it had not been for chapped skin, chronic coughs, hoarse voices, sore muscles, and an eighteen-day growth of beard to elucidate reality. I could not help feeling grateful that these were our only residuals, and of thinking about events we narrowly escaped such as frostbite, broken bones, gashed skin, and even fatality. All of these we had seen while on the mountain. It is highly likely that JC and I would have suffered some of those adversities had we not heeded warnings. I felt especially thankful for the ominous bite of that cloud at the Canaleta.

After the food and wine was depleted, we returned to the hotel where Jack, JC, and I sold or gave to Gabriel, Andriana, Federico, and Cesar a lot of the equipment we had brought from the United States. This not only facilitated our packing for the return flight but also expedited departing good-byes.

JC stayed in Mendoza a few more days, but Jack and I left the hotel at ten thirty the next morning for our noon flight to Santiago and Miami. When we arrived at the airport, Gabriel was there, but not to see us off. He had the handheld GPS receiver that I had brought him from the United States and asked if I could take it back. He had paid me to bring this set to him, and it worked admirably all the way up to Mount Aconcagua. We all were impressed with the way the device kept track of where we were and where we had been, but now back in Mendoza, the keyboard was inoperative. Of course, I took it and returned it to the manufacturer with a recounting of its experience. They said this was the first time that type of set had been at twenty-two thousand feet, so they would determine the cause of the malfunction. After a couple of weeks, I received from them a new set with a modified keyboard and an explanation that the seals that protected the keys collapsed from the increase in atmospheric pressure when going from twenty-two thousand feet to sea level. They thanked me for using their set on this expedition and sent some complimentary ancillary equipment and software as compensation.

Let me insert here an anecdote that may be of interest. Since Gabriel had requested a medical clearance before the expedition, I had a medical checkup that included a sigmoid colonoscopy. The results showed a polyp that should be removed promptly. I did not intend to allow this to interfere with my participation in the expedition, so I postponed an appropriate colonoscopy for after the trip. Three months later when the colonoscopy was performed, no sign of the polyp was found. Had it been misdiagnosed or disappeared through a natural body process such as physical exertion? Or could a mysterious healing have occurred through some physiological, psychological, or supernatural process? We do not know. We do know that emotions can influence a body's immunology and healing functions, but still, healings sometimes can only be explained as miraculous.

During the flight from Santiago to Miami, while reflecting on my recent experience, I realized that the reward for taking unnecessary risks and enduring hardships to climb to the top of a tall mountain can be more than searching for challenge, stimulation, or pursuit of a goal. Stories of mysterious happenings and reverence associated with a mountain can create a strong appeal. Those imposing edifices jutting up into the sky demand respect and create a sense of awe and mystery. There even seems to be some dynamic force on the mountain that causes feelings of contact with a mysterious unknown; something beyond our physical environment that might be called an esoteric connectedness, or an experience of a supernatural force that has or had a hand in our existence that could be called deity—a force that energizes our struggles to meet goals and pursue the ontological imperative. Is this only an emotional reaction of being in a stimulating and novel situation, or is it a glimpse of reality beyond normal perception? Might it be a combination of both, built on the human propensity for making meaning out of phenomena that evoke emotional arousal, and that seem beyond natural explanation?

Chapter 6
Awe: Emotions and Mysticism

After a strenuous day's climb, looking out from Mount Aconcagua over the mountains and valleys of western Argentina as the sun sets through brilliantly colored clouds was an inspiring experience. Adding to the inspiration was relief from rigorous physical exertion (particularly the weight of a heavy backpack), satisfaction from having endured hardships and gotten that far, and anticipation of an attempt at the summit. Then there was the feeling of being closely involved with nature and fully experiencing its impacts, a pleasant condition popularized by the famous sociobiologist Edward Wilson (2006) that he called biophilia, an innate attraction to nature. Also there was a feeling of great respect for a monstrous formation of rock and dirt that was the source of so many stories; and then, there was a strong feeling of accomplishment from being close to the culmination of an activity that had required months of planning and preparation, expenditure of considerable time, energy, and financial resources, as well as discomfort and hardship . All of this must have contributed to a mysterious feeling—an aroused emotional state that could well be called awe.

It is not necessary, though, to climb tall mountains to have these inspiring emotional experiences. They could be triggered merely by hearing moving music, seeing a colorful sunset, or experiencing an impressive event such as child birth or compassionate love. Humanistic psychologist Abraham Maslow (1971) called this "peak experience," and emphasized the value to health and well-being of being open to its occurrence. When was the last time you had such an inspired feeling?

Awe is defined as an emotion variously combining dread, veneration, and wonder that is inspired by authority or by something sacred or sublime.[1] It is a convenient term to describe the result of a sequence of events that starts with wonder about the cause of an impressive experience. When the nature of the cause is not known, a mystery results. Humans have always had a tendency to turn to supernatural explanations when natural explanations are not available and attribute mystical force to ineffable mysteries. Mysteries, then, stimulate a sense of wonder, apprehension, emotional arousal, and awe.

Much is known about emotions. They are always with us, varying according to our state of arousal as mentioned in Chapter 2, and a complex set of other factors such as pleasantness or threat of the situation, physical body condition, memories of related experiences, thought processes, and attributions of cause. A particular feeling can be an instantaneous automatic reaction or the result of a slower thought process. An abrupt change can cause a physical response before any thinking takes place[2] or a cognitive response with a somewhat slower process of mentally analyzing the impact of that abrupt change.[3] Both usually occur, but the instantaneous physiological response can be a startle reaction that triggers muscles to avoid or eliminate the cause and is called the fight-or-flight response. This seems to be built into us and was useful for our ancestors when suddenly confronted with a saber-toothed tiger. The evolution theory of emotions explains why some of our current reactions that helped ancestors are detrimental to us now, such as the repeated threats experienced when driving to work in rush hour traffic that triggers our saber-toothed tiger response and leaves us exhausted when we arrive at work.

An example of the slower cognitive response is the fear of high places that is now innate in humans because our ancestors were people who learned respect of high places and consequently lived longer and had more offspring than those who were less respectful and more vulnerable to serious falls. It explains why we experience fear, sometimes intensely, when looking out from the top of a high building even though there is no danger of falling and how we control the fear through logical thought processes. On top of a tall mountain danger and fear contribute to strong emotions that elicit both fast and slow reactions.

Experiences that have an impact on us are remembered. "Cognitive labeling" is a process by which memories are established to associate an emotion with the accompanying situation.[4] Thus, if one is in a religious sanctuary experiencing a pleasant emotional arousal because of beautifully moving music, stimulating coloring from stained glass windows, erythematic activity, and thoughts of a benevolent loving power, the emotion tends to be associated with the religious situation and stored as a memory that can exert a later influence without conscious awareness of the source. Neuroscience research has shown that subconscious emotional memories are located in the brain's limbic system and influence our perceptions and actions without conscious thought processes.[5] Have you ever had an uncanny feeling for no apparent reason? It was probably from a subconscious memory triggered by a situation associated with a forgotten experience. In any case we have a natural tendency to attribute cause to aroused feelings and latch on to the most immediately available explanation.

Errors can occur in attributing cause to events we experience and to our emotional reactions. Interesting research shows that once an intense response occurs and it lingers, cognitive processes tend to associate that response with whatever situation and environment that follows.[5] Thus, if a mountain climber's pleasant feeling after reaching a difficult campsite and unloading a heavy pack is intense enough to linger while the sunset creates eerie shadows, that emotion may be remembered as caused by or associated with the shadows. If the feeling was good, the situation would be remembered as desirable; and if the feeling was bad, it would be remembered for avoidance. If feelings are strong enough, an association tends to be stored in the brain so that a particular emotion will be triggered automatically when that situation is repeated or recalled. Many mysterious and maybe inappropriate feelings occur because of experiences consciously forgotten, but that linger in the hidden recesses of the mind.

Recent advances in neuroscience studies show interaction between emotional reaction and brain processes. Emotional arousal increases brain activity that focuses attention, resets thinking processes, and increases storage of long-term memories but decreases working memory and cognitive efficiency.[6] Research started by Andrew Newberg and Eugene D'Aquili shows that emotions associated with religious experiences that are similar to the awe and mystery experienced by mountain climbers are associated with decreased activity in the brain area that maintains external orientation and personal identity, and increased activity in the area associated with feelings of spaciousness and imagination.[7] Therefore, emotional arousal of this type facilitates the ability to respond quickly to a situation but may decrease ability to accurately evaluate the situation. Examples of increases in sensory acuity and imagination with decreases in objective reasoning can be seen in emotional reaction to sensory deprivation from isolation, in excitation from intense dancing or use of chemicals, and in decreased blood oxygen as occurs at high altitudes. These are some of the studies indicating that emotions experienced by many mountain climbers (and other adventurers) may be quite rewarding and arouse feelings of mystery, special insight, mysticism, and awe.

Awe is a powerful emotion characterized by a feeling of vastness that extends perception beyond its normal limits providing feelings of special insight and connection to a mysterious realm beyond our physical environment, a feeling so powerful that it calls for explanation.[8] Research has shown that such feelings are associated with mystical and religious experiences, creative imagination, deep satisfaction, and mental health.[9] These feelings of emotional arousal frequently defy objective analysis. Feelings of beauty, harmony, love, and transcendence involve passions more than intellects and can influence perceptions and override logic. We should realize that despite extensive knowledge about the mechanisms of emotional reactions, mysteries still exist about the formation of intuition, insight, and awe. None of this research negates the possibility that emotions can open a person to special insight, but it does bring into question the sources and validity of such insights.

Many times the situational associations and causal attributions (and misattributions) defy physical explanations and are filled in with convenient metaphorical explanations. "Anthropomorphism" is the term that describes the tendency we have to attribute human characteristics to mysterious phenomena. During earlier times when knowledge of nature was quite limited, important features of nature were given human like mental abilities, and just as people can be appealed to, important features of nature were appealed to and respected. This formed the ancient religion of animism introduced in Chapter 2 that provided not only explanation but also a feeling of being able to exert some influence on increasing positive environmental factors and decreasing negative ones. Feelings of certainty and control increased sufficiently to reduce anxiety of powerlessness. Research started by Julian Rotter has shown the extremes people will go to for a feeling that they can influence things important to them.[10] This is known as locus of control, and those that feel that they can exert influence as agent rather than being influenced as pawns have better health, well-being, and performance.[11] For our ancestors that were so dependent on the forces of nature, desire to influence them developed from awe to reverence and worship, and appeals developed into ceremony and ritual.

In those early times, animistic powers were conceptualized as deities residing in important features such as the sun, rivers, and mountains. Mountains acquired special power because of their imposing dominance of the landscape and stimulating sight; their association with the emotional arousal from physical exertion, reduced oxygen, and fear of height; and their projection into the sky toward the sun which was recognized as the most important feature of nature. In earlier times when the sky represented heaven and ultimate reality, mountains were considered mediators between people and that universal ultimate reality that must exist somewhere "up there."[12] The "cosmic mountain" was a place that connected the heavens with the earth, where people ascended to meet with gods that had descended to meet the people.[13] Whether or not there was anything "up there" is secondary to how such a belief filled the ontological imperative and provided answers or potential answers to the insatiable questions. The belief made life more meaningful and manageable but defied simple explanation. Metaphors, allegories, and symbolic representations were developed to make elements of belief easier to grasp and better to fill needs. Since mountains became associated in the past with sacred powers that helped fill important needs, could they still provide that function?

Even though the forerunners of Western culture modified animism about four thousand years ago with the concept of a single divine power, many elements of animism continue today and may account for the mysticism that draws people to the slopes of some mountains, and encourages a religious type of reverence for these features of nature. This has been supported and explained in detail by Edwin Bernbaum in his book *Sacred Mountains of the World*[14] and by Robert Macfarlane in *Mountains of the Mind*.[15] Many experiences that have been reported by inhabitants of sites on or near these "stone sentinels" indicate existence of more than merely a brain-based emotional reaction. Many traditions and cultures continue the belief that an unknown mystical type of force is associated with certain terrain features, especially mountains. Is there objective support for validity of belief in such forces? Or do these beliefs represent an epiphenomenon resulting from the human brain's propensity to seize onto supernatural explanations for emotional reactions that are not met by natural explanations?

Chapter 7
Mystical Points

Mount Heipori

Despite recent availability for tourism, Tibet is an area of the world that retains much of an ancient spiritual culture that purports manifestations of mystical forces. If such phenomena were based on more than brain based emotional arousal and subjective reaction, it surely would be observable in Tibet. As one of the most isolated countries bounded by mountain ranges and sitting on a plateau that averages about thirteen thousand feet in elevation, it has been relatively unspoiled by advancing material civilization (until just recently). Tibet is also one of the most mystical countries dominated by a religion called Lamaism that is a sophisticated combination of Hindu fatalism, Buddhist renunciation, and ancient Bon mysticism. The mysticism gives many mountains an important feature of sacredness. By Himalayan standards, Mount Heipori (sometimes spelled Hepo Ri) is not high, rising only about one thousand feet above the Samye Valley, but the base elevation of fourteen thousand feet makes it high for Americans who are acclimated to an average elevation of about five hundred feet.

In the eighth century when King Trisong Detsen wanted to propagate Buddhism among the Tibetan people, he invited the distinguished Indian Buddhist Padmasambhava (known as Guru Rinpoche) to come to Tibet and establish a monastery. Leaders of the traditional Bon religion objected to this, and according to traditional history, religious forces and demons thwarted Padmasambhava's progress. It was on Mount Heipori that he defeated these demons and established Buddhism in Tibet. The resulting Tibetan Buddhism incorporated much of the animistic Bon mysticism placing on Mount Heipori a combination of religious forces that made it an especially strong site of mystical power.

At the base of Mount Heipori, Padmasambhava started construction of Samye Monastery, and while it was being built, he lived in a cave on another nearby mountain called Chimpu. This mountain is higher than Heipori and more widely known because the cave and others nearby have become shrines for meditation and scenes of enlightenment for holy men.

I traveled to Tibet with a group sponsored by the Institute of Noetic Sciences for the purpose of exploring Eastern consciousness. The itinerary for this trip included a climb of Mount Chimpu, and a plan was established for me to sleep in one of the caves and climb to the summit of Chimpu. However, several complications interrupted this plan. One was the occupation of the caves by pilgrims, another was the reluctance of the chief guide to let anyone climb up the steep gravel slope that had been softened by rains, and finally there was a shortage of time. Three days had been lost from our itinerary because the Chinese embassy in Kathmandu, Nepal, held up the issuance of our visas causing us to miss the scheduled flight to Lhasa. That delay provided a wonderful opportunity to explore the Hindu and Buddhist influences on spirituality and consciousness in Nepal; however, it also shortened our time in Tibet.

The Chinese government had taken over Tibet in 1950 and attempted to destroy its traditional theocracy. They have now given up on trying to eliminate Tibetan religious life but have succeeded in replacing the government structure. Although China has relaxed its iron-hand domination, it is sensitive about authority and reacts aggressively to any criticism or defiance. Just before we arrived, a newspaper in Kathmandu had published an article critical of China's treatment of the exiled Dalai Lama, and in retaliation, the Chinese government closed their embassy.

While waiting for political channels to placate the Chinese embassy, our group stayed at the Happy Valley Guesthouse in a section of Kathmandu called Boudhanath. This is a pilgrim magnet because of the famous Boudha Stupa (Buddhist monument), which is the largest in Nepal. We visited Osley Gampa Monastery and had audience with Rinpoche Myngur, observed a cremation on the Bagmati River, toured Mother Theresa's Hospice, met with siddhas (Hindu hippies searching for enlightenment) at Pashapati Park, and traveled the harrowing road to Nagarkot in Eastern Nepal to interact with rural farmers and view the Himalaya Mountain Range. On the way to Nagarkot, we stopped at interesting places such as Baktapur, the old medieval capital of Nepal.

Climbing Higher

Boudha Stupa draped with prayer flags

The visit to Osley Gampa was especially interesting because it was the first mountain climbing experience for this trip. The monastery was built on a mountain about two thousand feet above Kathmandu Valley. The trail was 0steep, but all in our party made it. Rinpoche Myngur, who was the spiritual and administrative leader, met with us as a group and delivered a talk through an interpreter. His message was about how the key to happiness was divesting ourselves of material possession because they become encumbrances. Then we each had a private audience where he placed a silk prayer scarf (called *kata*) around our necks and gave a blessing. In the picture below, notice the material possession on the Rinpoche's arm—an expensive Rolex watch.

Answering Big Questions

Rinpoche Myngur giving kata blessing

On finally getting visas and rearranging flight schedules, we arrived in Lhasa and stayed at the Lhasa Hotel, which had been built by Holiday Inn and then taken over by the Chinese government. It was of good four-star quality and quite a contrast from other buildings in the area. The feature attraction in Lhasa is the Potala Palace, the former seat of the Dalai Lama theocracy, now a largely empty museum. Built in the seventeenth century, it was reported to be the largest building in the world (with more than one thousand rooms), and that title held until the Pentagon was built in Washington DC. An inspiring view of the Potala is available from the Jokhan Temple, which is the most sacred spot in Tibet and a major attraction for Tibetan Buddhists.

Climbing Higher

Potala from entrance gate

Getting to Samye from Lhasa is not difficult but does require fortitude. It is about one hundred miles southeast of Lhasa and can be approached in about two hours on one of the few paved roads in Tibet. However, the second leg of the trip, which also takes about two hours, requires crossing the Yarlung River with local pilgrims packed on a wooden barge that has to negotiate sandbars and other obstacles in the water (with occasional encounters). The final leg was an excruciatingly turbulent ride in a rugged Chinese truck that was endured with pleasure because the only alternative was hiking on foot. This adventure was not like going to Mount Everest; however, it provided firsthand experience of one of the most reputable sites of mysticism.

Answering Big Questions

Crossing the Yarlung River

My disappointment over being unable to climb to the top of Chimpu was overshadowed by the revelation that Heipori was even more sacred and could be a substitute. A local camp helper was recruited to act as a guide, and a plan was made for me to go with the local guide, Cheme, to Heipori the next morning while the rest of the group went in a truck to Chimpu.

While the main group left our tent camp before daylight for the trip to Chimpu, I waited until the sun came up to hike with Cheme through the settlement of Samye to the base of Heipori. It looked like a huge mound of rock and gravel forming a ridge with several peaks and felt the same way as we climbed. At the top of the first peak was a solid chorten about twenty feet tall. Chortens (similar to stupas) are of all sizes from a one-foot-high pile of rocks to a fifty-foot-high structure and usually contain religious relics that are symbols of the original Buddha or other holy men of the Buddhist faith. They are so numerous that it is rare for a chorten not to be visible either in a rural or urban area. Now, chortens are built as memorials to an important event and are considered power points for mystical energy.

The top of the main peak was festooned with prayer flags and housed a small stone temple and a bunker slightly off the summit. Cheme and I seemed to be the only people there—a refreshing situation since most holy places in Tibet are filled with local villagers, pilgrims, and holy people. The atmosphere also was refreshing because even though I had acclimatized to the high altitude, my nose and lungs tingled with a feeling of vitality despite the exhausting climb. The invigorating temperature, warm sunshine, and fresh air all seemed the most intense that I had experienced. This was a sharp contrast to the previous mountain I had climbed with our group at Drigung to witness a sky burial described later. That left a feeling of emotional drain subduing vitality.

In arranging for this climb, I made a point that I had a custom of gathering a few small rocks from the top of major mountains that I climbed, so as I was picking up a few pebbles, Cheme started a painstaking search of the area around the summit. After about fifteen minutes, he proudly displayed in his hand several small exquisite igneous-type rocks that seemed rather unusual for this sedimentary area. As a barefoot monk in a maroon robe approached, I realized that we were not alone. He took us into the bunker where Cheme handed him the rocks. The monk mumbled some sounds at them, at me, and then he handed the rocks to me. We exchanged the Buddhist "peace" sign, and with a feeling of renewed energy, Cheme and I prepared to descend. Later, I was informed that these were very special rocks containing divine power and should only be taken with a monk's blessing. How fortunate that a monk materialized at the needed time. I now keep the rocks secure and continue to treat them with respect.

Before descending, I took several pictures in an attempt to record this inspiring situation. To the southeast was the vast desolate sandy expanse of the Yarlung Valley. About three miles from Heipori was the lonely figure of a chorten that looked like a lighthouse rising out of a desert. To the northeast was the mountain range containing Chimpu, and to the west was an aerial view of Samye. This view of Samye was especially impressive because the mandala layout was clearly observable. In Tibet, mandalas are important symbols of the universality of existence and provide vehicles to assist in focusing on major aspects of Buddhism. Monks have traditionally spent much time making mandalas in various forms. During initiations, they are made on the ground out of different colored sand with a considerable amount of delicate labor, but then afterward, they are quickly destroyed symbolizing the impermanence of material things. When Samye was constructed hundreds of years ago, it was designed to have a ground plan that looked like a mandala. The central building, the Utse, represents the center of the universe with surrounding buildings, chortens, and gates representing elements of our physical environment. The spiritual environment where deities and demons compete is represented by the area outside the complex bounded by a stone wall.

Samye Monastery from Heipori

The Utse was intricately designed and constructed to represent not only the center of the universe but also the unity of universe components. The first three floors symbolize Tibetan, Chinese, and Indian cultures, respectively (all of the cultures known by them at that time). The third floor contains a balcony from which the monastery complex can be surveyed, and the fourth floor contains a sacred chapel. Of particular interest is a pair of twenty-foot-high golden Buddhas on the main floor. One is performing a bit of eroticism with a consort signifying the Tantric influence. While most schools of monastic life emphasize asceticism and celibacy, the Tantra school views physical pleasures as energy sources that can aid the progress toward enlightenment.

Answering Big Questions

Golden Buddhas in Samye Utse

We had numerous other adventures on this trip to Nepal and Tibet. In Nepal, they involved Hindu and Buddhist practices that had changed little from ancient times. Elaborate settings and inspiring ceremonies appealed to mystical forces considered true reality. They provided meaning for and acceptance of the hardships of daily life that seemed to satisfy the need to explain their feelings and difficult circumstances. Hindus were more accepting of their circumstances and more worshiping of deities than the Buddhist who relied on activities and rituals in an attempt to influence circumstances and prepare for their fate after earthly death.

In Tibet, Hinduism and Buddhism had been combined with the ancient animistic beliefs of Bon to produce what is referred to as Tibetan Buddhism or Lamaism. It uses sound and color extensively that create emotional arousal and sense of awe. At one time, about one-third of the population were monks, structured into a hierarchy with lamas at the top—a true theocracy ruled by the Dalai Lama and the Panchen Lama, who were considered reincarnations of Buddhist saints. The Cultural Revolution and dominance by the Chinese turned monks out of their monasteries and overthrew the theocracy, but the lama culture persisted and, with relaxation of Chinese control, is still visible. A good example of continuing traditional Tibetan culture is the sky burial ceremony. This we experienced in an adventure that involved climbing a sacred mountain about one hundred miles northeast of Lhasa.

We camped with tents in the Drigung Valley close to a small settlement called Mumba. To the north was Drigung Mountain on which an historic monastery was located about halfway up. From far and wide, families bring their deceased here for final disposition called sky burial. This is favored over cremation because the remains contribute more to nature, and firewood is conserved. After appropriate preparation and ceremony at the monastery, the oldest son carries the deceased usually at sunrise to a holy site on the mountaintop. Through special arrangements, we were allowed to attend a burial ceremony requiring ascent to the monastery in the middle of the night in order to join the procession at sunrise. The holy site consisted of a low circular stonewall about fifty feet in diameter enclosing a flat area lined with smooth surfaced rocks. On an adjacent field of about an acre in size was a flock of vultures that seemed to be sleeping. The nude body of the deceased was placed on the northern end of the stonewall, and after the son inspected the forehead for the hole from which the soul was supposed to have emerged, two men in white canvas robes proceeded to chop up the body with large machetes and spread the pieces over the rock area. Some type of signal was given to the vultures that scrambled into the rock circle and spent about five minutes devouring the flesh they picked off the bones. When the vultures had finished, they flew back to the adjacent field in a very organized manner. The white-clad men now picked up the bones and proceeded to smash them with mallets on a flat section of the wall. Barley powder was sprinkled on the bone fragments that were then thrown back onto the enclosed rock surface. Again, a signal was given to the vultures that scrambled into the rock circle, devoured the bone pieces, and respectfully returned to the field. It seems that they only eat bones that have been splintered and flavored with barley. In the meantime, food had been laid out on the west side of the circle, and we were invited to join in breakfast. Needless to say, we did not feel very hungry and started the trek back to camp.

Drigung sky burial site with vultures

Despite the Chinese domination and attempts to stamp out the ancient religious practices, Lamaism with its mystical culture continues and seems to be flourishing in rural areas. Sacred sites and ceremonies still evoke emotional arousal and sense of awe that stimulate feelings of "other worldly" supernatural presence. I felt this and recognized it as an emotional reaction to the sights, sounds, and activities, and I failed to experience any tangible indications of supernatural phenomena. For the local people participating in ceremonies, the emotional reactions reinforced and validated supernatural beliefs, and thus the ancient mysticism is perpetuated. Who am I to say they are only the result of emotional reaction?

Machu Picchu

Publicity of mystical sites in Peru was stimulated by Shirley MacLaine in 1983 with her book and movie *Out On a Limb*. Most famous is the Inca settlement built on the side of Machu Picchu Mountain (meaning "ancient peak" or "manly peak"). Remnants of the abandoned settlement are in a saddle between Machu Picchu and Huayna Picchu (young peak) at an altitude of 8,000 feet. These ruins are about 1,000 feet below the Machu Picchu summit and about 1,600 feet above the Urubamba River that forms a horseshoe around the two-peak mountain range. Nestled into a rugged section of the Andes Mountains, it is not surprising that the settlement ruins had escaped the public until 1911 when discovered by an American archaeologist looking for the traditional birthplace of the Inca people. It had even escaped detection by the Spanish conqueror Pizarro in the sixteenth century.

Answering Big Questions

Machu Picchu ancient ruins

The settlement was built in the fifteenth century as a royal retreat for the Inca ruler but was occupied for only about one hundred years. How and why it was built, how it was used, and why it was abandoned are not clearly known. However, there is no question about the astounding skills of its architects and builders and the importance of astronomical phenomena. A living area of about two hundred thatched roof buildings of precisely carved granite stone blocks is accompanied with an agricultural area, water supply, and assembly field. In the middle of the settlement that probably had a population of about one thousand, and on a raised mound is a column of stone called Intihuatana, Hitching Post of the Sun. It is perfectly aligned so that there is no shadow at the time of the solar equinox and is thought to be a ceremonial anchor spot for the sun. Other structures that must have also been used for ceremonial purposes are aligned so that the sun's rays enter in certain ways on certain solar events. Southwest of the settlement at a higher elevation on a saddle is Intipunku, the Sun Gate. At sunrise certain times of the year, light from the sun shines directly from the Sun Gate onto special spots in the settlement.

After an interesting tour of Lima, my wife and I flew to Cusco at an altitude of eleven thousand feet in the Andes Mountains. At one time, this was the capital of the Inca Empire and consequently was the scene of major conflict with the Spanish in the sixteenth century. Most impressive was Sacsayhuaman at an altitude of about fourteen thousand feet. This was a huge flat area the size of about ten football fields where annual assemblies were held. On the south was a complex of stone ruins that are the remains of temples and dwellings. The group we were with had arranged to meet with a shaman at a sacred site close by to participate in a Curandero ceremony.

The shamanic ceremony started with each of us placing on a ground cloth flowers, herbs, and trinkets that represent troubling things we wanted to get rid of. This was then placed in a fire and consumed in smoke accompanied with elaborate incantations. Later, each of us had the opportunity to stand individually in front of the shaman who, using bells and feathers, whisked away bad

Answering Big Questions

spirits and infirmaries. This personal treatment ended with a hit to the forehead and a loud chant. We all came away feeling shaken but renewed with energy and contentment. Aside from being tired, the only infirmary I had at that time was a degenerated disk in the spine, and since its pain continued, it was hard to evaluate the effectiveness of the ceremony.

From Cusco, we traveled by bus into the Urubamba Valley and visited the massive Inca fortress Ollantaytambo where the Spanish received their only major defeat in battle. As with other Inca settlements, a Temple of the Sun dominated from a high mound. Climbing to the top was exhilarating, and only the hardy in our group could do it.

The trip to Machu Picchu was a three-hour train ride winding through mountains and valleys to the village of Aguas Calientes on the Urabamba River about 8,000 feet above sea level at the base of Machu Picchu. We reached the Inca ruins by ascending about 1,600 feet laboriously in a rugged bus on a steep switchback road. We were fortunate to have a guide that could explain in detail the physical features of the ancient village and the activities and ceremonies of its residents. We were unfortunate to have cool damp clouds drifting through that gave a dreary feeling. The clouds dissipated late in the day allowing for brilliant sunset in the western sky over towering mountain peaks.

Switchback road to Machu Picchu ruins

The sky was clear the next morning, and the temperature was ideal for mountain climbing. Our guide said that climbing Huayna Picchu was too dangerous because of the previous day's rain and that the summit of Machu Picchu was restricted; however, a climb to the Sun Gate was in order. This is the sacred site close to the summit of Machu Picchu in a saddle on the ridgeline extending southeast from the summit. Its name was acquired because at certain times of the year the sun was seen from the village rising through the saddle. It also was important as the first place from which people hiking the Inca Trail from Cuzco could see the village. That was the only known access to the village back in its day. It was a moving experience to climb over the large stone steps and steep trail used by the Incas over four hundred years ago. At the saddle were the ruins of a stone gatehouse and a breathtaking view of the Inca Trail approach from the southwest. Access to the village would have been easy to defend from there.

To view the rugged Peruvian mountain peaks, walk in the paths of Inca warriors, touch astounding architectural achievements of Inca builders, and learn of their achievements and spiritual beliefs was an impressive experience. Their spiritual beliefs must have given them great power although not enough to survive. Was their belief system and its explanation solely the result of ancient animism, or was it based on special phenomena to which we do not have access? Aside from feelings of mystery and awe, I experienced no mystical activity. Does lack of mystical experience mean they do not really exist objectively?

Experiences in visiting mystical sites in Tibet, Nepal, and Peru aroused in me feelings that could be considered awe. Beautiful sounds, stimulating views, and mysterious activities contributed to eerie feelings of mysticism; however, my knowledge of the mechanism of human emotional reactions (see Chapter 6) provided me with natural explanations without the need to invoke supernatural factors. There must be more than a physical manifestation of a mystical force to account for the attraction. The question remains about whether supernatural explanations of mystical events beyond natural explanations are needed or are even valid. Could the supernatural explanation be designed into our brains by a transcendent force, or merely be a product of our thinking that has to "grope for straws" to "fill the gaps"? To answer these questions, let us look at how we make sense of our experiences and at the unique human ability to think about our own thinking process and to question the amazing products of that process.

Chapter 8
Personal Reality: Consciousness

It has already been established that people need to feel that their lives have purpose that gives meaning to their daily struggles toward goals and that there are explanations for their feelings, especially those associated with inspiration, mystery, and awe. Studies of history indicate that these needs, whether imparted by design or evolved by adaption, have been prevalent in human nature as far back as can be seen. Meeting them has formed cultures and advanced civilization, as well as contributed to wars and atrocities when people become overly proselytizing of their locally accepted explanation and use them for political purposes. Even when these needs seem to be met, questions linger because of the natural tendency to question the meaning of experiences and existence, and because of the fabulous ability of people to be aware of themselves and to be aware of thinking about these basic concerns. This takes us to the mental processes of thinking and awareness that relate brain, mind, spirit, and soul under the umbrella term, consciousness.

The terms "consciousness," "mind," "spirit," and "soul" are used in many different ways and sometimes interchangeably, but here specific definitions will be developed for each enabling explanation of the more accepted views of how people process information and form conclusions. This is not a comprehensive treatment of cognition or information processing because it focuses on mental processes used to find explanations for mysterious experiences and concerns.

All living things that react to their environment have some degree of consciousness. The controversial philosophy of panpsychism even claims that all things, including inanimate objects, have some form of consciousness or vitality. There is little controversy, however, that humans have a very sophisticated level of consciousness and that we are aware of having it and think about it; even think about thinking about it. Rene Descartes' ancient statement "I think, therefore I am" implies that thinking determines one's identity and even the world in which one exists. At this uniquely sophisticated level, people wonder why they are thinking, why they exist, where they came from, and where they are going, resulting in the concern referred to in the Introduction as the ontological imperative. They may set aside this sophisticated process because of more pressing needs such as survival, security, social relations, and esteem; however, such thinking has dominated societies and developed elaborate theories, speculations, and beliefs.

Prior to the development of objective science in the nineteenth century, consciousness was considered the property of philosophy and religion; and since its source and process was so mysterious, explanations were relegated to assumption, insight, and revelation. Many ancient religious beliefs that continue today view consciousness as God given and include a soul that in some form can be independent of the body and survive death. Religion uses a "top-down" approach (coming from an authoritative transcendent source) to support the role of deity that has recently been criticized as conflicting with research findings. Although the study of religion has now taken a backseat to studies of science, philosophy continues its involvement with religion by advancing theoretical concepts that attempt to incorporate new research results.

An early philosophical approach was idealism as proposed by the ancient Greek, Plato, and as promulgated by the British empiricist George Berkeley. It exists today in the view of consciousness as being the essence of reality — an idealistic monism. Our material world is the result of some form of mental activity. Eastern philosophy takes this further by suggesting that our perceptions of the material world are merely illusions of reality. In the seventeenth century, when more objective thinking was becoming popular, Rene Descartes proposed dualism: that consciousness was metaphysical and of a different nature than our physical body. Dualism continues today in many different forms and modifications. David Chalmers, who is a leader in consciousness studies, advocates a form of dualism that views mental processes as fundamental properties of the brain but separate from the brain.[1] Epiphenomenalism is a popular form of dualism that views consciousness as arising out of brain activity but completely dependent on the brain. Karl Popper and John Eccles take this view further by supporting a mind that arises from the brain and then feeds back to the brain, resulting in the concept of emergent interactionism whereby the mind can direct the brain.[2] In this view, consciousness is activity of the mind.

Other philosophers take a dim view of any theory providing a consciousness separate from the brain or a "ghost in the machine," proposing that only the physical or material has meaning.[3] A softer form of materialism called physicalism recognizes consciousness as a quasi-material product of the brain similar to the force of gravity or a property such as the color of an apple but still subject to scientific laws of physics. Particularly vocal about physicalism is Daniel Dennett who takes a strong approach using information about associated context to interpret reported subjective experiences—a process called heterophenomenology.[4] For example, a person's reported "redness" of an apple (called quale, a unit of subjective perception) would be analyzed considering surrounding colors, lighting, hunger, and etc. Consciousness is the system of qualia (plural for quale) currently being experienced and is influenced not only by the current situation but also by past experiences.

Much is now known about what consciousness does and how it functions, but little about how and why subjective experience arises out of physical neurological activity in the brain. How the perception of an apple's "redness" arises out of a person's sensory processes has defied explanation. This has become known as "the hard problem," a term coined by David Chalmers (1996) and considered a major continuing mystery (maybe forever beyond our grasp).

While philosophers are theorizing about how and why consciousness arises from the brain, scientists from many different fields have produced research results supporting aspects of a spectrum of consciousness theories. Many academic institutions have active study and research programs; for example, the Center for Consciousness Studies at the University of Arizona has held a number of international symposia emphasizing a role for quantum mechanics in explaining the "hard problem."[5] Stuart Hameroff, MD, has teamed up with Roger Penrose, PhD, to propose consciousness as the result of quantum effects in the small microtubules contained in brain neurons.[6] This is based on the popular quantum mechanics theory developed in physics that nicely explains observations of subatomic activity where particles are also waves that can exist in more than one place at the same time (superposition); that exist as multiple potentialities in a wave function until materialized (collapsed) by being observed or used, and that can be entangled (superimposed) with one another for immediate (nonlocal) interaction despite separation.

Quantum mechanics opened the door for many interesting studies of consciousness. Physicist John Wheeler from Princeton University claimed that consciousness reveals a fundamental constituency of our universe which can be considered information.[8] More recently from Princeton University are results of the Princeton Engineering Anomalies Research Laboratory's thirty years of studying human effects on physical objects which concluded that there must be another basic substance underlying matter and energy: information.[9] Other scientists are supporting consciousness as being a dynamic form of information that, in turn, is the basic constituent of energy and matter.[10]

Astrophysicist Bernard Haisch uses discoveries in physics to support an information system that is an intelligence underlying the universe, a form of consciousness or "great thought" that created reality.[11] Physicist Evan Walker proposed that our material universe results from the collapse of potentialities by a prehuman "quantum mind": "In the beginning was the Quantum Mind, a first cause, itself time independent and nonlocal, which created space-time and matter-energy."[7] This could be called Supermind or even God as the Great Architect that started things. It also could be called Great Observer who can intercede now at a quantum level. Thus, God could affect matter without violating physical laws.

Cosmologist Paul Davies has combined quantum mechanics with multiverse theory (ours is only one of many universes), string theory (nebulous multidimensional foundations of matter), and anthropic principle (our world is fine tuned for human life) in his book *The Goldilocks Enigma* (2006) to build a convincing case for consciousness consisting of mind that participates in the creative self-organizing formation of our existence. Consciousness is the central player in our evolving universe/multiverse. The implications of applying quantum mechanics and string theory to consciousness and our subjective experience of reality are rather spooky, but they provide support for the philosophy of idealism as well as dualism and physicalism.

Less spooky are implications about the hard problem coming from the relatively new field of neuroscience that combines disciplines such as neurology, biology, and psychology. Several researchers have written about how localized brain activity can explain consciousness processes,[12] and how the existence of unconscious processes imply that more is involved than just localized brain activity.[13] Brain surgeon Karl Pribram supports a dualistic theory by proposing that spiritual experience can be explained as a holographic type of resonance (a rippling effect from an overlapping of wave patterns) at the quantum level of neuron activity involving the whole brain and other body parts as well.[14] Neurobiologist Christof Koch has summarized the biological approach concluding that brain activity is necessary and sufficient for consciousness, but it is more than epiphenomenal because it feeds back to the brain. His neurological correlates of consciousness support the emergent interaction theory.[15] Other biologists such as Candace Pert[16] and Francis Collins[17] conclude that a personal consciousness is associated with a transcendent realm that relates to the concept of deity. Even the concept of soul as some survivable form of consciousness has been supported by physics studies of fractals (interference of overlapping wave patterns).[18]

The term soul is used here as an aspect of the mind that can exist independent of the body. It has been supported by research such as that started by psychiatrist Ian Stevenson at the University of Virginia about reincarnation[19] and that started by psychiatrist Raymond Moody about near-death experiences.[20] Also supportive are studies of remote viewing by physicist Russell Targ,[21] studies of mediumship by psychologist Gary Schwartz,[22] and studies of epigenetics and cell memory by biologist Bruce Lipton.[23] Respected neurobiologist Mario Beauregard has reported research indicating "there seems to be good reason to believe that mind, consciousness and self can continue when the brain no longer functions and that religious, spiritual, metaphysical experiences can happen when the brain is clinically dead."[24]

It must be recognized here that these concepts of soul are controversial. Many scientists and philosophers see no scientific justification in soul. This is summarized by cognitive psychologist Julien Musolino (2015) in his book *The Soul Fallacy*. He points out that most religions include belief in a soul that meets the important human need to avoid a meaningless life and complete annihilation upon death. Furthermore, he proposes that the personal comfort of possible continuation after death, and the social advantage of after-life accountability provided by belief in soul can now be provided by devoting effort to the "here and now" life rather than reliance on an assumed after-life existence. Whether or not it is real, a belief in some form of soul continues to help fill the existential need for immortality and continues to be basic in most religions.

Also controversial is the concept of spirit. Although not widely accepted, a number of psychologists have conducted reputable research supporting esoteric functions of consciousness. Dean Radin in his book *Entangled Minds* summarizes his and other research that supports emergent properties of consciousness that can extend beyond the brain and interact with both mental and physical events from a distance.[25] One example of this is the Global Consciousness Project that has demonstrated effects of the collective consciousness of many people independently perceiving a major event. This research has shown aspects of consciousness that can interact beyond the confines of the brain, supporting the concept of spirit.[26] Spirit as used here is an aspect of the mind that can send or receive extra-sensory signals external to the body. This is similar to "psi," a term used by many researchers that are convinced that extra-sensory perception (ESP) does exist even though it is difficult to control and is of questionable reliability.[26]

Studies of intercessory prayer have supported tangible effects of spirit.[27] Although some studies have failed to support external effects of prayer, there are now enough studies to support prayer as a spirit that exerts a force beyond a person's body.[28] This seems to be more the effect of personal intention rather than the intercession of a supernatural power.[29] While there is objective support for an interaction and effect of a personal spirit, similar support for a supernatural metaspirit such as deity is lacking. Deity has not been ruled out and continues to meet needs for acceptable explanations; however, support comes from subjective (personal feelings and experiences) rather than objective factors. Recent scientific research in psychology and neuroscience has been investigating indications of these subjective factors, but science in general has been unable to either support or disprove involvement of any form of supernatural power.

It is generally agreed that the waking state of consciousness people normally are in is optimal for managing activities of daily life. It is also agreed that people can experience altered states of consciousness (ASC) through sleep, daydreaming, meditation, chemical ingestion, and extreme emotional arousal or deprivation. Such experiences frequently give people the feeling of "other worldliness" and special access to information. During the 1960s and '70s, considerable research resulted from the possibility that ASC could provide special insight and access to alternate realities. However, experiments with mind-altering drugs, sensory deprivation, hypnosis, and psychedelic excitation have failed to confirm these possibilities.[30] Despite consensus that altering "normal" mental states decreases objective logicalness as discussed in Chapter 6, studies of ASC continue and show benefits of increased mental focus and creativity, potential explanations of some "paranormal" and anomalous phenomena, and effective therapy for some mental problems.[31]

This is by no means a detailed treatment of history, theory, and research about consciousness and cognitive processes. Voluminous writings are available reflecting a myriad of approaches from fantastic speculation steeped in colorful jargon to scientifically supported theories steeped in technical terminology. Susan Blackmore's book *Consciousness: An Introduction* presents an objective overview pointing out strengths and weaknesses of approaches,[32] while Jeffrey Mishlove's *Roots of Consciousness* present a comprehensive history pointing out studies of anomalous phenomena of continuing interest such as spiritual healing, psychokinesis (mental influence on physical objects), extra-sensory perception, and spirit communication.[33] Moreover, philosophers have written much about reality and mind supporting a full range of theories from naive materialism to sophisticated idealism. The treatment here is not complete, but it is a sufficient sampling to indicate a possible relationship between brain, mind, spirit, and soul, and to show a role for consciousness as the basis for the unique human goal of searching for explanations of perceived experiences that transcend the vicissitudes and shortcomings of the role supported by mundane secular authorities or the inflexible dogma of ecclesiastical authorities. When we consider differences between brain, mind, spirit, and soul, we are implying not only dualism but more accurately, pluralism—multiple natures with possible multiple realities. Theories of consciousness provide explanations of how people make sense of their feelings, experiences, and questions about ultimate reality. They can now be summarized in five categories arranged as follows from the most scientifically supported to the most speculative:

1. Materialism – Brain. Consciousness in humans is the activity of the mind. The mind is the operation of the brain. No brain, no mind, no consciousness. All aspects

of consciousness will eventually be explained as the physical operations of the brain.
2. Emergent Interactionism – Mind. More about consciousness can be explained by considering the mind to have creative ability that after emerging from the brain feeds back and influences brain functioning. The brain and the mind interact, but no brain, no mind.
3. Mentalism – Spirit. Some observed phenomena such as telepathy, psychokinesis, insight, and remote viewing can be explained by adding a capability of the mind to externally project and receive information or force through some presently unknown extra-sensory process. But still, no brain, no mind.
4. Supernatural – Soul. Prevalent in the history of most societies is a belief that some aspect of the mind can exist independent of the brain and can survive bodily death. This could not only explain mentalism but also aspects of such phenomena as near-death experiences, reincarnation, salvation, and spiritualism.
5. Idealism – Super Mind. Quantum mechanics, Eastern philosophy, and Western idealism explain the perceived world as the result of some form of ideation: personal, collective, or transcendent. Matter is a type of coalescence from some form of mentalism or consciousness that could be called supernatural, metaphysical, or divine. Personal consciousness is part of a universal consciousness.

(Note that the term metaphysical is many times used interchangeably with supernatural, but it also is used to refer to the philosophy of metaphysics which deals with the ultimate nature of reality, and also it is used sometimes referring to a divine power. To avoid confusion, this book will stick with the term supernatural even when the term metaphysical might be appropriate.)

There are objective research findings to support aspects of each of these theory categories, but none is conclusively supported or "proven." Any could be valid; any could be supplanted; however, the more inclusive a theory is at explaining consciousness, the weaker is its scientific support. Despite which theory one may subscribe to, the concept of consciousness helps to explain why and how people persist in striving for stimulation and challenge (Chapter 2), establishing and pursuing goals (Chapter 4), becoming influenced by emotional reactions (Chapter 6), and thinking about ultimate explanations. Anyone who has looked at the stars on a clear night and wondered about what was beyond their sight, or who has been mystified by watching a brilliant sunset, or who has been inspired by the sound of patriotic music, cannot help from experiencing emotional arousal and a desire for explanation that triggers the ontological imperative. That imperative can be ameliorated by knowing about these theoretical formulations providing potential explanations.

Consciousness provides for a personal view of reality that varies considerably among people. Each of the theories providing explanation continues because it helps to provide a personal reality that gives meaning, manageability, and coherence to human life. Shortcomings and conflicts usually exist in any view one has of personal reality, so questions of validity, universality, and ultimate nature either lurk in the background or become an important concern.

Could it be that these many different views support belief in supernatural force, supermind, or deity as a natural part of consciousness resulting from the common need for explanation and meaning of experiences and emotions as proposed in Chapter 6? One thing that seems common in consciousness processes across cultures is the concept of sacredness—that is, acceptance of and respect for something beyond or deeper than our current view of nature. It may be part of nature not yet known, or it may be of a different reality, something in a supernatural realm. In any case, our sense of awe stimulates a respect for the unknown "something" that stimulates a sense of sacredness. Since sacredness is attached to many mountains, it might be helpful to look for the sacred in sacred mountains. Many examples of sacred mountains are in the United States, and most are associated with lore originating with Native American tribes. Blanca Peak is revered by the Navajo Indians, and Mount Humphreys is especially revered by the Hopi people.

Chapter 9
Sacred Points

Blanca Peak

Even in today's materialism, there are many mountains in the United States that are considered sacred and still the sites of mystical experiences associated with belief in divine force. One example of this is a mountain peak looming up from the east side of the San Luis Valley in the Sangre de Cristo Range of southern Colorado. The Ute, Pueblo, and Tewa people have a long history of visiting the area frequently and holding the mountain sacred. The Navajos also include it in their culture and named the mountain Sisnaajini. It is now known as Sierra Blanca Peak or Mount Blanca, located in the south central part of Colorado, thirty miles northeast from the town of Alamosa.

View of Blanca Peak from the south

Climbing Higher

The Navajos believed holy people had transformed Sisnaajini into the eastern pillar of their sanctuary. The north was marked by Dibe Nitsaa near Durango, Colorado; the west by Dook'O'Oosliid near Flagstaff, Arizona; and the south by Tsoodzil near Grants, New Mexico. When Navajos die, their spirits return to heaven through one of these mountains. Sisnaajini now anchors the boundary for the Colorado counties of Alamosa, Costilla, and Huerfano and marks the southeastern edge of the Rocky Mountain peaks.

Getting to Mount Blanca is not difficult. We left from the motel in Alamosa about nine in the morning and drove to the base of the mountain range at an elevation of about eight thousand feet in twenty minutes. Since one of our vehicles was a four-wheel Land Cruiser, we were able to continue driving up the rocky trail about one more mile where we parked and started hiking. The Land Cruiser had to make two trips because our party consisted of seven men ranging in age from sixteen to seventy-two. The Land Cruiser belonged to a navy pilot from San Diego; the others had driven from St. Louis in two cars.

The plan was to climb four miles on a rocky trail to an elevation of 11,800 feet and camp at a scenic lake called Como. All went well for about three miles when rain clouds started threatening. The four younger members quickened their pace in an attempt to get to the base camp location before the clouds opened up. They made it, and two started back to help the older members who were caught in rain and were putting up a tent when they met. As the rain slackened and youth prevailed, everyone made it to the camp about four o'clock. Dry air and a little "fire starter" overcame the rain effects, so that a campfire was able to provide warmth and light for the evening's activities. Where the temperature had been about 90°F in Alamosa, it was about 45°F at Lake Como.

After organizing camp and woofing down hastily prepared freeze-dried delicacies, a few branches of sage were ignited at the campfire, and the group used a Native American custom to show respect for those that had used this location for spiritual purposes. Wafting into one's face the smoke from smoldering sage is a ceremony used by American Indian tribes before engaging in an important event to show respect and elicit the cooperation of nature. With the difficulty of the climb ahead and the threat of thunderstorms, we needed any available help, but more important was our desire to express appreciation for having gotten this far and to better experience the tranquil beauty of the surroundings. We also expressed thanks for mosquito repellant and drinking water filters.

It rained again during the night, so we did not get the early start that had been planned. But by eight, breakfasts and personal matters were completed, and with light daypacks, the group set out for the summit. Two miles of hiking along a discernible rocky trail with relatively gentle climbing past several lakes put us at the base of a steep slope of rocks and boulders. Rocky peaks towered in all directions. To the north was Ellingwood Peak (14,042 ft.), to the south was Little Bear Peak (14,037 ft.), to the east was Blanca Peak (14,345 ft.), all connected with high ridge lines. A ragged layer of clouds that obscured the tops of the peaks caused an enigmatic atmosphere. Looking back, we could see Crater Lake and Blue Lakes, but a ridgeline blocked the view of Lake Como. The pine trees at Lake Como had given way to sparse brush at Crater Lake, and now there were only rocks of all sizes with scree mixed in between boulders.

This was the tough part. We were able to follow a faint trail part of the way; however, even on that, it was necessary to scramble over loose talus and use hands to climb around boulders. It took more than an hour to reach the saddle at

Climbing Higher

about 13,800 feet on the ridge between Ellingwood and Blanca peaks. However, on reaching the ridge, feelings of exhaustion were subjugated by the astounding view. After looking at rocks only a couple of feet away for about an hour, it was traumatic to suddenly be looking at mountains, valleys, and plains that stretched out to infinity. The narrow ridgeline dropped off like a cliff on the other side, and I found myself clutching at the closest boulder while struggling with an uneasy dizziness. The feeling of height and insecurity was breathtaking. Forcing deep breaths helped the lungs, and dizziness was subdued by focusing on the rocky ridgeline and its distant peak. Looking up is more comfortable than looking down.

View from Blanca Peak summit of ridge to Ellingwood Peak

The final climb to the summit required free scaling techniques because of the rugged rock configurations. Loss of a foothold or handhold or a slip would be disastrous. As we struggled on to the summit, the clouds dissipated and the beam of sunshine and calm breeze made the thirty-eight-degree temperature comfortably warm. The older members of the group had planned to meditate for five minutes on the summit to experience any possible influence of native spirits. After sitting quietly for a few minutes, a large gust of cold wind hit the summit jolting all to the realization that dark clouds were building and that descent should begin quickly. Was that cold gust the native spirits telling us to start moving down if we wanted to return safely? Sometimes it is best not to linger long contemplating situations.

Descending seemed much more difficult than ascending. It was not as strenuous, but firm footing and balance required more effort, and the downward view was more distracting. Where it had taken about four hours to climb, it took about three hours to return. The last leg from Blue Lake to the base camp seemed much longer on the return than it had been earlier, but the sight of Lake Como was the third best view experienced that day; the first being the view from the Blanca Peak summit, and the second being the view of infinity from the Ellingwood–Blanca ridge.

The return to camp was not too soon, for as we once again were woofing down some freeze-dried delicacies, thunder and lightning started. This would not be the time to be close to Blanca Peak summit. Before taking cover in the tents, we took time to ignite what was left of the sage bundle, wafted the smoke, and expressed appreciation for having gotten to the top of Mount Blanca, departed at just the right time, and arrived safely at camp. Now it could rain, and the spirits be at rest.

And that it was. Showers and thunderstorms continued, and no one climbed Mount Blanca for the next few days.

Nature cooperated with us, though, because we were able to break camp the next morning and make it back to the motel in Alamosa by about five in the afternoon. The hike from Lake Como to where the Land Cruiser was parked was without untoward event, but it was tough. Going downhill used special unconditioned muscles that compounded the difficulty of finding good footing on loose rocks. While the three older members were struggling with their packs and feet, three of the younger members moved down all the way to the trailhead to save the Land Cruiser from making two trips. The navy pilot was worried about getting his vehicle out of the rocks before the next rainstorm, so he too surged ahead. When he determined that the vehicle was safe, he hiked (jogged) back to help the older members. He even shouldered one of their packs and some of their other equipment. Of course, everyone knows that navy pilots are invincible.

It was about six when seven weary mountain climbers (having showered, shaved, etc.) assembled in the motel Jacuzzi with bottles of champagne and a case of beer. Stories and congratulations were exchanged boisterously, and conflicting comments were made about native spirits and navy pilots, but all agreed that it is good to have both of them on your side. Did native spirits influence the events, or were the feelings of influence merely coincidences interpreted with conscious or subconscious interests in features considered sacred? More investigation was needed.

Humphreys Peak

The western anchor for the Navajo sanctuary is another mountain in the United States that has acquired the reputation of being sacred. This is Dook'O'Oosaliid now known as San Francisco Mountain consisting of several peaks formed by an ancient volcano. This area is part of the Coconino National Forest located just north of Flagstaff, Arizona. The tallest is Humphreys Peak—the highest point in Arizona with a summit at 12,633 feet. It is connected by a saddle to the next highest peak, Agassiz with a summit at 12,356 feet. The entire range is a focal point of sacredness for the Hopi people who call it Navatukaovi.

Agassiz Peak has been involved in great controversy that continues even after a US Supreme Court decision that allowed the construction of a ski slope on the west side. The Hopi still actively oppose this use of their sacred area. They believe that spirits called *katsinas* living on the mountain slopes in spots called *kivas* control forces of nature. In addition to guarding vegetation that yields medicinal herbs, katsinas descend at certain times of the year into the villages and participate in ceremonies and celebrations. They can become manifest in special people and dolls. Out of respect for the Hopi, the National Forest Service enforces strict restrictions to designated trails and areas while the Hopi are allowed access to their native sites.

In preparation for experiencing this sacred area, JC, Steve, and I made extensive attempts to arrange for a Hopi that would guide us up the mountain allowing us to visit sacred sites. When this met with no success, we planned to spend a couple of days on the Hopi Reservation about ninety miles northeast of the mountain to try further. We stayed in the Hopi Cultural Center motel at the village of Second Mesa and had interesting discussions with local people. The legal officer at the Hopi tribe office was particularly gracious, but he was more concerned with countering efforts to expand the ski slope on Agassiz Peak and water rights than with helping us visit Hopi areas on the mountain. Therefore, we completed plans for our expedition without their local help.

The San Francisco Peaks form a horseshoe around a volcanic crater with a lower rim on the northeast side. Since the Hopi Nation resides to the east, that side of the peaks is most sacred to them. Many of the devout still start the day by facing to the mountain and paying homage. Fortunately, there is an authorized campground called Lockett Meadow on the eastern slope at an altitude of 8,600 feet accessible by a rugged dirt road. We decided to camp there two days and explore the eastern approach to Humphreys Peak. For the summit climb, we planned to use the Humphreys Trail that starts at the base of the Arizona Snow bowl ski slope on the west side of Agassiz Peak. That route requires a climb of about 3,100 feet vertically for a distance of about 4.5 miles taking about three hours. Not the way the Hopi did it, but convenient and time effective.

It was just at sunset when we got camp set up at Lockett Meadow, providing perfect timing for a twilight hike up the inner basin trail to what is left of the eastern rim of the crater and through sacred Hopi territory. It may have been wind rustling the tall aspen trees, the dancing shadows of moonlight, or the faint howls of lonely animals, but all three of us felt the presence of some unexplained force. As we returned to camp, the wind became bitingly cold, so it was with comfortable anticipation that we lit the campfire and settled down to preparing freeze-dried dinner. We had not seen a katsina (also called kachina) or kiva, but we must have been close, and a longer hike in tomorrow's daylight might be more successful.

After breakfast the next morning, we started up the Inner Basin Trail and, in about an hour, reached a ridgeline that overlooked the crater with Agassiz and Humphreys peaks looming up on the other side. The elevation was about 9,500 feet. At this point, JC was having some trouble breathing and decided to return to camp while Steve and I explored further. The trail continued ascending around the southwestern rim, alternating between open grass fields and dense aspen forests. It was just east of Fremont Peak where the Inner Basin Trail joins the Weatherford Trail that we decided to turn back and check on JC. It had been an exhilarating hike, but no sign of kiva or kachina. The following morning, we did some more exploring before breaking camp and driving to the northwest side of Flagstaff. There we swallowed our pride and checked into a motel that was conveniently located on the road to the Arizona Snow Bowl sky slope on Agassiz Peak.

Humphreys Peak from Inner Basin Trail

Because of his breathing and heart palpitation on the Inner Basin Trail, JC decided not to attempt the summit climb, so he acted as chauffer and drove us to the Snow Bowl parking lot where the Humphreys Peak Trail starts at an altitude of 9,200 feet. He was going to visit the Lowell Observatory while Steve and I represented him at the summit.

The Humphreys Trail was easy to follow, and for the first hour, we ascended on a gently rising switchback trail through a dense forest of pine and aspen. After passing the tree line, the trail was steeper with rocks of all sizes. It was probably about ten o'clock when we reached the saddle on a ridge between Agassiz and Humphreys peaks. The trail north along the ridgeline was difficult because of large rocks and boulders that dominated the route. Three false summits made this part of the climb seem excessively long; however, once on the real summit, all was well. To the north at a distance, the Grand Canyon was visible, to the east were Sunset Crater and the Painted Desert, and to the west was the vast Coconino Plateau. To the south was Agassiz Peak with parts of Flagstaff visible around it. The horseshoe configuration of the peaks was clearly seen with a center on the Inner Basin remnant of the ancient volcano crater.

View from Humphreys Peak summit to east over the Inner Basin

The relatively flat area of the summit was about one-third of an acre with several stonewalls that served as wind shelters. Ten other climbers were already there, many in a jovial mood, so all enjoyed friendship. Wind was light, sky was clear, and sun was warm. Steve and I joined the others in sharing food items and mountain climbing stories. Since August was a time for afternoon storms, we stayed only about thirty minutes before starting the return trip.

Going down was difficult for me because I had to overcome old habits. This was the first climb I had been on since having a knee replaced, and I kept forgetting that my right leg would not bend as far as it used to. Climbing up was not so bad since the steps were rather deliberate, and I adjusted to leading with the left leg that bent all right. But now, going down required faster footwork and hard concentration to lead with the right foot. The pain of bending an artificial knee too far is quite distracting. We made it back to the trailhead in less than three hours, and JC was there with the van to whisk us back to the motel and the comforts of civilization.

Before returning to our homes, we visited many other sacred sites in the area. Notable were Sunset Crater, which was about ten miles east of Humphreys Peak and Walnut Canyon, which was about ten miles south. These are sacred to people that trace ancestors to the Anasazi, Pueblo, or Sinagua tribes. Although exact dates and tribe composition are unknown, these sites were home to ancient people intermittently from the first through the twelfth centuries. Now, many descendants periodically visit these sites because they believe that the spirits of their ancestors are there and desire respect and acknowledgment. While we were at the Walnut Canyon Visitors Center, a Sinagua couple checked in for permission to visit the ancient cave dwellings. They had pouches of corn and eagle feathers to leave for the spirits. Unfortunately, we were not allowed the same privilege.

More impressive was Chaco Canyon in New Mexico. Anasazis and their descendants developed elaborate settlements here over a period from the first until around the thirteenth centuries. Their "great houses" were like our large apartment building complexes with up to nine hundred rooms (other settlements to the north were even larger). Their society was something of a theocracy since its culture was dominated by belief in spirits of nature and ancestors. All settlements had large structures called kivas that served as ceremonial centers and clubs, and usually they contained a hole into the ground through which spirits emerge. While exploring the Una Vida great house, we met a couple that was visiting and paying homage to what they thought was their ancestral home. They said they were from the Pueblo people and that this was their religion. We stayed in that area into the night and, after watching a colorful and inspiring sunset, felt the eerie presence of what could have been the respected spirits. Unexplained sounds contributed to this experience; however, they may have come from distant animals of some sort.

We had now visited two sacred mountains and several other sites steeped in lore about divine spirits and supernatural force. At many of them, each of us experienced feelings of mystery, awe, and supernatural presence, but no tangible activities that would support stories of physical manifestations of spiritual forces. Could it be that such stories are the result only of expectation or of anticipating perceived manifestations of sacred spirits that are part of a local belief system or culture? Or could they result from the appeal of mysticism resulting from an innate tendency to attribute supernatural explanations to phenomena unexplained by objective knowledge? Or is there really a supernatural or unknown natural force behind this lore? We are looking for the sacred in sacred mountains—sacred phenomena beyond assumption, speculation, and belief.

Chapter 10
Ultimate Reality: Beyond Ourselves

To find the sacred in sacred mountains and the importance of such an endeavor, we must move from personal meaning to a generalized or universal meaning, and transition from the personal appeal of arousal and excitement, goal pursuit, emotional reaction, and mental processes into a realm of reality beyond the personal realm. This involves explanations that extend beyond our individual consciousness, beyond ourselves. Research started in the 1950s showed that people are, by nature, scientists and naturally search for explanations of their experiences and those of other people.[1] Underlying this is the need to be able to predict with reasonable certainty what is going to happen as well as the need for meaning and cause of experiences. The immediate (proximate) cause is usually readily available; however, the cause of awe, mystery, and mysticism is not readily available and requires looking beyond immediate experience for a deeper (distal) cause.

Research showed that since people have a strong need to know reasons for their experiences, they will go to extremes in attributing causes.[2] Natural explanations of science have always had limitations, so when natural explanations are not available, supernatural explanations were frequently invoked to fill the gap going beyond a personal immediate view of reality. Before geology, meteorology, and physics had provided natural explanations for many of the forces of nature on which people were so dependent, it was reasonable that the supernatural explanations of animism (belief that supernatural forces resided in nature) would be developed as discussed in Chapter 6. It was a satisfactory and convenient way to account for unexplainable observations and emotions, and for the mysterious source of the environment. Some aspects of animism carry over into many religions and belief systems of today. High-altitude mountains still stimulate a sense of mystery and awe, and still are held in reverence for many people as being associated with mysterious divine powers. People living close to mountains are quite proud of lore about the associated supernatural forces or spirits, and derive comfort and benefit from perpetuating supporting beliefs. Remnants of animism still fill in many gaps left by science.

Science has given us knowledge about our environment that has improved health and longevity, provided marvelous technology, and produced unparalleled comforts. This is not enough, though, for thinking people. They also want knowledge about where they came from, why they are here, and where they are going. This is an extension of the need to make sense of experiences and emotions described in Chapter 8 as the process of searching for distal cause, ultimate explanation, ultimate reality, or ultimate truth. The term "ultimate concerns" has been applied to this search.[3] The term ontological imperative was proposed in the Introduction to describe the source of this search, which also is a source of uncertainty and ambiguity because of its ongoing never complete nature. People are uncomfortable with ambiguity, want a feeling of control and predictability, and have a natural tendency to attribute cause to observed phenomena. Science reveals cause reliably for phenomena that can be studied objectively with results that recur under the same situations (replicable) and are agreed to by all observers (consensual), but cannot answer questions about ultimate concerns that are beyond the reach of objective research. Religion, on the other hand, directly answers ultimate questions by organizing subjective explanations in an acceptable way using personal experience, revelation, insight, and faith in established beliefs.

Ultimate reality is defined here as the most basic nature of our existence and its original cause. Its study is something of an oxymoron because if it is ultimate, it is beyond our knowledge and grasp. Wesley Wildman (2017) at Boston University shows that the term is normally used to focus on the most ultimate cause we can grasp which becomes either creative deity or spontaneous evolution. The origin of neither can be studied objectively because they both are beyond scientific investigation (and maybe beyond our grasp); but, the impact of this concern has been important for the development of civilization, and attempts at objective study are now being made. Recent information from the study of history and science help explain the nature of sacredness and its relation to our search for distal cause--ultimate reality.

Studies of history and anthropology indicate the importance of this concern about ultimate reality as a starting place for religion. It was present in the earliest known records of human activity. Exercising the concern has facilitated social adaption and phylogenetic (human species) development of religions over the ages.[4] Studies of psychology and sociology indicate that this concern also involves religious development over the life span of individuals, and can be considered ontogenetic (individual) development.[5] So, this concern is important for the development of civilization as well as of individuals. The term "spirituality" nicely captures the nature and ramifications of this concern at a level more basic than religion.

Ubiquitous Spirituality

The further astronomers can look out in space, the more they see; and the further physicists can look into the atom, the more they see. The limits of outer space, the "macrocosm," studied by astronomers and the limits of inner space, the "microcosm," studied by subatomic physicists expand with the increase in observational capabilities, indicating that space and time extend farther than what is now observable and may even be infinite or eternal.[6] (Logic supports the idea that in a realm of infinity, not only could anything exist, but somewhere everything probably does exist.)

A reasonable conclusion is that there is more than what is now known, maybe even realities beyond our comprehension. Moreover, people make this observation from their own experiences even when not aware of the sophisticated scientific findings and theorizing. That there must be something beyond our personal physical "life space" was popularized by psychologist Carl Rogers (1961) who found it useful in assisting people wanting help in managing stresses of life. This gets us into a realm beyond science that opens a door to possible supernaturalism. Whether there is or is not a supernatural reality beyond our proximate reality, people seem to have a need for such a belief, or at least a provision for such a possibility.

Psychiatrist Robert Cloninger effectively supported "self-transcendence" as a personality characteristic innate to all of us. This is a desire to reach out beyond oneself and learn about the mysterious realm of the unknown.[7] The ontological imperative, then, pushes that person to attribute cause for the desire. Attribution theory research supports our natural propensity to attribute cause to the things we experience, and a pervasive question concerns the cause of our existence. How did it start and why do we persist in struggling through hardships and discomforts for it to continue? The term "perennial philosophy" captures what seems to be a universal attempt to provide answers to these questions by religions, philosophies, and cultural traditions that have developed a common thread positing an ultimate goal of transcending our current state of existence.[8]

Behavioral geneticist Dean Hamer has actually located activity in the brain indicating that even though existence may be a dominant concern, this desire to experience and understand esoteric self-transcendence is genetically based and inherent in our mental processes.[9] Neurobiologist Kevin Nelson[10] and radiologist Andrew Newberg[11] have independently drawn similar conclusions about physiological brain activity associated with spiritual experiences. It should be noted here that even though many spiritual experiences have been related to abnormal brain activity such as seizures, oxygen deprivation, and chemical alteration, the possibility is not ruled out for the occurrence of special insight or contact with some kind of supernatural "mind stuff" in a transcendent realm. However, biochemist Stuart Kaufman in his bestselling book *Reinventing the Sacred* (2008) showed how the naturally occurring process of self-organization leads to the emergence of a human complexity that gives rise to a sense of sacredness without need for a supernatural force or a transcendent realm. Abrahamic religions (Judaism, Christianity, Islam) are not yet ready to entertain these questions; although many growing religious movements such as Ethical Society, Universal Unitarian Church, Theosophy, and Religious Naturalism recognize a sacredness arising from awe and beauty in nature without the constraints of traditional religion.[12]

With the growing recognition of the continual increase in complexity and sophistication of our known universe and its living organisms, emergence has become a popular topic for both researchers and philosophers. Nancy Adams who is the wife and colleague of astrophysicist Joel Primack has summarized research about emergence in her book, *A God That Could Be Real* (2015). She defined emergence as the creation of something new and more than the sum of its parts when complexity has increased enough, and she shows how spirituality emerged from the human mind as the brain complexity increased, and that the concept of God emerged from the resulting species-wide collective development of human consciousness. It seems that just as the mind emerged from the increased complexity of the brain, it is possible that the deity/deities emerged from increased complexity of the mind. This is one example of many theories about an ultimate reality behind fundamental human motivation that are becoming more and more popular because of the growing population dissatisfied with the unyielding dogma of traditional religions. Many people now claim to be "spiritual but not religious."

Another example of a reputable system proposed by notable philosophers and researchers is panentheism that is associated with process theology. This has been explained by Philip Clayton and Stephen Knapp (2011) as viewing God as the ultimate Creator that is continuing to develop with the development of humans. Theistically oriented people that dislike questionable supernatural claims of religions are being attracted to such belief systems because they are more accommodating of research findings and more consistent with personal experiences.

Even Christian theologians are developing ways to make religious dogma more compatible with experience and science findings. A good example of this is the work of the noted theologian Gordon Kaufman (2006) that calls for thinking of God not as the creator, but as the mysterious creativity that made possible the emergence and development of humans. This Creativity is not an explanation of the ultimate mystery of existence but is a descriptive term for the process. In his book, *Jesus and Creativity*, he summarizes shortcomings in the dualistic picture of Jesus (material and divine) and emphasizes the teachings that were so radical at that time. At the present time a new culture is needed based on Jesus's radical teachings to subdue instincts of self-preservation and self-defense with a spirit of self-sacrifice for the well-being of humanity that can dominate our personal and organizational lives. This does not negate Jesus's divinity, but makes it a part of the ultimate mystery of creativity.

Even though use of the term spirituality seems new, its ubiquitous nature can be traced to ancient history. An example of this is the ancient movement of Freemasonry which traces its history to King Solomon three thousand years ago. It developed as a major organization after the seventeenth century Enlightenment when many people were attempting to shake the shackles of ecclesiastical dogma and political dominance that were creating hardships and subduing a sense of freedom and advancement. It has become a major fraternal organization. Its only dogma is that there is a master Great Architect of the universe who exemplifies truth. Truth is symbolized as the "Master's Word" and a major goal is attainment of knowledge about the Master and the Master's Word. Freemasonry uses truth in two different ways. One as a tenet advocating honesty and correctness, and the other as ultimate reality symbolized as the Master's Word which has been lost and is the object of search. Because of the allusive nature of the ultimate reality of truth, allegories and symbols with rituals and ceremonies are used that provide structure for abstract ideas making the pursuit enjoyable and meaningful. There are many interpretations about the meanings of the symbols and rituals providing a varied and tolerant approach to divinity. Even though these interpretations are varied because of an oral tradition, an authoritative summary was assembled by Albert Mackey (1921) in *An Encyclopedia of Freemasonry* that is still in use.

Since activity is emphasized in Freemasonry, one interpretation of its three-degree initiation process categorizes three levels of development. First is the earthly pursuit of wisdom, strength, and beauty that enables recognition of a need for something beyond the self. Second is the mental pursuit of knowledge about this need, climbing through a winding staircase of information that leads to understanding, performance, and reverence. The third level, then, is the recognition of the finitude of life on earth and importance of the search for truth and its source—ultimate reality. The attraction of Freemasonry through the years is an example of the universality of this search and the attractions of associated activities such as comradery, fraternity, pageantry, charity, and feeling of constructiveness.

The term spirituality is increasing in stature at the present time because of growing dissatisfaction with both institutionalized religion and its opposite, militant atheism. It allows treatment of religious concepts in conjunction with objective findings of history and science without the limitations of dogma, religious faith, or scientism (worship of science). Much is now being published about spirituality; however, most is of esoteric or inspirational nature. The major textbook *Psychology of Religion* devotes a few paragraphs in the first two chapters about spirituality being an aspect of religion and in a later chapter about its role in mysticism, but little about it as a basic psychological characteristic of people.[13] More detailed information about spirituality and its relationship to religion has been presented in the *Handbook of the Psychology of Religion and Spirituality*[14] and *Psychology, Religion, and Spirituality*.[15] The reader is referred to these text-books for additional details and support. Although the information presented here is brief and selective, it probably is representative of reputable information and is consistent with other reports of scientifically based research results.

Spirituality has been defined and measured in many ways. One widely used measure focuses human activities such as the seeking of meaning, purpose, and transcendence.[16] Other measures were developed using standard statistical psychometric techniques focusing on characteristics of personality related to common aspects of leading spiritual traditions. Studies using these measures have supported spirituality as being an independent personality factor related to other established personality factors and spiritual activities.[17] As a personality factor, it has been related to health, longevity, religious activity,[18] and feelings of well-being.[19] Neuroscientist D. F. Swaab (2014) in *We Are Our Brains* summarized supporting research about spirituality and concludes that it is a characteristic that everyone has to a variable degree.

More directly, though, spirituality can be defined as an attitude of concern about an unknown realm that transcends our personal selves. Some people are more conscious of this concern than are others. Some accept a belief about it on faith in an established religion or belief system. Some set it completely aside. But throughout history it has been a major force. "Spiritual intelligence" has been proposed as the ability to recognize this basic need and to effectively deal with it.[20] Attempts to obtain replicable information about the validity of spiritual phenomena is an ongoing effort that could be called "ontological research," with "ontological engineering" being attempts to apply this information for oneself and for the benefit of other people. These are aspects of spirituality that combine science, philosophy, and religion.

Despite the tremendous capabilities of human intelligence, they are limited, and there is a tendency for individuals to latch on to the products of their limited personal experience and handed down information, and to fixate on them for guidance and answers to every day questions as well as for questions of ultimate concerns such as meaning in life and the nature of ultimate reality. These questions about ultimate concerns have been studied in many different fields. The only major conclusion from science (that can be objectively supported) is that the goal of human existence is to exist and to further existence by pursuing what seems most useful for continued existence, happiness and reproduction. Spirituality causes us to think that there must be something more. Proposals are limited only by the extent to which it is considered. Some of the proposed goals receiving objective support include self-enhancement, epigenetic emergence, increasing complexity, development of potential, and personal flourishing, none of which require a transcendent deity. Fulfillment, though, has been so difficult that most cultures have historically supported a deity-like supernatural realm with transcendent goals that could be interpreted as doing God's will, growing closer to a deity, pursuing ultimate creative force, developing through esoteric reincarnation, or unfolding divinely. These ultimate goals grow out of the goal orientation discussed in Chapter 4 and need for a sense of purpose and meaning discussed in Appendix A.

Many answers to ultimate concerns come from the field of philosophy that mediates between science and religion. Philosopher Owen Flanagan (2009) has made a commendable attempt to show that supernaturalism is not necessary with his concept of eudaimonic flourishing (see eudaimonia in Chapter 4). In his book, *The Really Hard Problem*, Flanagan proposes that if the hard problem about consciousness is how subjective experience arises from neurological brain activity, the "really hard problem" is how people are conscious of meaning in an apparently meaningless material world. From his work with neuroscience, he concludes that meaning, spirituality, and transcendence are part of nature and are best met by flourishing—that is, by living the "good life," experiencing beauty and awe, accepting ultimate explanations as possible myths, having a focus outside one's self, and feeling meaningful and constructive.

Philosopher Loyal Rue in his widely read book, *Religion is Not About God* (2006), provides support for a general theory of religion based on natural factors that provide personal wholeness and social coherence as unique human needs. This is close to the concept presented here about spirituality, and he proposes this as the universal factor underlying most religions.

Psychologist Gordon Allport's concept of "religious sentiment" (1955, p 93) captures this tendency and has expanded it to include "quest," which emphasizes the search for a framework of belief that provides for an ultimate goal.[21] Most research about religious belief focuses on the content or end product of belief as opposed to the search or seeking process. Seeking requires openness to new information and ideas while maintaining sufficient focus and faith to prevent unproductive confusion and vacillation. It is increasingly being recognized that spirituality is basically an ongoing striving process—a quest.

A notable attempt to restore spirituality as an essential human striving is the publication of *Spiritual Evolution* by the famous Harvard medical researcher and psychiatrist George Vaillant (2009) who has spent a career studying human development and health. He points out how spirituality evolves as a process for stimulating positive emotion through three avenues: biologically over millions of years of brain development, culturally over thousands of years of social development (phylogenetic), and individually over a person's lifetime of personal adjustment (ontogenetic). He concludes that people are hardwired to generate positive emotions which are the source of our essential spiritual being and cultural progress.

Dimensions of Human Spirituality

Although spirituality is proposed here as a universal human characteristic, it is manifest in many different ways resulting in many forms of commitment. In addition to the impact of varied experiential and social factors, genetic and biological mechanisms have been found to affect the spiritual activity of individuals. Among animal species, humans have a very sophisticated mental capability that seems to be unique. This is the tendency to think abstractly about what is beyond immediate experience and to be concerned about meaning, purpose, the unknown, and the hereafter. Psychologist Rollo May described this as the "human dilemma" which is a major source of anxiety that can be treated with existential therapy.[22] Since existence comes first, many people become bogged down in their own personal immediate needs, fears, desires, and pleasures to such an extent that they suppress their sophisticated mental capabilities and avoid thinking about these abstract topics. As psychiatrist Erich Fromm explained in his concept of "existential dichotomy," we have a tendency to subjugate our higher human creative abilities and needs in order to meet our animal needs resulting in an "existential dilemma—conflict between basic physical needs and higher intellectual needs."[23] For Dr. Fromm, this is a major source of anxiety and other mental health problems.

A useful explanation of spiritual activity involves filling one's personal needs according to their immediacy. These range from Maslow's "deficiency needs"—physical sustenance, security, social relations, and self-esteem—to actualizing "metaneeds" such as beauty, order, justice, and meaning.[24] (see Chapter 4.) Any of these needs may exert a force on the individual; however, thought and action are frequently dominated by the deficiency needs because of the requirements of daily living. This is a basic dimension where filling spiritual needs is secondary activity and frequently experienced as insatiable yearning for nebulous satisfaction. It may be relegated to the unconscious mind.

When deficiency needs are met sufficiently that a person can devote more thought and activity to metaneeds involving helping others and benefiting society, focus can be made on a second dimension. This involves the application of spirituality and requires investment in a conceptual belief system that provides a foundation for action benefiting others as well as oneself. For most people, an already established system is accepted because of cultural and social experiences. The activity was called ontological engineering.

A third dimension involves making one's belief system sensible and compatible with experience and knowledge. Activity involves recognizing shortcomings in established belief systems and in recognizing conflicts between them and other information. Attempts are made to define and operationalize (define in concrete measurable ways) concepts so that hypotheses can be formulated and tested, and information developed that can be used for the benefit of oneself and others. This is a refinement that was called ontological research.

The most abstract or fourth dimension involves recognition that our cognitive ability, understanding, and knowledge are limited and that there is a vast unknown that extends beyond the observable physical environment and may contain some form of transcendent or supernatural realm. This was exemplified in a 1949 letter by Albert Einstein who wrote, "I do not share the crusading spirit of the professional atheist. I prefer an attitude of humility corresponding to the weakness of our intellectual understanding of nature and of our own being."[25] Activity in this dimension involves a need to accommodate that realm, to pursue knowledge of it, to experience it, to approach it, to contribute to it, and to contribute it to society. For success, it requires not only dedicated spirituality but also creativity, charisma, and a variety of abilities.

Dimensions of Spirituality

1. Existence: Filling one's own needs
2. Engineering: Helping others fill needs
3. Research: Organizing information to facilitate need fullfillment
4. Ideation: Developing resources

Dimensions 2, 3, and 4 involve activities that Maslow referred to as actualizing. He also provided for a difference between nontranscendent and transcendent actualizers in writings published in 1971. The difference is that activity of the transcendent actualizers is focused on the dimension 4 where activities have not been selling well in our society. Involvement does not make much money, so those people that pursue them must have independent resources as well as a strong conviction of the importance. Despite our society's dominance with the dimension 1, the others exert a force that may be out of conscious awareness, stored in the unconscious mind. The large percentage of the US population that support established religions are focusing on dimensions 1 and 2 because they are trying to meet metaneeds by using a specific belief system and accept that system's application and meaning. Thus, they recognize a higher-level metaneed and are attempting to fill it and help others. The conceptualization, development, and pursuit of transcendent needs dominate dimension 3 activities. For people focusing on dimension 4, ideation (focus on underlying ideas) overrides worship and faith, and the mechanisms of religious practice become flexible and even superficial.[26] It seems that people investing to some degree in all dimensions have greatest well-being, but the investment of activity and process seems to be much more important than the success or end product.

This structure of spirituality is fairly consistent with results of extensive research by Lawrence Kohlberg (1984) about moral development and James Fowler (1995) about religious faith development, except that their structure is based on sequential stages rather than dimensions. The term "dimension" is used here to avoid a qualitative judgment about levels or stages of development, because dimensions coexist as opposed to being sequential.[27] This is illustrated by newborn infants that reach out to explore and learn even when physical needs are met and before they become aware of rewards and punishments.[28] There are many theories about levels of moral or spiritual development culminating with an ultimate stage,[29] but it must be emphasized that these ultimate levels can exist in anyone and may even be prepotent to such an extent that physical needs or other prior sequential stages are overridden. Spirituality may lie dormant in one person and be a dominating activity in another person, but it is inherent either consciously or subconsciously and is an unavoidable force behind development of religious types of belief systems. All dimensions exist in everyone, but the degree to which they are manifested is quite varied.

Personal Religion

When an individual develops or acquires a sense of spirituality that is well enough conceptualized to elicit faith and to be shared with others, it comes under the general term "religion." Religion is defined here as an organized belief system about a metaphysical or supernatural force that has influenced and/or is influencing human existence, and that can be shared with others. Because of the elusive nature of ultimate concerns, people turn to others that seem to have more insight and knowledge than they do. Adults frequently rely on childhood learning. Also, people tend to accept beliefs of their own social group to form their personal religion.[30] Beliefs become social enterprises incorporated in culture. They tend to fill the ontological imperative, but rely mainly on faith and mystical subjective experience for justification. Personal belief systems come in many forms all the way from theism to atheism, with many in between such as animism, totemism, paganism, spiritualism, pantheism, panentheism, and agnosticism.

Where established religion does not fill the imperative, other systems develop. Some, such as Freemasonry, reflect a progressive search; some, such as Nightingale-Conant, focus on self-help; and some, such as Rosicrucian, use ancient mysticism. A proliferation of quasi-religious organizations has come and gone, and at the present time, there are many that exist as business enterprises under the guise of both commercial and nonprofit organizations. Many use pseudoscientific information to bolster their philosophy; most use self-help techniques, but all capitalize on the human restlessness and longing for satisfying answers to their questions of ultimate concerns. The popularity of books and magazines about spirituality and religious mysticism attest to questions not met by mainstream belief systems and to a continued yearning for alternate explanations. It is important to recognize the religious nature of these movements, and that information is now available to analyze their characteristics and impacts. Objective science cannot answer questions of ultimate concerns as does religion; however, many attempts are now succeeding to objectively study the subjective and anomalous phenomena that result from and on which religion is based.

Psychology, as an objectively oriented study of human nature, has supported the concept of needs to usefully account for the beliefs, attitudes, and values that underlie the actions, reactions, and well-being of both individuals and societies. For example, M. D. Faber has recently built the case supporting God as filling our need for the "great mysterious caregiver" that we all had as infants, but then lost as we learned about our caregivers and about our existence.[31] Prominent among the needs of people that have been supported by research and clinical experience are predictability and certainty,[32] community and belonging,[33] control,[34] object of authority and worship,[35] transcendent functioning,[36] religious sentiment,[37] sense of coherence,[38] and sense of purpose.[39] This latter need of a purpose that gives meaning to one's life was discussed in Chapter 4, and is so strong and obtuse that it is frequently met abstractly by attributing it to a mystical source. A major strength of religion has been to usefully provide for these needs, as well as for others such as social support, charity, acceptance, stimulation, harmony, salvation, forgiveness, and aesthetics.

As an individual's spirituality develops into personal religion, is used and shared, it takes on a social life and structure. Current major religions can be grouped into three categories: western, eastern, and naturalistic. All of these center on the concept of a supernatural (nature extension), or transnoetic (unknowable) realm for the source of existence with a basic need to accept and accommodate that realm. In the United States, our culture is based on the western system that traces lineage to a Judeo-Christian concept of God as the key to life and salvation. Middle Eastern culture is based on a similar lineage focusing on Allah as God and on His dominance. Eastern systems are based on a concept of esoteric reincarnation with a purpose of progressing through material phases to achieve transcendence to "true" reality. The force here is not God, but consists of the drive to transcend this earthly existence and unite (or reunite) with a transcendent reality. Naturalistic systems are based on respect for and supplication to the forces of nature — extensions of animism and naturalism. Purpose lies in attunement and cooperation with forces that are represented by or inhabit the features of nature.

It is interesting to note that many belief systems include the philosophy of idealism; that our physical phenomena are the result of thought, some kind of "mind Stuff" — a bold idea for our materialistic culture. Chapter 8 pointed out that most religions and philosophies in the eastern category hold that our physical phenomena are illusionary or the product of mentation. This relates to the "Copenhagen Interpretation" of quantum physics introduced in Chapter 8 that implies material phenomena are determined by observation, use, or measurement. A "post-Copenhagen interpretation" that is gaining momentum in physics views information or consciousness as a force underlying energy and matter.[40] (See Chapter 8.) These support the theory that information, knowledge, and consciousness are non-physical or supernatural things that could underlie our material world, and could be related to a deity worthy of belief.

There are many different systems of organized beliefs, but most have objects of devotion and worship, tenets of faith, provision for afterlife, and procedures of prayer that have many similarities. It seems that the ultimate concerns of humans involve an innate universal need for devotion, faith, and prayer that develop into systems according to social interactions and cultural support.[41] Because of the abstract elusive nature of these ultimate concerns, they become represented by symbols, signs, allegories, metaphors, icons, and anthropomorphisms (having human characteristics, Chapter 6) that can more easily be grasped and used. A feature of Christianity is the incarnation of God in Jesus, a human form of God that can be more meaningful than God as the "great I am." Although these representations facilitate the use of abstract concepts, when combined with emotional reactions and cognitive expediency they frequently become substitutes as idols and icons that obscure underlying concepts. For many people, this fits in with the acceptance of dogma and authority of institutional religion. However, for others, such acceptance is not satisfying and spirituality as a more basic generic form of religion dominates. A person may accept the comforts of religion without being consciously aware about pangs of doubt; however, lurking somewhere is an uncertainty that stimulates a searching associated with the individual's naturally occurring predisposition of spirituality—concern about something beyond current knowledge. It is an unavoidable consequence of being human.[42]

Institutional Religion

Since religion becomes a social enterprise, it takes on accouterments of social structure. Leaders emerge that vie for power; hierarchy is established with rank, and unquestionable dogma is formed. Institutionalization develops with churches, synagogues, temples, mosques, etc., that assume the role of spiritual (and many times physical) caregiver and moral authority. The earliest known system of animism placed explanation and power in forces of nature and related deities, and relied on the good will of those mystical forces. This was augmented with personal revelations and insights of charismatic leaders for sustenance, health, and well-being. As more immediate (proximate) explanations developed and greater personal control of nature was acquired, people became less dependent on mystical sources, mystery decreased, and personal power increased such that the belief systems became diverse, complex, and profuse. As social systems developed, direct experience of mystical forces gave way to use of shamans with special insight about nature and supernature; then to priests who acted as mediators with special connections to deity; and then further to preachers and pastors that had special knowledge about deity.[43] Most of the major current religious organizations are follow-ons to systems started long ago by brilliant charismatic leaders and have become institutionalized into a hierarchical social structure that continues to meet many human needs. They provide explanation for existence and motivation for human activities, even such things as climbing mountains.

Institutional religion has been dominant in most recent societies, particularly in the United States, but its role is currently decreasing. While membership in traditional churches is decreasing, non-traditional churches are increasing indicating the persistent role of spirituality. Explanations for feelings of awe and mystery continue a concern for sacredness and a transcendent realm with a supernatural force despite decline in institutional religion. Can it be scientifically supported that there is some type of supernatural force that is the source of the awe and mystery we feel rather than an adaptive creation of the human mind? It has already been pointed out that humans need to believe that there is meaning and explanation, particularly for the arousals of personal feelings. We recognize that despite the vast knowledge available, there is still much unknown and mysterious, and maybe even realities beyond our comprehension. A convenient concept that provides explanation for all of this mystery is the existence of a supernatural divine power, but can it be supported objectively?

It has been said that attributing ultimate cause of human life to a deity is less mysterious and more probable statistically than attributing the cause to unguided evolution. Physicist Stephen Unwin reported in his book, *The Probability of God* (2003), the use of Bayesian mathematics to show the probability of a deity as 67 percent, and the probability of "no God" as 33 percent. It is interesting that the factors he used did not include the two emphasized in this book as being the most important. One is findings from psychology, sociology, and neuroscience indicating that religion fills many important human needs mentally, socially, and biologically; and the other is from history and anthropology indicating that humans as we know them have always had religious types of belief and activity.

The prolific science writer Clifford Pickover (2002) in *The Paradox of God* summarizes many examples of information and theories supporting belief in a divine power. One example supporting belief based on logical thinking is the famous "wager" proposed by the seventeenth century mathematician Blaise Pascal based on the assumption that God has the power to reward a believer with Heaven or punish a nonbeliever with Hell. If a person believes and God exists, reward occurs but if God does not exist, it does not matter; and if a person does not believe and God does not exist, it does not matter but if God exists, punishment occurs. So, just to be safe, it is wise to believe. An example base on function was the relative advantage of being in a world where everyone believes in a judgmental God but that God does not exist, or being in a world where no one believes but God does exist. More people choose the former because belief would make people more humane and dependent on each other. All of these are controversial but for many people they help fill spiritual needs.

Many sets of recent polls report the popularity of and extent to which people in the United States are concerned about a supernatural force behind their existence. In surveys conducted over the past fifty years, professed belief in God or a higher power has never been below 90 percent.[44] Praying on a daily basis was reported by 67–75 percent; membership in a church or synagogue was 69 percent with 40 percent reporting regular attendance, and 82 percent stating a personal need for spiritual growth.[45] Attendance in traditional churches is decreasing, but that in modern non-traditional churches is increasing. There is an increasing popularity of other religious type organizations such as Eckankar, Spiritual Frontiers, Scientology, Theosophy, Unity, Universal Unitarian, Mind Science, Soul-Esteem, and Baha'i. Moreover, publicized now is a plethora of pseudoreligious or nonreligious systems such as Avatar, Arica, Cafh, Rosicrucian, EST, Silva Mind Control, and Ethical Society.

Much more information is available about religion, but that is not the focus of this book. Rather, the focus here is on primary human motivation: why at a fundamental level people do the things they do, especially difficult things like climbing mountains. At that level, spirituality and religion become important and seem to hold the keys to the well-being of individuals and of civilization. Religion is also becoming more important because of growing independence and mobility of individuals, and reduction in the nuclear family and local neighborhood cohesion, resulting in loss of traditional social structure. Religious institutions have always helped to fill this need for social structure. They must recognize their importance and adjust to changing situations in meeting their traditional role of helping the primary motivation of individuals (pursuing the ontological imperative) in an age of science and individualism. The circumstances under which ancient religions developed are different from the circumstances now, so it is reasonable for modern religions also now to be different. The United States population exemplifies this trend, but it applies to other populations globally as well.

Religion has been important in most studies of history.[46] People have traditionally tended to aligned themselves with religions of their time as either followers or leaders, and even the unaligned were influenced by the beliefs in their community. Belief systems develop as religions and in turn, are major influences on development of individual societies. They range all the way from determinism established by a theistic force to existentialism that relies on nature. Most people subscribed to a belief system within that range that provided for answers to their basic concerns through some form of intellect higher than that of their personal self. The differences in belief systems have created and destroyed societies raising many questions, for example:

1. Are there qualitative differences in the various forms of religious belief that makes one (or some) "better" than others? Or is belief such a personal thing that its "appropriateness" depends on the individual person? In either case, the validity of the belief is not as important as the belief's function and impact, and societal well-being may be best pursued by studying the impacts of various beliefs, and stimulating tolerance of alternative beliefs and the process of the pursuit. But is one better than another?

2. What is the nature of the "higher intellect"? Is it an epiphenomenon of brain activity whereby one's mind grasps an explanation? Or is it an omnipotent determining power that controls and can respond to our requests? Or is it an initiating power that no longer directs? Are we trying to use a cause that is not really there?

The answers have been so nebulous that many organized belief systems hold that the true nature is unknowable, but they usually take strong stands on answers for which these questions may be examples. Extremely different ways of living go with different systems. Would it be better for societal well-being if people were seeking answers rather than attempting to sell their beliefs or those that have been sold to them? And could a better job be done of studying impacts of these questions?

For many people, visiting sacred sites provides insight or enlightenment that seems to support positive answers for them personally. In addition to providing stimulation, challenge, goal accomplishment, and ecstatic feelings, visiting sacred sites and climbing mountains steeped with folklore, myths, and beliefs about supernatural forces provides a potential for gaining information about ultimate concerns, satisfying the spiritual quest impulse. So, this may be a reason that many people are attracted to mountains revered as sacred. The best example of a widely accepted sacred mountain is Mount Moriah, the centerpiece of The Holy Land in Israel visited annually by millions of people.

Chapter 11
Most Sacred: Mount Moriah

By Western standards the most sacred mountain in the world is Mount Moriah, even though it is not really a mountain by our definition. It is an elongated hill in Jerusalem at the east edge of Israel rising about five hundred feet above valleys to the south and east. To the north and west are even higher hills, and across the Hebron Valley to the east is the Mount of Olives that is higher. At one time Moriah probably was higher, though, because over the past four thousand years it has been cut, scarred, scraped, and leveled many times. It has changed hands many times also, and although Israel now controls Jerusalem, the Palestinians, by joint agreement, now control Mount Moriah with the golden Dome of the Rock as its centerpiece. The agreement by which both parties respect the other's interests is tenuous.

Mount Moriah view from Mount of Olives over Hebron Valley

All three of the major monotheistic religions consider Mount Moriah of major importance to their history, culture, and tradition. Abraham, who was a founding father of all three, had two sons: Ishmael and Isaac. Jews and Christian trace lineage to Isaac, and Muslims trace lineage to Ishmael. According to tradition, Ishmael as the firstborn should have received Abraham's inheritance, but it was given instead to Isaac.[1] This is background for a competition that continues today among some of the descendants.

Jewish and Muslim tradition both believe that a stone on Mount Moriah was the first material emergence when God created the earth. That rock is still there and is frequently referred to as the Foundation Stone. To create Adam, God used dust from Mount Moriah. It was on Mount Moriah that Noah built his ark before the great flood. According to the Bible[1], Jacob was sleeping on Mount Moriah when he had the dream of climbing a ladder into heaven. The authenticity of these events is questionable and dates somewhat obscure; however, around 2000 BCE has been established as the time that Abraham took his favored son on to Mount Moriah when he thought sacrifice was called for. After that, numerous settlements developed in that area, the most notable being the City of David around 1100 BCE where King David established a capital for the Jewish tribes he had united. In 968 BCE, his son, Solomon, started building his famous temple on Mount Moriah, and Jerusalem was established as a major government center.

King Solomon's Temple was a focal point of the Jewish people for about five hundred years until a force of Babylonians destroyed the temple and took the Jewish people as captives back to Babylonia. When the Persians conquered Babylonia in 538 BCE, they allowed the Jews to return to Jerusalem where they started the arduous work of rebuilding the temple on Mount Moriah, which became known as the Temple Mount. This Second Temple had become somewhat run-down in 63 BCE when the Roman army took over the area. The Romans had selected Herod from a Jewish tribe friendly to the Romans to be king. King Herod was not very popular; however, he obtained some loyalty by remodeling and enlarging the temple. This fabulous structure required leveling and extending the hilltop by constructing walls around the slopes. This became known as King Herod's Temple and sometimes is referred to as the Third Temple. This is the temple Jesus visited and attempted to decommercialize in his last days on earth. By 70 CE, the Jewish people had revolted and caused so much trouble to their rulers that the Roman Legions slaughtered or dispersed the people, leveled Jerusalem, and destroyed Herod's Temple.

Mount Moriah was covered with rubble in 621 CE when Mohammad was gaining power in the southern land of Arabia. According to Islam tradition, one night Mohammad awoke to be confronted by the archangel Gabriel, who placed him on a winged horse that whisked him north to Mount Moriah. There he made an ascent into heaven and met many prophets to include Jesus, Moses, and Abraham. When the prophets told Mohammed that he should pray fifty times a day, the Moses suggested he negotiate.[2] This he did, and God said, OK you need to pray only five times a day, so those are the instructions Mohammed took back to his people in Mecca. This established Mount Moriah as a sacred site for the Muslims (and their use of five daily prayers). After Mohammed died, his succeeding caliphs occupied that northern land and built a memorial over the Foundation Stone in 691 CE.

This is the Dome of the Rock, whose golden dome dominates Jerusalem today. It was designed to be more conspicuous than the memorials erected under the guidance of Constantine in the third century CE to memorialize the life and death of Jesus. Since Christianity had been declared the official religion of the Roman Empire and subsequently spread throughout Europe, pilgrims descended on Jerusalem. Muslims resisted that influx causing armed intervention. During the Crusader days in the tenth century CE, the Dome of the Rock was turned into a Christian church; but after the eleventh century, when the Crusaders were finally defeated, it was returned to being a sacred Muslim shrine.

Mount Moriah continued to be controlled by Muslims, except for a brief period after the 1967 Israel-Arab war when Israel conquered the West Bank, including East Jerusalem, and reclaimed much of Jewish historical territory. Jerusalem is now the capital of Israel, but as a concession to the Palestinians, they gave up control of Mount Moriah. The Israelis have unfettered access only to a portion of the Western Wall that had been part of the foundation of King Herod's Temple. This has become known as the Wailing Wall, where pilgrims and tourists can visit entering through a large heavily guarded plaza.

Climbing Higher

Wailing Wall and Plaza on western side of Mount Moriah

I had travelled to Israel as part of a tour group that visited Jerusalem, Sea of Galilee, Dead Sea, and sites in between that comprise what is known as the Holy Land. I was informed that non-Muslims were only allowed on Mount Moriah at special times, so I arranged my itinerary to meet one of those times on a Wednesday morning at seven thirty right after the morning prayers. Entrance would be at the Dung Gate on the southern wall surrounding the Old City of Jerusalem. (The Dung Gate was so named because in earlier days, garbage and waste was removed from the city through this gate.)

My thirteen-year-old grandson and I were billeted at the Ritz Hotel about one mile north of a main entrance to Old Jerusalem called the Damascus Gate. We estimated hiking to the Dung Gate would take about an hour, so we set out at six. After clearing a metal-detecting security station in the Damascus Gate building, we emerged onto the main north–south street called Ha Gay. I would call it an alley;

however, even at this early hour it was a beehive of activity lined with vendors, shops, and bazaars. Picking our way through this maze emerged us at the Wailing Wall Plaza to an impressive view of the western side of Mount Moriah with the golden Dome of the Rock dominating the skyline. The plaza was in the Jewish Quarter, so at the south end above the Dung Gate, we cleared another security station. It was seven fifteen, and we were prepared to climb through the gate up a causeway leading to the western slope when guards there said, "Sorry, but no one is allowed to enter today." The businesslike attitude and display of weapons indicated that protests were not appropriate despite our disappointment—a disappointment that not even climbing on the Great Pyramid in Egypt could ameliorate. Mountain climbers recognize that sometimes the summit is not achievable, but in this case, the ascent was not even begun. My flight schedule out of Tel Aviv precluded an alternate time, so I had to be content with pictures of the Dome of the Rock and the Foundation Stone.

This was unfortunate, but since I was not Muslim and would not be participating in an Islam ceremony, a significant experience may not have occurred anyway. I had better fortunes in Egypt where I was impressed with a feeling of reverence, respect, and awe when visiting the Mohammed Ali Mosque. The preparation of washing, removing shoes, and then repeatedly kneeling and standing with the sensing of melodious sounds and soft colors suggested the possibility of a divine force demanding supplication. Experiencing this five times a day as is customary for Muslims could make the feeling of a divine force seem real even without prior belief. Looking at these experiences objectively indicates that situation, activity, and anticipation influence perception and interpretation of experiences so that the cold objective approach might interfere with esoteric phenomena, while a warm subjective approach might stimulate such phenomena. The validity of esoteric phenomena is questionable when it is only the product of private feeling and thought. Despite the lack of objective support for esoteric beliefs, we must be careful about dismissing such beliefs because of needs and possibilities discussed in Chapter 10.

The time set aside to climb Mount Moriah was used to trace the Via Dolorosa, known as the Way of the Cross. My background in Christianity filled me with anticipations of esoteric experience when tracing this path taken by Jesus carrying his wooden cross from where he was convicted and sentenced to crucifixion to the site on Golgotha where he died. It was a winding route of narrow streets through a dense section of Old Jerusalem. Every few yards there was a shrine or church commemorating an aspect of Jesus' walk, and throughout were shops, vendors, and bazaars selling everything from wood trinkets to gold icons. Golgotha (also known as Calvary) is now enclosed in a complex of structures dating back to the third century CE when Constantine declared Christianity the official religion of the Roman Empire and sent his mother, Queen Helena, to supervise building memorials to activities of Jesus. An altar was constructed over the site of crucifixion with a rock underneath that was cracked during the geological disturbance that occurred at the time of Jesus' death. Further underneath is the burial site of Adam's skull. Close to the entrance of the complex is the Stone of Anointing where Jesus' body was laid when taken from the cross. In the center of the complex is the Holy

Answering Big Questions

Sepulcher where Jesus' body was entombed. This is an ancient structure within a large more recently constructed rotunda. Altogether, the complex is known as the Church of the Holy Sepulcher. All branches of Christianity are represented, but most conspicuous are the Eastern and Greek Orthodox sects with regalia of elaborate ornaments and icons.

Holy Sepulcher in rotunda of Church of the Holy Sepulcher

Crowded on the Way of the Cross were tourists, pilgrims, vendors, and clerics; most of whom were worshiping and supplicating before the symbols of Jesus' last days. At the Wailing Wall were similar groups reverently performing rituals of the Jewish faith. Although I did not witness it, I understand that on Mount Moriah a more select group also performs similar rituals of the Muslim faith. All of this resulted from belief in a transcendent God that influences human destiny. To walk the path of Jesus, pray at the Wailing Wall, and observe the Dome of the Rock covering the Foundation Stone were moving experiences personally; however, they failed to elicit in me any special insight, nor did my emotional arousal sufficiently justify the mass of violence, conflict, and combat that has occurred in the past two thousand years over devotion to and exclusivity of these sites. Jerusalem and Mount Moriah represent ages of tremendous hardships as well as of positive social advances. They exemplify the historic role of belief, faith, and worship in human nature. Did a great creator design these into humanity, or are they the result of evolutionary adaption that facilitated existence?

A sense of sacredness seems to be built into us and is a foundation of religion, but does it have a useful function in explaining why people persist in overcoming obstacles in pursuit of difficult goals? And also, does it provide more benefits than decrements in the advance of civilization and human well-being? Civilization seems to be at a turning point now where both the sacred and religion are losing their ability to satisfy the hunger for sensible answers to questions of ultimate concerns. This is similar to the Reformation that took place in sixteenth century Europe to undermine the stifling dominance and intolerance of church power. The beginning of science and awakening of liberty stimulated a revolt against religious constraints. As science advanced further revolt occurred against church and political constraints resulting in the eighteenth century Period of Enlightenment that radically changed Western culture. Are we again at a time when new information is calling for change in church, religion, and faith beliefs—a Second Reformation leading to a Second Period of Enlightenment? This could result in a major change in accepted explanations of ultimate concerns that, in turn, could result in major change in explanations of human motivation.

Chapter 12
Existential Reality: Conflict, Dilemma, and Paradox

We all have beliefs, and we all have faith. They are basic to navigating our personal existence. Both involve assumptions that certain things will happen in certain situations with sufficient consistency that we can manage our lives with an acceptable degree of coherence, predictability, and meaning. Optimal management is provided by another thing we seem to have: a built-in need to believe that there is something beyond ourselves, something bigger and better than ourselves that got things started and that provides meaning, consistency, and sacredness. An ultimate goal would be to strive for knowledge about this and use it in our daily activities—to accommodate it. Sharing of beliefs and faith about this has created religious institutions that provide a supernatural power such as God offering not only explanation of existence, but also other things such as comfort of a continued existence instead of the abyss of nothingness and futility for life's struggles. Increasingly, though, the dogma and revelations of religion that were useful in ancient times conflict with newly acquired objectively based information, and have contributed to dissatisfaction with the institutions that had been so important in advancing civilization and ameliorating the ontological imperative.

Religion has also come under criticism recently because of terrorism, atrocities, genocides, inhumanities, and immoralities perpetuated in its name. The famous author

Michael Shermer (2015) has shown many examples of religion retarding the advance of civilization; for example, Christian Crusades and inquisitions, and Islamic terrorism. Also publicizing current problems caused by religious beliefs are Daniel Dennett (2006), Victor Stenger (2003), and Sam Harris (2004) among others.

Belief in a deity such as God can be vulnerable and insecure when based solely on faith in religious dogma and childhood learning. Current media coverage and emphasis on rationality magnifies inconsistencies between religious beliefs on one hand and newly available objective information and logical reasoning on the other hand. Joseph Campbell showed how myths develop from beliefs and become vehicles that perpetuate and enhance their own power[1] similar to what are now called memes—culturally established concepts that continue because of their social momentum rather than objective logic. This does not mean that religious dogma, writings, and mystical experiences are invalid or unimportant. For many people, they are sufficient to support belief satisfactorily, but for many others their social momentum must be augmented with moral, social, emotional, and economic factors to fit in with current events. Such augmentation justifies beliefs as usefully functional but reduces their sacred foundation, emotional appeal, and unquestioned truthfulness.

Then comes scientific information indicating that there is insufficient objective support to make supernatural beliefs logically reasonable. Religionists claim that such information is irrelative because beliefs are beyond objective investigation and can never be proved or disproved. They have to be taken on faith, and science is seen as an attempt to find out about God's creation rather than an attempt to find a more reasonable source of that creation. Scientists, on the other hand, have trouble formulating testable hypotheses about supernatural beliefs and ultimate reality, so generally avoid prove or disprove efforts. Where aspects have been tested objectively, results were conflicting, inconsistent, or otherwise explainable. The result is discontent without resolution.

For many years I have followed the work reported by (and maintained memberships in) many organizations dedicated to investigating alternate forms of religious types of phenomena that are more compatible with objective observations such as Institute of Noetic Science, Edgar Cayce Foundation, Society for the Scientific Study of Religion, Association for Transpersonal Psychology, Institute on Religion in an Age of Science, and Templeton Foundation. I have also followed organizations supporting such phenomena as psychic ability, near-death experiences, out-of-body experience, remote viewing, reincarnation, extraterrestrial beings (UFO), and consciousness. Each has its own publication such as *Journal of the American Society of Psychical Research, Spirituality & Health, Zygon, and Journal for the Scientific Study of Religion* that reported their work and those of similar investigators. The more structured research is reported by the Society for Scientific Exploration, Parapsychology Foundation, and various psychology organizations such as the American Psychological Association divisions of Humanistic Psychology and Psychology of Religion and Spirituality. All of these have reported research supporting validity of anomalous phenomena that may involve a supernatural realm.

Research about psychic phenomena has gained considerable credibility by the publication of *Varieties of Anomalous Experience* by Cardena, Lynn, and Kripner[2] and of the *American Psychologist* report by Bem and Honorton (1994) entitled "Does Psi Exist? Replicable Evidence for an Anomalous Process of Information Transfer." These are examples of reputable reports supporting validity of psychic phenomena sufficiently to be scientifically accepted. Research in parapsychology and consciousness studies has moved beyond demonstrating that psychic and mentalistic phenomena occur to attempting to use and explain the effects. Even though objective research supports validity of some phenomena that are still considered mysterious or mystical, it does not yet support validity in deity, discarnate spirit, or extraterrestrial being (see Chapter 8).

Psychologist Charles Tart, who has spent a lifetime career studying psychic phenomena, presented a well-balanced summary of research related to spirituality and supernatural belief in his book *The End of Materialism* (2009). Even though he said he had not had a deeply mystical experience himself, he shows the prevalence of such experiences and their impact on culture. He concludes that the "paranormal" is actually "normal." His experiences are similar to mine, having been acquainted with religion and attending church during childhood followed by academic and professional work in scientific fields that led to big questions about human nature, life, and the supernatural resulting in efforts to find answers. This seems to be a common pattern for many people and a potential for everyone—an effort beyond that of meeting the pressing immediate needs of everyday life.

Many individuals and groups of individuals have had subjective experiences they report as substantiating belief in a supernatural deity; however, objective analyses of these experiences have failed to provide support. All of my years in following this research (and conducting some of my own) have likewise failed to reveal sufficient objective support for "proof" of a supernatural force that could be considered deity. Meditation and introspective exploration have provided glimpses of insight for me as they have for others, but no objective support for supernatural deity beyond private personal subjective experience. Even though there is support for an as yet unknown medium that can produce "nonlocal," psychic, or healing phenomena, it does not reliably support existence of deity. This does not negate or rule out a divine force, but suggests that support must come from other sources such as personal experience, respected knowledge, reliable authority, or insightful revelation. There is something there, but its nature is elusive and depends on what is meaningful to individual people personally.

Anomalous experiences continue to receive some scientific support that reinforces belief in systems providing supernatural frameworks, idealistic objects of devotion, tenets of faith, and procedures of prayer. These help to fill innate universal needs for framework, devotion, faith, and influence that have developed into religious belief systems and organizations according to social interactions. One of the most fascinating patterns that permeate human history is conflict between communities because of, or in the name of, religious beliefs. It comes in many forms from "mine is the only true God" to "your God is an outdated primitive concept that must be eliminated." The secular humanism and militant atheism movements propelled by Paul Kurtz,[3] Richard Dawkins,[4] and others have been effective in showing the inconsistencies and illogicalness in many institutional religions, but still polls show that most people adhere to these religious beliefs that include some form of transcendent being (see Chapter 10). The continued popularity of such beliefs indicates that they fill important needs.

Science

By using an inductive or bottom-up approach, science investigates speculation, theories, and assumptions about observable phenomena, and discards or modifies those that are unsupported or faulty. This eliminates investigation of ultimate reality and deity because they are not observable or falsifiable (capable of being disproved), leaving these topics to the vicissitudes of human thinking. Scientific activities have been producing reliable information that conflicts with some dogma advocated by organized religions resulting in doubt about belief foundations. Examples are: age of the world, human evolution, sanctity of life, spiritual healing, and resurrection. For some religious people this is either explained away or ignored, but for others it sows the seeds of doubt and interferes with their commitment. For non-religious people, skepticism is heightened. Much has been published about the sociology and psychology of religion, and information is being generated about the growing population alienated from organized religion but still concerned about ultimate reality beyond the reach of science; for example the growing group claiming to be spiritual but not religious.

Another example is religious healing. Science writers such as Richard Dawkins (2006), Sam Harris (2004), and Daniel Dennett (2006) have shown that many healings previously attributed to mystical divine intervention can be explained as the result of the body's extensive powers of generation and regeneration; that meditation can have the same beneficial physical effects as prayer; and that church attendance alone (independent of belief) is related to better physical health. Many phenomena labeled as miracles that were previously explained by divine intervention and used to support belief have now been shown to be explainable as naturally occurring physical activity. New discoveries in physics and biology indicate a natural explanation for many "mind over matter" phenomena used to justify belief in divine power. The need for a Creator as first cause has even been brought into question because of recent support for multiple universes, cyclic universe, and infinite space, indicating the possible absence of "beginning." However, science is still unable to make conclusions about ultimate cause, and even though these developments question religious dogma, it must be realized that they do not rule out a divine creator that could have started these processes and may even continue to influence their courses.

Chapter 10 emphasized that science provides revelations in a different way than religion in that they are tested for replicability and consensual validation in an attempt to separate them from inaccurate assumptions and mental confabulation (internal dialogue melding spurious information). Research started by Elizabeth Loftus demonstrates the creativity and questionable accuracy of information people use to make judgments.[5] In interpreting sensory input, the human mind modifies, augments, and reduces that input to such an extent that perception can be a distorted view of what is really "out there." The human mind has great powers of confabulation, by which perceptions are manufactured and appear as insightful revelations but are merely amalgamations of information (both valid and invalid) already stored in the brain. This frequently results in a disjointed faulty conclusion. Neurological studies of meditation, prayer, awe, and sensory alteration mentioned in Chapter 6 revealed a mechanism in the brain that diminishes activity in centers of external orientation and increases activity in centers of internal attention and emotions, indicating that inspired states may be accompanied with a reduction in objective validity.[6]

Many anomalous experiences interpreted as resulting from psychic or spiritual realities can be explained as mental aberrations resulting solely from brain activity. An example of this is the effect of DMT (dimethyltreptamine), a psychedelic chemical produced in the brain's pineal gland that shifts neurological activity from the thinking cortex to the emotional limbic system. This is associated with vividness in dreams, out of body experiences, and possible information from an esoteric realm similar to that reported in ancient lore by prophets and shamans.[7] Although validity is controversial, it is possible that this shift in brain activity makes for better receptivity of reality beyond normal perception.[8] Reputable interpretations of quantum physics findings even support the philosophy of idealism (Chapters 8 and 10) indicating that care must be exercised in dismissing the possibility of divine reality.

In order to account for observations of subatomic phenomena, the science of physics has developed the theory of quantum mechanics introduced in Chapter 8. This is about the microcosm where the process of observation intermingles with objects observed. At that level, only potentialities seem to exist until they are observed or used (Chapter 10). Objective observations seem to be influenced by subjective intentions of observers, raising questions about reliability and giving support for interpretations considered mysterious or mystical. This does not replace the classic laws of physics that continue to explain phenomena at the everyday super atomic level. However, at the subatomic level, a door is opened for the possibility of a "Supermind" that can intervene there without violating classic laws as discussed in Chapter 8. A door is opened for a divine, prehuman Great Observer or a Great Experimenter who originally collapsed potentialities resulting in our material world.[9] Quantum mechanics does not prove the existence of deity, and is still controversial, but it does provide support for a mysterious source based on objective observation rather than only subjective ideas. This results from science rather than religion and is considered objective observation rather than divine revelation.

There are many theories and beliefs about deity that can be questioned. Writings such as the Torah, New Testament, Koran, Book of Mormon, and Course in Miracles are examples of products of human minds considered divine revelation, and although they were inspired and contain inspiring passages with beneficial guidance worthy of study, they came from a human mind (or minds) and not necessarily directly from a divine source. Many examples are available of mediumship where an individual seems to channel information from a discarnate source, but none has been conclusively supported as coming from a deity. Therefore, it seems appropriate to test revelation and faith and be aware of their foundations. Trouble and damaging conflict continue because of uncritical acceptance of some particular written passages or interpretations thereof attributed to divine sources and are used to support espousal of exclusive knowledge of Truth. Many of these belief systems not only claim a true deity, they claim others are wrong and should be subdued or completely eliminated. Violence and terrorism results.

It should be noted here that writings considered sacred scripture provide an important need for both believers and societies whether or not they not come directly from a divine source. This is the need for an established authority not subject to the whims of society, vocal minorities, or powerful leaders. Like a written constitution, a sacred scripture may contain something objectionable, but its guidance is better than a lack of stable reliable authority. It establishes a morality that can be counted on for consistency.

Science has brought on questions about belief in divine cause as the basis of existence and human motivation that cannot be ignored. Astounding comforts of entertainment, health, longevity, and well-being have come from technological advances; but at the cost of many comforts of religion. Physicist Marcelo Gleiser (2014) in his book, *The Islands of Knowledge*, summarized a vast amount of scientific information leading to this situation. In drawing conclusions about ultimate cause and answers to fundamental questions of existence, he supported theories of uncertainty, transcendental naturalism, and cognitive closure that indicate an inability of the human mind to see beyond a "horizon" or to understand ultimate reality or consciousness. Ultimate truth is a phantom, and "what we call real is 'contingent' on how deeply we can probe reality." (p. xx) So, the comforts of science do not eliminate need for the comforts of religion, and many times fail to provide suitable substitutes after shaking religion based comforts discussed in Chapter 10.

Paradox and Dilemma

As spiritual belief becomes a social enterprise providing meaningfulness and belongingness it is reinforced by dogma, scriptures, revelation, ritual, and worship requiring acceptance as a religion. Doubt is discouraged. Faith in the religion, then, is not to be questioned, and because of its nature, its foundation cannot be investigated for falsification or objective support. As knowledge of the world increases and provides physical explanation that conflicts with the dogma, more doubt occurs that if not out in the open as a conscious issue, may be repressed and form a subconscious pocket of internal energy that can influence people without their awareness.[10] (Freud's ideas about this have been substantiated.) Even if dogma is accepted and pangs of doubt are subdued, doubt cannot be completely eliminated because of the recognized importance of science. The provision for ultimate reality from religion is questionable because of science, but can science do any better?

For some people the pangs of doubt can be alleviated by recognizing that science deals only with observable physical phenomena where religion goes farther by dealing with mental non-physical ideas and revelations. The famous paleontologist and science educator Stephen Gould (2006) coined the term "nonoverlaping magisteria" to show that religion and science each deal with separate domains of knowledge that contribute to civilization. Thus, both approaches are needed to get a comprehensive view of reality.

Gould's nonoverlaping magisteria has recently received a lot criticism because a large number of scientist and philosophers consider science and religion to be inherently incompatible and forever in conflict. A good summary of this conflict is given in *The Religion and Science Debate* edited by Harold Attridge (2009). Neither religion nor science by itself provides satisfactory answers to questions of reality. For many people, this magnifies their naturally occurring yearnings of spirituality. A paradox is that both are needed: science based on objective information and religion based on subjective faith. Combining religion and science has the potential of forming complete answers; however, this has not occurred in the past, and the current state of human mental processes indicates it will not happen in the near future. This reinforces a paradox of believing religious explanations but also doubting their validity. This can be called the "great paradox."

Chapter 10 mentioned Clifford Pickover's (2001) summary of many paradoxes that have been associated with religious beliefs and theories of ultimate reality. As reliable information about nature has increased, conflicts have also increased with information about nature that had been considered sacrosanct and previously accepted on faith. However, the great paradox proposed here emphasizes the need and function for both sides of most of these paradoxes. It takes paradox to the fundamental level of having belief in a supernatural power while also harboring a disbelief—a truly great paradox.

Human nature dislikes paradox and tends to align with one side of the conflict to reduce dissonance. This produces the "great dilemma." A dilemma occurs when one is faced with a difficult or irreconcilable choice that is uncomfortable, and can lead to frustration and anxiety. The dilemma here is that one feels that a choice must be made between belief and doubt, or between consolidation of faith and search for truth. Some people have abandoned institutional religion because of this dilemma.

Related to the great paradox and the great dilemma is what can be called the "elusiveness paradox": the need to strive for a seemingly inaccessible goal. The nature of ultimate reality has been so elusive that it seems beyond our ability to grasp at the present time, and maybe never. However, we cannot escape the need to continue in search even if the goal seems unattainable and the process is subjugated to belief. What a difference our world would be if all societies were oriented to this search instead of trying to impose their set of beliefs on others.

Although much has been written and said about ultimate reality, none has emerged as being completely satisfactory. It seems that in our current state of intellectual capability, the answer is inaccessible. Furthermore, the ugly possibility arises that there may not be an answer since history indicates that despite advances in knowledge about the material environment, no real progress has been made about knowledge of ultimate reality. Indeed, we seem to have regressed in our knowledge and use of a divine force (or forces) that seemed to be more active in earlier times. The acclaimed science writer John Horgan has published several books about our inability to understand origins of the human mind and the universe. His book, *Rational Mysticism* (2003), builds the case for the inexplicability of ultimate reality or of a divine realm. However, the need is still so great that even though we cannot see the end goal and realize that it may be unattainable, we continue the search, and when pursued, a wondrous sense of adventure, awe, and sacredness can open up.

So how can institutionalized religion continue to meet the human need for meaning and ultimate truth, yet also accommodate conflicts with science and support a continuing quest? Some attempts are currently underway. Notable is the call for a "bottom-up" approach to theology.[11] Some attempts using this approach have been made by researchers such as Ursula Goodenough,[12] Candace Pert,[13] Francis Collins,[14] and Gary Schwartz.[15] Advocates of process theology, panentheism, theobiology, neurotheology, and others also contribute; however, unresolved conflicts still occur. In general, all of these approaches start with the "top-down" process and attempt to support sacredness and ultimate truth with objective information, resulting in scientific minutia, philosophical obtuseness, or theological abstraction becoming theology masquerading as scientific inquiry.[16]

The conflict occurs where the top-down and the bottom-up approaches intersect. The strict bottom-up approach publicized by Daniel Dennett,[17] Richard Dawkins,[18] Sam Harris,[19] Victor Stenger,[20] and others finds no support or need for supernatural explanations.. The top-down approach is based on faith in a supernatural deity, concepts of which are limited only by imagination and interaction of a complex set of needs. It is at the meeting place of these two approaches that attempts to reduce conflict result in movements such as religious naturalism or theistic atheism. It seems that the best way to minimize an oxymoron situation is to admit that both approaches are useful. The need of providing for the mysterious unknown can be conveniently met by accepting already established beliefs and focusing on beneficial effects while adjusting those beliefs to absorb new research findings. For many people, the need to believe and accept appears stronger than the need for objective explanation. For others, the need for objective explanation dominates. However, for most, both are needed: a top-down religion to believe in and a bottom-up quest for logical explanation.

It seems logical that by extending objective knowledge resulting from doubt with subjective knowledge from belief, a dialectic tension would occur that can energize development along the path to meaning and purpose. A belief incorporating knowledge acquired through observation, learning, and experience must be flexible because the knowledge on which it is based is recognized to be changeable where belief based only on dogma and faith is inflexible. New information adds to the former but detracts from the latter. It can follow that there may really be some force beyond our current knowledge and transcendent to our personal lives that could be regarded as a deity that set in motion the developing complexity of our world. At the present time, the true nature of this deity seems beyond our grasp. We have need to believe that there is such a transcendent force while recognizing that such a belief may be assumption based on questionable information. We are seekers and believers, so if we accept one and set aside the other, an unnatural repression occurs that can boil to the surface at an inappropriate time. If we can accept both, seeking can continue while the comforts of belief can be experienced without serious interruption.

The assumptions of religious beliefs started because of needs and situations that existed at the time, so those needs and situations constituted objective information at that particular time. If we recognize that needs and situations have changed, beliefs can be modified. This is difficult to accomplish, though, when religious beliefs are unquestioned. Psychology research about cognitive dissonance has demonstrated that people can change beliefs when faced with conflicts between their actions, feelings, and beliefs.[21] And they can ignore information to justify actions. For example, if a person believes smoking is bad for health but smokes anyway, the person tends to modify the belief to "smoking is not that bad." Even though this process may involve rationalization whereby logical analysis is ignored, it shows that beliefs can change, particularly when actions change. Are religious beliefs subject to such modification? Mark Taylor in his book culminating a series about religion and postmodernism has effectively pointed out that not only is it possible, it drove the Reformation and early development of Christianity.[22] He also points out that unquestioned religiosity and morality are more dangerous than the beliefs they are designed to uphold.

According to evolutionary psychologist Jesse Bering, perceiving the supernatural is an organic function of the brain, and God evolved from that function as an adaptive concept similarly to the emergence presented in Chapter 10. Furthermore, Dr. Bering concluded that a person can still enjoy God while considering the concept an illusion.[23] Having both belief and doubt in a deity may seem new, but it was justified in the 17th century by the famous French scientist Blaise Pascal (see Pascal's Wager earlier in this chapter) who concluded that it is rational to believe in and live to please God even if He does not exist.[24] Is it possible to live as though there is a transcendent being and at the same time doubt its existence? Can we have it both ways?

The respected social psychologist and educator David Meyers, in his book, *A Friendly Letter to Skeptics and Atheists*, intimated the usefulness of believing and doubting. He professed belief in Christianity based on passion rather than intellect and justified continuing prevalence of religious belief on its ability to fill human needs for social support, meaning and purpose, acceptance, and hope. He summarized the results of his experiences and research with the belief that "(1) there is a God and (2) it's not me (and it's not you)--and that we should hold our own untested beliefs tentatively, assess other's ideas with open minded skepticism, and when appropriate, use observation and experimentation to winnow error from truth." [25]

The debate about religion versus science can be traced back to the sixteenth century when Copernicus proposed that church dogma was wrong about the earth being the center of the universe. Then came indications that humans were not created fully formed. Debate about such issues have continued since then.[26] Many theologians and some scientists claim the two sides of the issues are compatible, with both seeking to understand ultimate reality but using different complimentary approaches (nonoverlaping magisteria). Many other scientists, theologians, and philosophers claim the two are fundamentally different and irreversibly conflicting because they start with different assumptions and languages, and use approaches that conflict—religion assumes existence of deity while science assumes only observables have meaning. We have surveyed background information about the importance of these issues and ramifications about how they relate to our daily lives. Let us now look back on the preceding chapters that presented that brief survey and look at the associated mountain climbing examples in an attempt to relate the ontological imperative to current human affairs. Is the conflict between explanations provided by science or religion really important? Can the adverse effects of the conflicts be alleviated for the benefit of individuals and their societies? Can useful conclusions be made?

Maybe another mountain climbing story revisiting earlier experience would be helpful.

Chapter 13
Traditional Climb: Mount Fuji

Climbing mountains can have both literal and figurative significance. I have climbed many mountains for many reasons, but the reason that seems most significant to me is the urge to explore; to reach out to something beyond everyday life that might reveal unusual information--something that might ameliorate the ontological imperative. It seems that we all have this urge, but for many it goes unfulfilled because of the consuming demands of immediate existence. The importance of this urge for me resulted from my experiences, study, research, and teaching of psychology that started when I retired from military service. It really started long before that, though. My encounter with Mount Fuji as a brash young soldier was a milestone in a concern that started early in life and one experienced by most people as they wonder about their existence. At the time of my experience on Mount Fuji, I did not realize there was a paradox of goals: to believe in a transcendent realm associated with the mountain, yet to question and challenge that belief. Is it possible my survival then may have been because of belief? Could that climb have had a beneficial effect on my life?

As explained in the introduction, working with people all around the world in many different capacities from follower to leader impressed me with the impact of the beliefs people have. After all these years of study and experience, do I know any more about these beliefs now than when I first became interested in their impact? Maybe climbing Mount Fuji (Chapter 1) again would provide some insight. I had often thought that such a climb in traditional manner with Japanese people during their proper season would not only show interesting differences with the first climb, but might provide some of the spiritual enlightenment the locals seem to experience. It might help tie together the mass of disparate information to form a helpful theory or philosophy beneficial for me and maybe also for my society.

My youngest son had accompanied me on several climbs (Aconcagua in Argentina, Whitney in California, and Blanca Peak in Colorado), so I proposed that he go with me to Fuji. I arranged with the Japanese Travel Bureau to join a local group scheduled to make a standard two-day trip to the Fuji summit. It was to leave from the Shinjuku Station in Tokyo at 7:30 a.m. on July 25, traveling by bus to reach station 5 on Mount Fuji at 11:30 a.m. There are now four main trails to the summit, the most widely used being the Yoshida Guchi trail that leads from the Kawaguchiko Station 5. This is the same one I used in 1959, but now it is one way, so descent from the summit to station 5 is on another trail. The plan was to eat lunch at station 5 and then climb to station 8, where we would have supper and sleep until 11:00 p.m. Then we would climb to the summit in time for sunrise and goraiko. A breakfast box was to be provided at the summit before descending to station 5 for lunch and bus ride to a hot bath spa and then back to Tokyo.

We made contact with an English-speaking guide by phone from the hotel the day before the scheduled climb. He reminded us to have a light backpack to carry a fleece jacket, gloves, hat, headlamp, and two liters of water. In addition, we were to bring a change of clothes to use after the hot bath when we come off the mountain. The temperature in Tokyo was about 80°F, but it could be close to freezing at the summit. Have a good night's sleep and a hearty breakfast before meeting the next morning.

Streets were quiet that Sunday morning at six thirty when we started the taxi ride from our hotel in downtown Tokyo to Shinjuku about five miles northwest. We had estimated forty minutes, but it took only twenty, and the only activity was people emerging from nightclubs. Jack and I were two of six that met an English-speaking interpreter who merged us with the larger group of thirty. The tour guide spoke in Japanese for about five animated minutes, and our interpreter said, "She said we are now going to board the bus." In addition to Jack and me, there were only two other Caucasians—mountain climbers from Moscow.

In 1959, the road leading to station 5 was gravel single lane. Now the road was paved double lane with passing zones for buses. Where station 5 was a three-room hut with a small gravel parking area, now it was a village with three multistory hotels, five restaurants, and numerous shops and venders surrounding a five-acre paved parking and assembly area. We were looking down on a fluffy layer of clouds and invigorated with a temperature of about 65°F. A red torii gate sacred to Shintos led to a Shinto shrine where many climbers, including ourselves, sought good omens. After lunch and purchase of wood walking sticks (one thousand yen each with two hundred yen for a station 5 stamp burned on the wood), we thirty-six climbers assembled for the first leg. A mountain guide had now taken charge and spoke to us in Japanese for about ten minutes. Our interpreter said, "he said that we were now going to start the climb."

Station 5 hotels (compare with view in Chapter 1)

The trail to station 6 was a shallow ascent around the mountain through trees and vegetation. It was gravel about six feet wide so that faster climbers could easily pass others. Some had on traditional white clothing of Fujiko pilgrims, and all were in a jolly festive mood. At station 6, vegetation had thinned, temperature dropped to about sixty, and scattered clouds skidded by. As with all stations, a wood worker was there to burn onto the walking stick (for two hundred yen) the Japanese stamp symbolizing presence at the station. From station 6 the trail was steeper with more switchbacks and sections of solid volcanic rock.

Trail to station 6

From station 7, gravel gave way to rock, and climbing became more difficult and slowed to what is known as the Fuji shuffle. Breathing was harder and breaks more frequent. The trail was still wide enough that groups could leap frog by one another. This was fortunate because there was a solid stream of people ascending. There was still a festive and social atmosphere, and we all seemed to be united with camaraderie into a fellowship of joint effort. Some of the Japanese climbers spoke English, so during the breaks, I was able to learn that they still believe in the divine nature of Fuji-san and felt that its spirit energized their climb. "Yes, it's part of our culture, and besides, it is a lot of fun."

The last 100 feet into station 8 at 9,548 feet was tough, but we made it at about five o'clock emerging on top of a cloud layer. The rather large one-story building was accompanied with a separate toilet building (one hundred yen per visit) and had a one-hundred square-foot wooden platform assembly and eating area and several bunk areas for sleeping. Supper consisted of soup, rice, vegetables, and raw fish and was served in traditional Japanese style requiring sitting on the floor with legs crossed. This was not only uncomfortable for me; it was impossible due to my artificial knee and degenerate spine. Graciously, the proprietor provided a beer case for the elderly American to sit on.

Trail to station 8

As supper ended, the sun was setting and temperature had cooled off to about 40°F. Men were taken to a large bunkroom and arranged like sardines in a can on a wooden platform. Spacing was so close that when I turned over I would bump into the person on either side. Women were similarly packed on another platform. Needless to say, those used to moving during sleep and that did not snore failed to get much sleep. At ten, we were aroused and told that there were many people on the trail and that we should get started to make it to the summit by sunrise. Everyone had headlamps in order to see what was immediately in front. This precluded seeing in the darkness down the slope and minimized fear of height, because now the climb was quite steep over both loose and solid rock requiring some hand-over-hand scaling. For me, the walking stick that was so useful before was now an impediment. The cool night air was noticeably thinner, so breathing was much more difficult. The slow pace and frequent rests were welcome. The camaraderie and social support kept many of us going. Some had brought small bottles of oxygen, but I did not see any being used.

On approaching the summit, I summoned enough courage to look down the slope and was amazed at the line of light marking the zigzag switchback trail. It was a continuous line of headlamps disappearing into the cloud layer below. In 1959, when I was warm enough to see at the summit, there was no shelter and only rock and ice. The crater of the dormant volcano was about five hundred yards in diameter with a small weather station hut at the opposite side. The rim of the crater could be traversed in about one hour. This time, the summit greeted me with a brightly lit hotel complete with restaurant, assembly area, sleeping facilities, and a veranda for watching the sunrise.

We arrived about four with plenty of time before the four forty sunrise to eat the breakfast of rice and raw fish wrapped in seaweed. As the sky began to lighten, our mountain guide made an excited announcement that was interpreted as saying that a cloud was hanging over the summit, and that we had to quickly descend about one hundred feet to see the sunrise. I did not have time to explore the summit and fortunately was just below the cloud as the sky progressed from purple to red, then orange as a brilliant spot of gold burst forth from the black horizon. It was an exhilarating experience, and I felt what seemed like the force of purification tugging at my body. It is possible that was the force of gravity because the descending trail was more attractive than the ascending trail back to the summit. Therefore, I did not explore the summit to compare its scene with that of 1959.

Sunrise from Fuji Summit

The trail down was mainly volcanic scree, which, together with the comfortable daylight, made going down much faster than the climb up. Passing a torii and snow chute added interest to the descent; however, most interesting was the view back up the trail of the steady stream of pilgrims. It was easy now to believe the estimate of five thousand climbers being on the mountain on a good day during the climbing season.

Descending Trail from Fuji Summit

It was about ten when Jack and I reached station 5. At a hotel restaurant, he had vegetables with noodles, and I ate spaghetti. The group assembled at eleven thirty, and a thirty-minute bus ride put us at the Yamanakako spa. This modern version of the public hot bath preserves the traditional rejuvenating benefit of relaxing in hot water with new conveniences such as coin-operated lockers and electric hair dryers. This spa had a choice between indoor or outdoor soaking, and of course, males and females were segregated. No one seemed to mind the nudity and lack of privacy.

We arrived back at the Shinjuku Station on schedule at six thirty and, after bidding fond farewell to our fellow climbers, we boarded the subway for return to our hotel in downtown Tokyo. (Fare was about two dollars each versus thirty dollars for the previous day's taxi fare.) We proudly displayed our Fuji walking sticks that were appropriately admired by other subway riders. Although tired, a little sore, and groggy from lack of sleep, a delicious sukiyaki dinner in the hotel dining room culminated a meaningful experience with a feeling of enlightened development—a good feeling, but was it anything more than an emotional reaction? Did anything occur from this challenging activity to support a mystical benefit?

I had accomplished a difficult goal filled with anticipation and meaning. The spirit of Fujitsu was surely there, and I felt its presence, but not once did it reach out to touch me. Furthermore, I did not observe it touching any of my fellow Japanese pilgrims. A stimulating adventure, but still no objective experience to support belief in its associated esoteric traditions. A beautiful experience, though, that in itself supported traditions. It is possible that once again scientific objectivity won out over subjective phenomenology, limiting the view of transcendent possibilities and supporting the Great Paradox.

An old Japanese saying is, "A wise man climbs Mount Fuji once; a silly man climbs it twice." Maybe this should be changed to "A silly man climbs Mount Fuji once; a wiser man climbs it twice." Our destiny seems to be the pursuit of wisdom and understanding. A major way of doing this is through repeating experiences that embrace challenges and explore difficult paths. Many times that seems silly, but then, silly is a relative term that can be applied to many human activities with varying results depending on the depth of the consideration. More important, though, is the realization that this pursuit logically leads to the paradox of believing and questioning explanation and meaning of existence at the most fundamental level. The benefit for me personally seemed to be realization that the quest of the ontological imperative provided significant meaning and purpose for my life, and since that seemed to be a benefit for my fellow Japanese climbers and their society, it may help other societies as well.

Incidentally, the nightclub center that used to be in the Ginza has now been replaced by the Roppongi district. To make this trip to Japan complete within the ten-day allocation, we took an afternoon tour of Tokyo to see the Imperial Palace and Tokyo Bay. I also saw the Dai-ichi Building that was the largest building in Tokyo when I was first there in 1953—now it nestled among towering skyscrapers. We also took a night tour to see modern nightlife and a one-day excursion to Kamakura for seeing the Great Buddha and the ancient Shinto headquarters. The Great Buddha was the only thing that had not changed since 1953.

Chapter 14
Pragmatic Reality: Coherence and Conciliation

Now we have stories about nine mountain climbing experiences. They were personally meaningful for the author, but what was accomplished? What do they mean? Climbing mountains is physically stimulating, emotionally appealing, and mentally challenging and also can be viewed as symbolic of the course in human life— overcoming obstacles in striving for something higher than current existence. Our intellectual capacity for abstract thought causes us to look for meaning and significance in our observations, experiences, and existence leading to the ontological imperative. It is a challenging course fraught with dilemma, paradox, and mystery that make it a sacred effort when carefully considered. The ubiquitous intrigue of mystery and mysticism that has dominated human history and contributed to sacredness is unavoidable for those not consumed by daily existence. To meet the ontological imperative, objective knowledge of science goes only so far and subjective knowledge involving a sacred transcendent realm seems necessary.

A major thread apparent throughout history is the commitment to belief systems that involve some form of supernatural power; a power transcendent to humans, that created the world and still exerts an influence on it; a power generically referred to as God in Western society. This has been an effective way to fill the unique human need to provide for the mystery of existence and the nature of ultimate reality; how and why this existence started and what its future is—the ontological imperative. Why are there so many different answers producing so many different belief systems? Why do so many people become so heavily invested in a particular system that alternatives and conflicting information are ignored, while other people subscribe only superficially, ignore or reject them, or continue searching for more satisfying explanations? Why do the religious beliefs that so effectively fill many needs become so narrowly focused that consideration of conflicting information, alternatives, or modifications is reduced to such an extent that the striving process to seek understanding and coherence is frustrated and conflict is magnified?

The most viable answer to these questions is simply, "human nature." It is the way we are, either as we were created or as we evolved. Many explanations of human nature have been given. A good example from Chapter 10 is the subconscious desire for the "great mysterious caregiver" that we all had as infants, but then lost as we learned about our existence.[1] No animal is more dependent on a caregiver in its early days than a human, and his or her days of dependence are the longest. As we learn from experiences, a complex set of psychological needs develop that interacts with physical needs and biologically based temperaments that are never fully satisfied. The interaction of needs, fulfillments, and beliefs continues to make human nature controversial.

A Scientific View of Human Nature

Although much about human nature is still unknown and controversial, a paradigm has been developing to which many researchers agree. It sees humans as complex, sophisticated, complicated living organisms that have many important common characteristics, yet many characteristics so varied that each person seems to be unique. These characteristics result from an interaction of biological, environmental, experiential, and situational factors. They can operate subconsciously to produce rapid, instinctual actions that may appear without thought; however, vast conscious mental powers provide objective and logical control that usually dominate. People not only react to situations; they create and influence situations and their perception of them, and attribute meanings while searching for explanations. Thought processes emerge from the brain and generate concerns about the past, present, and future that do not exist in other organisms. It seems unlikely that this intricate organism is the result of happenstance and undirected evolution, but there is no proof that it is the result of a supernatural source. Such source has not been disproven, though, and many needs are alleviated by such a belief. Normally thinking people develop or adopt a system of assumptions, values, beliefs, and speculations to meet needs that make their existence manageable and meaningful.

As George Kelley showed (Chapter 10), we are all scientists. We have a need for an understanding of our existence. Science with objective knowledge provides that understanding only as far as observation and research can go. And that does not extend to the meaning of our existence or provide for what started it all. Complete understanding requires assumptions and beliefs that result in religions and philosophies. Spirituality provides a link between religion and science, but problems occur when religion fails to incorporate scientific findings that conflict with dogma, and when science makes unwarranted conclusions about dogma. Science uses objective logic that deals only with observable phenomena whereas religion uses subjective experience that deals with revelation, assumptions, and speculation. As previously discussed, serious conflicts occur.

Conciliation

Resolution of these conflicts seems unlikely; however, conciliation is possible with the potential of consilience for the long-sought unified theory of human nature if it is recognized that this conflict facilitates the continued development of human life. The conflict provides energy for creative thought and constructive activity. Success in accepting and living with this conflict and its uncertainty rewards individuals with a feeling of progress and the satisfaction of pursuing a process leading toward a meaningful goal. For societies, the reward is release from the competitive and violent efforts to impose certain beliefs on others. The great paradox becomes acceptable, and the great dilemma is eliminated (Chapter 12), rewarding individuals and societies with a sense of coherence that unites pursuit of discovery with comforts and benefits of religious faith. Resolving these issues represents a major milestone toward developing an acceptable unified theory of human nature and explanation of fundamental human motivation. This is what E. O. Wilson (2006) describes as consilience.

The time seems right for a second Enlightenment. A time similar to that in eighteenth century Europe when people revolted against the constraining dominance of the church and government. In the United States people are calling for reduction in political dominance and increase in religious belief systems that make sense in light of new knowledge and experience. Here are four suggestions that reasonably follow from the preceding information that may help. The first is to recognize and manage one's own characteristics, adapting those parts of their nature that can be influenced and adopting to those that cannot. Aspirations should be consistent with both personal characteristics and current situation. A key is to know one's capabilities and have a realistic view of one's situation.

Five-Factor Spirituality

The ancient saying "know thyself" is wise advice. However, when people become interested in the fundamental question of "what am I?" they can easily become overwhelmed with the complexity of their nature. The question usually boils down to "out of all of my different characteristics, which ones have important impact on my life?" This has been a driving force in medical and psychological science. The first major set of important characteristics is attributed to the Greek physician Galen who about two thousand years ago proposed that four "body humors"—blood, phlegm, yellow bile, and black bile—were related to a person's health and ability. More blood made one aggressive, more phlegm made one sluggish, more yellow bile made for irritability, and more black bile made for sadness. He called these temperaments sanguine, phlegmatic, choleric, and melancholic respectively. Since that time, hundreds of terms have been proposed[2], and extensive research has arrived at five that most usefully describe important characteristics (personality factors) related to health, well-being, and performance: extraversion, agreeableness, conscientiousness, openness, and neuroticism/emotional stability.[3]

Chapter 10 supported spirituality as a personality factor, a characteristic that exists in most people to a variable degree and that can be measured. It can be related to the "big five" personality factors that form a useful vehicle for analyzing its components. Appendix F is a short self-evaluation by which you can get an indication of how you score on these five factors with respect to spirituality. Rather than good or bad, scores indicate a state to be aware of and manage. Participation is most useful if done before reading the following explanation that relates each of the five factors to effective spirituality. (Complete the short exercise in Appendix F before reading further.)

> 1. *Sociability.* We are social animals, highly dependent on fellow members of our species. There are times we all want to be alone; however, the more interpersonal relations one has, the more satisfied and happy one is. Extraversion, as opposed to introversion, has been associated with "surgency" or feelings of positive well-being. Spirituality, likewise, is more satisfying when shared with others. This characteristic has a strong genetic base, consequently is difficult to modify.
>
> 2. *Agreeableness.* Focusing on points of agreement as opposed to points of conflict sets an atmosphere for positive interpersonal relations as well as positive

internal feelings. The constructive nature of spirituality is more effective with less disagreement, competition, and hostility. Conflicts are inevitable and, when accepted with tolerance, are vehicles for growth and positive relations.

3. *Conscientiousness.* Fortitude and persistence in pursuing a task is related to success and is the most important characteristic sought by employers looking for good job performance. It is a general characteristic that carries over to most tasks including exercise of spirituality. Pursuing knowledge of ultimate concerns is more satisfying than pushing the concerns into the background.

4. *Openness.* Appreciation of aesthetic experience and tolerance for alternate views with curiosity and interest in new experiences, ideas, and information has been associated with intellectual capacity and creativity. Development of spiritual abilities is facilitated by these characteristics when augmented with emotionally appealing activities and patience.

5. *Stability.* Some people are more reactive than others are and may have less control over their emotions. When this interferes with effectiveness, it is called neuroticism. Emotional stability and balance are needed to maintain a constructive spiritual development, and likewise, spiritual development enhances stability

Despite the risk of narcissistic self-centeredness and hubris, it is important for people to be in touch with themselves, and to relate the mechanisms of daily experiences and social demands to their inner feelings and desires. These five characteristics form a convenient vehicle for viewing other people as well as oneself. Recognizing one's own important characteristics is one thing, but probably more important is recognizing how they impact oneself and other people when ultimate concerns emerge. Next, people must realize that they do not yet know the true nature of ultimate reality despite knowledge of one's self and one's environment.

Nognosticism

Chapter 10 pointed out the limited nature of knowledge about reasons for our existence and motives; and Chapter 12 pointed out that even though science has provided knowledge resulting in astounding comforts, capabilities, health, longevity, and well-being, ultimate cause remains a phantom. We recognize that our knowledge and perceptions are limited and that there is more than what is in our current awareness. We think in terms of cause and effect, so we like to think that there is some cause or reason for our existence, for feelings about our life, and for our continued struggles in the face of hardship and unpleasantness. There should be something beyond our current knowledge transcendent to our personal lives that set in motion the developing complexity of our world. This force could be natural or supernatural. At the present time, it is questionable that anyone knows its true nature. We seem to have a need to believe that there is such a transcendent force while recognizing that such a belief may be speculation and worthy of doubt--the great paradox.

It may be a thankless task to believe in a transcendent force as ultimate reality, yet continue to seek substantiation or alternatives because of lingering doubt--the elusiveness paradox. Agnosticism holds that it cannot be accomplished because this ultimate reality cannot be known and dooms us to the fate of Sisyphus, the Greek king who was condemned by the god Zeus to spend eternity repeatedly carrying a large rock to the top of a high hill and watching it roll down.[4] The ancient field of apophatic theology confirms a deity type of ultimate reality, but holds that it cannot be described or named—it is forever a mystical mystery. Nevertheless, the continued advance of knowledge indicates that just because it is not now known, that does not mean it is unknowable.

The paradox of believing that yes, there is, but no, it may not be creates an uncomfortable uncertainty which is the price paid to avoid the depressive pessimism of eternal ignorance. A later chapter attempts to show the feasibility of accepting that there is something beyond our current knowledge that may include a deity, but at the present time it is theory that has not been confirmed. A key is to accept that we just do not know. This is "nognosticism," a term used here to represent an alternative to agnosticism, atheism, deism, and theism. It recognizes that any or all of these may be true. We really don't know, nor is the nature of ultimate reality known. These are beyond our grasp at the present time, and we cannot escape the need to continue the search even if its goal seems inaccessible and its process seems remote and difficult.

Science and religion may converge someday, but it will not be anytime soon. In the meantime, for optimal well-being and health, we must recognize the need for both and work toward the "great conciliation" of religion and belief with science and doubt, striving for a seemingly inaccessible goal while living in the world as it seems here and now. The third suggestion is that while having belief in "our own system," and realizing that it may not be the absolute truth, we should be tolerant of other belief systems, even if we disagree.

Ecumenical Humanism

The term "ecumenical humanism" implies a philosophy that places humans at the center of existence and sees them as holistic, creative, specially endowed organisms that are oriented toward a goal of developing increased understanding of reality that extends beyond immediate physical phenomena and into a possibly transcendent realm. Humans are at the center because their minds know best the products of their own limited perceptions—perceptions that form their own sense of identity and place in the world. They have a universal need for a belief system that provides a satisfactory explanation about all of this for themselves while recognizing that other people may have other belief systems that likewise are satisfactory for them.

Different religions fill this need for different people through different beliefs about some form of transcendent existence or force. For Christians, this is God as manifested in Jesus Christ and as explained in the New Testament. To fit in with most Christian churches, one must accept Jesus as a divine power and the avenue to salvation. Other religions have even more stringent dogma. Most emphasize faith that requires subjugating further inquiry to acceptance. Such acceptance stymies further search into the purpose and meaning of one's existence and life in general. Truth, then, is not something to search for because it is revealed through faith, and faith results from acceptance of a particular belief system.

Despite the large number of established religions, many people have not found any church or organized system with acceptable tenets of faith. For them, belief in a transcendent force that provides for and explains existence by supplementing the limitations of science would be more satisfying if they supported a continuing search encompassing scientific information, personal experience, and objective analysis rather than only religious teachings of faith. Their destiny seems to be a quest for development. Paleontologist Teilhard de Chardin said this from a philosophical viewpoint,[5] and psychologist Martin Seligman said this from a scientific viewpoint.[6] Yes, revelation and faith are important; without them, we would flounder in ambiguous solipsism. However, people are so complex and sophisticated with ideas that result from such a complicated interaction of temperaments, experiences, values, attitudes, and beliefs that spiritual ideas are rarely the same for any two individuals. Social interdependence brings people together into societies that stimulate the sharing and adjustment of personal ideas to produce organized group beliefs and culture. Such is the history of religion, but despite the universality of human needs and the desire for harmony and coherence, many different belief systems have been organized, each purporting to be the only one of true validity.

It is not necessary to accept all religions as true or equal or give up one's own belief system in order to tolerate the existence and function of other belief systems. We can be tolerant of other religions without losing faith in our own. (That is, as long as the other religions are tolerant of ours.) As used here, the term "ecumenical humanism" recognizes that each religion has reason for existence if it ameliorates the ontological imperative and improves human welfare. It is a melding of secular humanism and religion based on tolerance of alternate views. And, the fourth suggestion is to recognize our innate need to strive for knowledge about cause and meaning of our existence—the ontological imperative.

Pragmatic Pluralism

It is a tall order to find a belief system that is based on the ontological imperative; that accepts the possibility of alternate realities beyond our present knowledge; that accepts the need to both believe and doubt the existence of a higher intellect while seeking its nature; that tolerates and cooperates with multiple belief systems; and that lives constructively in the here and now. Shortcomings exist in all of the currently available belief systems such theism, deism, pantheism, agnosticism, and atheism; or the more recently formed panentheism, theological humanism, or religious naturalism. Some of the latter come close but none explicitly advocate belief in a divine power while also doubting certainty of its existence and knowledge of its nature.

The term "pragmatism" implies practical usability and requires maintaining contact with the needs of existence and well-being as they seem at the present time. It recognizes that even though anything may be possible, we must consider what is logically probable and useful in the current situation. The term "pluralism" implies recognition of possible validity for multiple realities and ultimate causes with tolerance of alternate views. Maybe the term "pragmatic pluralism" would be acceptable to people aware of their need to believe in a higher intellect and to share it with others, but are dissatisfied with the limitations, irrationalities, and conflicts imposed by institutional religions and militant atheism. They would be aware of unlimited possibilities but live with probabilities of what is practical "here and now."

It should be noted that the term pluralism is used here to indicate possible multiple forms of reality, not just multiple views. The term pragmatic pluralism has already been used in the philosophy fields of ethics, politics, and religion. The imminent Finnish philosopher, Sami Pihlstrom (2013) has summarized that use for integrating multiple views, approaches, and methods for social issues while emphasizing usefulness and practical application. The term "practical ontologic pluralism" might be more descriptive of the unique concept proposed here and might reduce the baggage associated with pragmatic pluralism. Also it might better relate to the ontological imperative in explaining why people persist in pursuing difficult tasks, but it would lack the rich philosophical implication of pragmatic pluralism which is used here in a basic sense. Pragmatic pluralism is hereby defined as the philosophy of life that recognizes that realities different to our own with alternate laws of nature and different forms of life may possibly exist including a transcended realm containing a deity. However, we must live in our own world as we see it here and now according to practical probabilities.

Implications

As thinking humans, we are concerned with why we are here, where we came from, and where we are going. We recognize that our knowledge is limited and that there is a mysterious unknown. Anything may be possible, but we must live in the world that presents itself to us and realize that not everything is probable.

We do not know for sure that there is something in the way of a deity or supreme being, and whether there is or is not, whether we believe or not, we would do well to recognize the benefits of living as if there is. For social justice, we need a moral authority that transcends the vagrancies of human judgment. For personal coherence and happiness, we need the possibility that there is a purpose that provides meaning for our existence. We need to think that there may be some continuation after personal death. We need to feel that there is some way to atone for our missteps. We need to be aware of our subconscious dependence on a mystical caregiver. We need an object of devotion and source of unconditional love. We need social support with a sense of belonging. And finally, we need to recognize that we don't know everything and that in the realm of the unknown, anything may exist—even plural realities and the divine supreme being of our forefathers.

Since no one knows for sure, most people subscribe to the most expedient belief system available. Despite individuality and creativity, this tends to be a social endeavor that acquires a life of its own. The leaders and activists propel it to an elite status calling for supplication and faith. If we remain aware of the system's origin, we will recognize the paradox and dilemma involved and tolerate them as well as those of other systems. Aggression and proselytization can give way to cooperation and development. Prejudice and conflict can give way to assistance and exchange. That is, if we can believe and doubt at the same time. Thus, if we can believe without closing our mind to alternatives and if we can doubt without losing coherence, then we can best develop both individually and collectively. It facilitates climbing high mountains, running great races, and feeling useful. Through faith, hope, belief, and reason, people can experience life as being manageable and meaningful despite an uncomfortable uncertainty.

Chapter 15
Uncertain Climb: Mount Kilimanjaro

So, we live in a world of paradox facing dilemma, conflict, and uncertainty. Is it better to put on the rose colored glasses and ignore this unsettling situation, or is it better to try to adapt and live with it? Maybe one more mountain climb fraught with uncertainty can explore the feasibility of living with uncertainty of the great paradox. And a good study of this question would be challenging an 85 year old man, frail, tired with worn out joints and deteriorated muscles to climb to the summit of a 19,000 foot mountain.

Kilimanjaro is a widely known mountain made famous by Ernest Hemingway and Gregory Peck (see preface). It is the highest free standing mountain in the world and the highest in all of Africa with a top elevation of 19,340 feet. It is one of the most popular mountains with an estimate of 35,000 climbers each year. Technical skill is not required, but it is grueling for even experienced mountaineers requiring about 20 miles of hiking to reach a base camp at 15,500 feet on the shortest route. It consists of three volcanic peaks with the tallest and largest in the center. The rim of the main volcanic peak is reached by a steep 4 mile 8 hour climb into subfreezing temperatures with another hour of steady ascent along the rim to reach the summit. The Kilimanjaro Park Service estimates that 41% of the climbers reach the summit. It is highly uncertain that an elderly frail man would succeed.

Answering Big Questions

Mount Kilimanjaro in Tanzania, Africa

We have already established how psychology shows that people by nature need stimulation and challenge. Too little and they are bored; too much and they are overwhelmed with stress. They are goal oriented, setting up tasks and deriving pleasure from accomplishment. Plus, they have a natural desire to reach into the unknown and acquire new experiences and information that has potential for filling in the mysteries of existence. But, they live in a world dominated with immediate needs. Not everyone is consciously concerned with the whys and wherefores of their activities and existence, and where climbing a mountain may be beyond the meaningfulness of one person, it may be of special significance to another.

There were several reasons I wanted to climb Kilimanjaro. First was the need for another mountain climbing story to round-out this book that alternates chapters of climbing experiences with chapters about why people undertake such difficult activities. A second reason for this climb was to experience a distinctly uncertain situation and explore "living with the uncertainty of paradox." Can an 85 year old frail elderly person with worn out joints and muscular deterioration achieve an important but unlikely goal? This goes back to psychology that clearly shows a major factor in personal health, particularly for older people, is activity—both mental and physical. Unfortunately, many older people give in to their aches, pains, and weaknesses becoming couch potatoes that wither away. And then a final reason to attempt this climb was the neat idea of establishing a new record for the oldest person to successfully reach the Kilimanjaro summit.

An agent in Boulder, Colorado, arranged for my youngest son, Jack (46 years old) and me to make the climb in the September dry season. My climbing experiences and those of Jack were many years ago, but even now as a corporate pilot, Jack stays in good shape with running and mountain biking, so no special preparation was required for him. For me though, there was work to do. Surgery for the replacement of my second knee had been in January and there was a question about regeneration of the leg muscles.

In St Louis the closest thing to mountain climbing is hiking the Chubb Trail in West Tyson Park. It ascends only about 400 feet, so seven laps are required to simulate a 2,800 foot climb (the average ascent for a day's climb on Kilimanjaro is 3,000 feet). Meeting people on the Chubb Trail was a fascinating experience of making friends with interesting St Louisians, but when the temperature and humidity rose to the 100 range and Missouri mosquitos emerged, it was so difficult I sought alternate ways for conditioning. I found it in the local Club Fitness gym that had a stair climbing machine that accomplished the same workout in air conditioned comfort. Enough so that I felt encouraged about maybe being adequately strong for the September climb.

After two days of frantic airline flight segments, Jack and I arrived at the Kilimanjaro Airport and were met by Tanzania Journeys representatives that drove us about an hour to a hotel in the village of Moshi close to the Kilimanjaro Park entrance. After supper, a good night's rest, and buffet breakfast the next morning, our guide, Rashid, oriented us on what to expect and went over our clothing and equipment pointing out what to take and what to leave at the hotel. After another good night's rest we drove in an overloaded van about an hour to the Marangu Gate entrance to the Kilimanjaro National Park at an elevation of 6,700 feet. In a large parking lot our party assembled and organized. For Jack and myself as climbers there was a guide, assistant guide, cook, and eight porters who carried our camping gear and food. One porter carried a portable toilet and another carried oxygen equipment. What luxury—never before had I had such help! It was interesting that the porters were limited to carrying 55 pounds each and were inspected and weighed by park rangers before being allowed to start.

Climbing Higher

Marangu Gate Parking Lot at entrance to Kilimanjaro National Park

The first day's hike started at 11:00am and was quite enjoyable ascending about 2,100 feet over a linear distance of 7 miles through rain forest complete with monkeys and native wildlife. About 1:00pm the guides broke out box lunches consisting of blackened charcoaled chicken, boiled egg, pastries, and fruit, and our picnic lunch was supplemented with interesting explanations of the local wildlife.

Answering Big Questions

Rain Forest Trail from Marangu Gate

At 4:00pm, we arrived at Mandara Camp (8,875 feet elevation). This was a group of unheated A-frame huts with bunk beds. One hut served as a dining room shared with other friendly climbers, and where we had a delicious supper of cucumber soup, blackened charcoaled fish, vegetable casserole, and fruit. The next morning we were awakened by a porter bearing hot ginger tea for eye opening and hot water for washing. Breakfast was porridge with pancakes, scrambled eggs, bacon, toast, and fruit. After preparing our day packs with fresh water and rain gear and repacking everything else in the duffle bag for the porters to carry, we started a 7.5 mile hike at 8:20am ascending 3,400 feet to reach Horombo Camp (12,200 feet) at 3:30pm. This leg was kind of tough, but mostly in rain forest shielded from the hot sun with a pleasant temperature. Day 3 was for acclimatization at Horombo. Jack went on a scenic hike with guide Rashid, but I elected to rest in the warm sleeping bag. On day 4, a 6 mile hike started from Horombo at 8:20am, ascended 3,300 feet, and reached Kibo Camp (15500 feet) at 2:50pm. This leg was tough, but enjoyable because we broke out of the jungle growth and could view distant features. This took us through a saddle between the main peak and a secondary peak to its east, both of which were impressively visible. Kibo Camp consisted of dormitory style huts with bunk beds and many climbers milling around and sharing stories. They were from many nationalities with the most vocal being from France

Mandara Camp at 8,875 feet Elevation

Day 5 was for acclimatization at Kibo, and once again I chose to rest in the warm zero degree sleeping bag while Jack went on a scenic hike with Rashid. Sleeping was sporadic because of climbers returning from summit attempts—some did not make it and all were exhausted. Day 6 started on day 5 at 11:00pm when we departed on

Answering Big Questions

the night climb to the Kilimanjaro crater rim to arrive at sunrise. This was the toughest part—three miles up 3,000 feet on steep rocky switchbacks where all of my effort was needed to continue putting one foot ahead of the other and maintaining balance with the limited view of a headlamp. The temperature was below freezing so Jack and I wore light and medium weight under garments with insulated outer wear and down parka, augmented with balaclava, hand and toe warmers. By the time we got to the crater rim and daylight was breaking, my lungs ached, my legs hurt, my back was sore, but somehow my feet continued to work. What a relief when I saw the sign that said "Stella Point" and the sun was peeking through the layer of clouds far below. For some climbers, this was far enough and marked their turning point, but to reach the summit, another hour of steady ascent along the crater rim was needed to reach "Uhuru Peak" Summit at 19,340 feet. The going was slow but we arrived at 7:20am. Rashid said that the steep climb was usually made at night so that climbers would not be distracted by the imposing view ahead or the scary view behind, and effort could be focused on foot work. That could account for my being able to summons enough energy to continue to the summit.

Uhuru Peak Summit at 19,340 feet Elevation

Despite the fatigue of utter exhaustion, sight of the Uhuru Peak sign, created a jubilant surge of energy that was shared with other climbers competing for photos in front of the sign and sharing exclamations of awe about distant views. On one side was a drop-off into the ancient volcano crater and on the other side was a drop-off into a billowy cloud layer covering the southern part of Africa. The air was cold, probably about 15 degrees Fahrenheit, but the bright warm sunshine made it comfortable. Although there was no snow on the summit, a huge glacier on the left side reminded of past snow and ice. What a pleasant feeling of inspiration, but breathing was difficult causing an overwhelming desire to start down soon.

South Glacier from Summit

With renewed energy, we started the descent on the same path as our upward climb. That energy was quickly dampened because of the difficulty in clambering over rock formations and stones on the steep slope. We reached Kibo Camp at 11:20am, wearily ate some porridge, and conked out for a short nap. We departed from Kibo at 2:00pm and arrived at Horombo Camp as the sun was setting at 7:00pm. After a short night's sleep, we departed Horombo on day 7 at 9:20am. It was cold and sleet was stinging my face as we picked our way down the trail. We were now under that layer of clouds whose tops looked so inspiring from the summit. Sleet, freezing rain and light rain fell during most of this leg of the descent. (If this is the dry season, what happens in the rainy season?) We arrived at Mandara Camp at 3:00pm, ate a box lunch, and immediately proceeded on the last leg to Marangu Gate. This was tough for me. Stepping over rocks and tree roots was excruciating for my knees and aggregated a state of physical exhaustion. Fortunately, assistant guide Rama stuck close by me and was quick to provide a steadying hand when I would stumble. Most of this leg was in the dark, so head lamps were needed allowing us to arrive about 8:30pm at the Marangu Gate.

Although the park office was closed, a ranger was there to present us with certificates for a successful climb. The porters were already there and had our personal gear loaded in the van. Our whole climbing team was there, so after breaking out a bottle of champagne, we exchanged good-byes and distributed tips. The drive back to Moshi was subdued—we all thought only of a hot shower and bed rest.

Two nights in the hotel before starting the homeward flights had been arranged for. This was fortunate because early on our climb, I had stumbled causing an abrasion on my right forearm that had become infected, and now I was able to have it treated at a local clinic and started on a course of Egyptian anti-biotic. This extra day also provided an opportunity to see the local area, shop, and carefully select a tanzanite pendent to take home to my wife. Tanzanite gems are unique to this area and as bluish versions of diamonds are distinctly valuable tourist items. Another unique item is a small painting of Kilimanjaro on banana leaf—a must souvenir.

As a departing celebration, we invited Rashid and Rama to join us for a memorable dinner at the hotel. We had been through a lot together creating a lasting bond similar to those I had developed when serving in the U S Army. Jack and I had much to think about during the long series of flights back to the United States. Success in climbing Kilimanjaro did seem to add to a comforting feeling of moving "higher" in life and there seemed to be some increase in knowledge that could be considered enlightenment, but the task now was readjustment of our biological clocks and digestive systems.

It is amazing that no major adverse events occurred and no climber experienced any symptoms of altitude sickness. Oxygen was available, but not used. Diamox (altitude adjustment medication) was used and probably helped. It is amazing that an 85 year old body could live with the uncertainty of such a demanding challenge and resolve it, thus demonstrating the ability of people to maintain vitality in old age, and to accomplish difficult goals such as providing a new mountain climbing story and setting a new world record. Although difficulties and discomforts had occurred, uncertainty was not only tolerated, it was rewarded.

The snows of Kilimanjaro had been surmounted without adding any more frozen carcasses. The epigraph at the beginning of this book is about a leopard that became a frozen carcass after reaching the mountain's top and was presented by Ernest Hemingway as a riddle for the story's hero. Why would anything climb so high that it froze to death? The story did not provide a specific answer; however, the hero died in pursuit of the riddle. He had waisted his talents and thus failed to climb the mountain of life symbolized as Kilimanjaro. The implication is that climbing to a high level is a natural goal that requires constructive use of one's talents and fortitude in meeting challenges and uncertainties. Mount Kilimanjaro is thus a symbol of life's purpose.

Chapter 16
Living with Paradox

A final comment should now be made about a major theme of this book—the great paradox of believing in a transcendent power and at the same time questioning its validity. It is easy to say and to justify our need to accept and manage uncertainty of the great paradox, but it is more difficult to accomplish. Paradox involves conflict, uncertainty, dilemma, and confusion that can be summarized under the term ambiguity. People are uncomfortable with this, find it difficult to manage, and have varying success in dealing with it. Difficulty in living with ambiguity is considered a major source of the anxiety and depression that are prevalent today in our society. It has also been the source of violence both within and between societies. How can we best deal with this conundrum?

First, it is helpful to recognize that ambiguity is a natural part of human life. We all are continually faced with the need to make choices and decisions when the best solution is unclear or subject to conflicting information. Philosopher David Cosby has published several books showing the inevitability of ambiguity.[1] He proposes this issue as being a major factor in the development of religion. It is very comforting to believe that an omnipotent, omniscient benefactor is behind all events and that allowing "thy" will to be done will produce the best outcome. It alleviates the burden of shouldering responsibility all alone, provides meaning and purpose, and is a major provision in all of the Abrahamic religions. Throughout known history humans have turned to belief in a supernatural force for survival and comfort in a dangerous and mysterious world, thus reducing ambiguity but it has also contributed to the great paradox of believing in a force that conflicts with objective observation and experience.

In his book, *The Paradox of God*, Clifford Pickover (2001) showed that paradoxes of free-will, consciousness, belief, and divine force are among the most profound and perplexing arenas of human thought. He presents 16 historical examples of paradox that have been faced by society and managed in an acceptable way. For solution he relies on innate human characteristics such as pattern-seeking and brain neurology as predispositions toward belief in an all-powerful supernatural force that makes paradox more tolerable.

While turning to a religious faith can reduce the conflict and uncertainty of many ambiguities, many philosophers such as William James, Mikhail Bakhtin, and Gianni Vattimo have proposed value in uncertainty. Certainty leads to faith and commitment in authoritarian rules that may deaden a believer's attempts to resolve conflicts and explore, thus reducing beneficial effects of religion.[2] There is a history in Christian tradition that an "uncertain naiveté" is recognized as essential for a satisfying dynamic religious faith.[3] Religion Professor Mark Taylor goes further in his book *After God* by showing that recognizing a paradoxical faith of affirming possibility in the face of impossibility produces an uncertainty that leads to the creative emergence that has fostered human evolution.[4] Belief in certainty provided either by religion or science has been shown to stimulate passivity whereas recognizing uncertainty stimulates action and inquery.[5] So, uncertainty is beneficial even when relying on supernatural deity.

Dr. Cosby demonstrated that comfort with uncertainty can furthermore be achieved without belief in a supernatural deity if one can recognize intractable ambiguity as being an inevitable and meaningful part of nature.[1] Nature seems to have provided some relief from ambiguity through constructive life experiences that are independent of belief. Studies about the sense of well-being in individuals found that people with constructive life experiences have a more mature stage of psychological development; accept conflicts and difficulties in their lives; and take steps to ameliorate problems.[6] At this stage a person accepts the dynamics of life even while realizing that its meaning may remain elusive and irrelevant. Even if one has not reached this level of development, knowing of its the possibility makes acceptance of current conflicts easier and more meaningful, and facilitates further development.

Research has shown that tolerance and management of ambiguity is related to health and well-being.[7] Health and well-being have also been associated with the experience of awe as discussed in Chapter 6. Awe is usually a rewarding experience involving mystery, wonder, emotional arousal, and feeling of contact with a higher realm. However, this rewarding experience would not occur without feelings of uncertainty and ambiguity.

A comprehensive survey of research from social psychology and cognitive science about ambiguity was published by Jamie Holmes in 2015. This research was triggered by the famous work of Leon Festinger in the 1950s about cognitive dissonance that was used in Chapter 12 to explain a mechanism for change in beliefs. Holmes showed that we all have a "need for closure" and an "intolerance of ambiguity" that causes us many times to jump to conclusions before considering appropriate information, thus resulting in faulty decisions. The antidote is to create a culture that respects ambiguity and stimulates people to recognize its prevalence thereby avoiding hasty decisions. Also emphasized is the role of ambiguity for encouraging creativity and innovation in individuals, and for advancing science and culture in societies.

A more applied approach has resulted in many reports about conflict resolution, negotiation, mediation, management, and motivation. Success in all of these is built on recognizing existence of opposing factors and considering alternate views. Sometimes motivation to resolve conflicts must be developed and value of effort versus payoff must be weighed with tolerance. Practical solutions without emotionally laden bias are the key to this non-ideological approach of overcoming ambiguity resulting from conflict. A realistic view of factors relating to an ambiguous issue with subjugation of emotions seem to provide the best solution.[8]

Techniques for allowing creative and productive results to come from the inherent uncertainties of life are presented by Jonathan Fields (2011) in his book *Uncertainty: Turning Fear and Doubt into Fuel for Brilliance*. Out of many techniques to capitalize on uncertainty and to prevent vulnerability for fear, doubt, and anxiety, these are emphasized: accept uncertainty and its risks as a small price to pay for creative accomplishment; develop solid foundations to which uncertainties can be anchored; and create rituals that provide feelings of stability in the face of confusion.

Psychiatry and clinical psychology have organized many ways to help prevent adverse effects of mental conflicts and to alleviate suffering providing techniques useful for people faced with ambiguity. Most popular is the approach known as cognitive behavioral therapy that attempts to elucidate factors precipitating a difficulty, view those factors realistically, and then tailor steps to change their impact.[9] Although these ways were aimed at persons with mental problems, they have contributed to alleviating discomforts of ambiguities and conflicts experienced by most people on a daily basis. Since these discomforts produce stress, research about stress management has produced many techniques for alleviating their adverse impacts.[10] These are widely supported and practiced by organizations as well as individuals.

The paradox of believing and questioning the existence of a transcendent force in a realm beyond the current view of existence can be seen as a natural part of our life. It is a "state of affairs" that can be accepted along with other ambiguities and managed in a thoughtful manner. Instead of being viewed adversely, these ambiguities can be viewed as challenges that energize progress in personal development, that improve sense of well-being, and that stimulate scientific advances. Thus, the ontological imperative can be pursued effectively recognizing that there is knowledge we do not yet grasp, that conflicting ideas are natural, and that we can enjoy life here and now despite unknown possibilities. A feeling of purpose in the struggles to overcome obstacles of existence, and a feeling that life is meaningful and manageable provide a comforting sense of well-being for individuals and a more cooperative attitude between societies.

Epilogue

Not all mountain climbing adventures are started for personal reasons, but these too can have enlightening effects. My experience in climbing Mount Naze in Taiwan did not start with the goal of reaching a summit for any personal reason. It was to retrieve the body of a pilot that had crashed on an isolated mountain top. I was on a military tour of duty with the Military Assistance Advisory Group (MAAG) working with Chiang Kai-shek's Republic of China Army as an advisor for aircraft maintenance. An additional duty was maintenance officer for the small flight detachment we had at the Taipei Airport. We had several airplanes and helicopters to transport MAAG staff around the island of Taiwan and to places such as Hong Kong and Okinawa.

It was Sunday morning and I was sleeping late when the phone call came saying that an airplane crash had been reported and the plane was determined to be one of ours. One of our pilots had left on an early flight from Taipei to Tai Chung in a U6 Beaver, and an air traffic controller traced the flight path to that mountain site. A local village rescue team was at the crash site on a mountain twenty-five miles southwest of Taipei and there were no survivors. Our emergency procedures called for the maintenance officer to organize rescue actions, so I was off. Flying a light helicopter, I picked up a medical officer but the weather was so bad that after about ten miles we had to turn back. He arranged for a medical crash truck and again we started out. On arriving at a village at the base of the mountain we were led on foot for a climb to the crash site at 6000 feet elevation. It was a tough climb from an elevation of 1000 feet through a cold light rain. The local rescue team was at the crash site and had extracted the charred remains of the only occupant. Yes, I could recognize that it was John alright despite the extensive burns. All that was left of the airplane was the tail section. Now the task was to get John's remains back to Taipei where his wife and two children would be waiting.

Remains of U6 Beaver

The accident investigation failed to determine the cause. John had filed a flight plan to proceed from the Taipei Airport west to the PO radio beacon and then south to his destination. It is possible that he took a short-cut by departing from the path to PO and flying visually to Tai Chung, an acceptable but risky action because of the high probability for clouds to limit visibility. He could have lost sight of the close-by mountains and got too close to one of them. Less likely was malfunction of navigation instruments, and then there is the possibility that the accident was intentional because of the spat he had with his wife the day before.

This was not the first time I had been confronted with death, but it was stirring because of our close working relationship. He was the advisor for aircraft procurement, parts, and supplies so we not only worked closely together, we backed each other up frequently, and shared activities with our children and wives. Death is an event we all will experience and what happens to our physical body is well known, but what happens to our consciousness can only be theorized as done in Chapter 8. Many answers have been proposed. For religion it is based on revelation. For science it is inconclusive because no reliable results are available for the "ultimate experiment" that takes place at the time of death. For psychology, philosophy, and literature it is based on experience, speculation, and the development of a person's life. If that life had developed with meaning and purpose, death likewise could have meaning and purpose.

Human nature is built on overcoming obstacles, reducing uncertainty, and developing resolutions for issues of life that vary from meeting immediate needs to searching for ultimate reality and truth. One of the most useful explanations of this process is the psychosocial theory of development originated by the notable psychologist Erik Erikson (1964). This is based on research showing a pattern in the way people change their actions and reaction as they advance over their years. Their years can be divided into stages characterized by different typical major concerns that become critical issues, and how they resolve these concerns create psychological turning points. This pattern helps to explain why the ontological imperative has different ramifications for different people in different stages of life.

An infant is concerned largely with meeting physiological needs and because of dependence on caregivers, the critical issue is development of trust that these needs will be met rather than a mistrust that can come from experience of unmet needs. In early childhood (about 1-3 years of age) self-control is a major concern and successful resolution results in a feeling of autonomy rather than a feeling of shame and doubt. From about 3-6 years the issue is usually development of initiative instead of passivity with feelings of guilt. From about 6-12 the issue is a feeling of industry versus that of inferiority. For adolescents, identity is critical, then in young adulthood (20-30) resolution of social intimacy is critical to prevent a feeling of isolation. Adulthood from about 30-65 is concerned with being productive and generative versus stagnating without accomplishment. The final stage comes when people slow down and retire from previous activities. That is when their life is up for review and a feeling develops either of despair or integrity, where life is seen with failure and meaninglessness or as productive with a feeling of meaningfulness and satisfaction about accomplishments.

For people fortunate enough to reach that final stage, the feeling of integrity is determined by their view of having meaning, purpose, development, and contribution. It is too late then to go back and change what was done, but it is not too late to avoid despair by finding meaning and purpose in previous and continuing activities. This is also important for people that reach the end of life prematurely, that are faced with the prospect of dying before a full life span is completed. How can despair be avoided? That is the purpose of this book.

It proposes that we recognize that our knowledge is limited and that there is an unknown realm beyond our current grasp. In that unknown realm there must be something bigger, better, and beyond our personal physical existence. This something could be anything. It may have gotten things started and may even continue to influence things. We do not really know, and furthermore, we do not know what the relationship is between that unknown realm and our personal selves. Is there something in each of us (such as consciousness or soul) that joins that realm when we have completed our physical life? We do not know, but it is possible enough that we can look forward to getting the answer one way or another at the time of our physical demise. In the meantime we can build experiences supporting a sense of well-being by pursuing our personal growth and contributing to that of others, by respecting the diverse beliefs of other people without compromising our own beliefs, and by trusting that the unknown benevolent realm does exist.

Knowing whether God or any other esoteric power really exists becomes unimportant if we are living effectively. We can try to draw conclusions from experiences and accumulated knowledge with a sense of respect and wonder about the unknown that creates a feeling of awe and reverence. So, what does all this mean? What is its impact? We can be content with the realization that even though we don't know, we can enjoy pursuing the ontological imperative, the quest, with a feeling of emerging, advancing, and flourishing...

"And the night shall be filled with music,
And the cares, that infest the day,
Shall fold their tents, like the Arabs,
And silently steal away."
          (When Day is Done, Longfellow)
This may not be the best recipe for happiness, but it provides a sense of contentment, accomplishment, knowledge, and respect for the unknown...

"He went like one that hath been stunned,
And is of sense forlorn:
A sadder and a wiser man
He rose the morrow morn."
          (Rhyme of the Ancient Mariner, Coleridge)
In the meantime happiness comes from enjoying the mysteries of life and realizing that we can...

"...live in a house by the side of the road
Where the race of men go by-
The men who are good and the men who are bad,
As good and as bad as I.
I would not sit in the scorner's seat
Nor hurl the cynic's ban-
Let me live in a house by the side of the road
And be a friend to man."
          (The House by the Side of the Road, Foss)
The main thing we can hope for is to leave...

"Footprints in the sands of time,
Footprints that perhaps another,
Sailing o'er life's solemn main,
A forlorn and shipwrecked brother,
Seeing shall take heart again."

(A Psalm of Life, Wadsworth)
And when it is all over…
"… When my work is done,
My course on earth is run,
May it be said, well done,
Be thou at peace."
        (West Point Alma mater, Reinecke)

Endnotes

2-1 Hebb, 1955.
2-2 Zuckerman, 1979.
2-3 Eysenck, 1982.
2-4 Friedman & Rosenman, 1974
2-5 McClelland, 1965.
4-1 Little, 1999.
4-2 Cantor, 1990.
4-3 Allport, 1954.
4-4 Maslow, 1968.
4-5 Emmons, 1989.
4-6 Lazarus, 1991.
4-7 Adler, 1997.
4-8 Minninger, 1957.
4-9 Jung, 1938.
4-10 Crumbaugh, 1973
4-11 Battista, 1973.
4-12 Wong, 1998, Markman, Prouix. & Lindberg, 2013.
4-13 Steger, Frazier, Oishi, & Kaler; 2006.
4-14 Wheeler, Munz, & Jain; 1990.
4-15 Wheeler & Haywood, 1995.
4-16 Seligman, 2002.
4-17 Flanagan, 2009.
5-1 Ibarra, 1996.
6-1 Collegiate Dictionary, 2003.
6-2 Zajonc, 1984.
6-3 Lazarus, 1991.
6-4 Schacter & Singer, 1962.
6-5 Zillman, 1983, Bargh, 2014.
6-6 Barrett, Nienderthal, & Winkleman; 2005.
6-7 Newberg & D'Aquili 2001.
6-8 Emmons, 2005, Schneider, 2004
6-9 Hood, 2005, Mikulak, 2015
6-10 Rotter, 1975.
6-11 DeCharms, 1968.
6-12 Bowker, 2002.
6-13 Hamblin & Seely, 2007.
6-14 Bernbaum, 1997.
6-15 McFarlane, 2003.
8-1 Chalmers, 1996.
8-2 Popper & Eccles, 1977.
8-3 Ryle, 1949.
8-4 Dennett, 2005.

8-5 Hameroff, Kaszniak,& Chalmers; 1999.
8-6 Hameroff & Penrose, 1996.
8-7 Walker, 2000, p 326.
8-8. Wheeler, 1990.
8-9 Jahn & Dunne, 2011.
8-10 Grassie, 2010.
8-11 Haisch, 2010.
8-12 Gazzaniga, 2008.
8-13 Ornstein, 1977.
8-14 Pribram, 1999.
8-15 Koch, 2004.
8-16 Pert, 1997.
8-17 Collins, 2006.
8-18 Lipton, 2005.
8-19 Stevenson, 1997.
8-20 Moody, 1975.
8-21 Targ, 2004.
8-22 Schwartz, 2011.
8-23 Lipton, 2005.
8-24 Beauregard & O'Leary, 2007, p 166.
8-25 Radin, 2006.
8-26 Tart, 1992.
8-27 Dossey, 1996, May & Bhatt, 2014
8-28 Hodge, 2007.
8-29 Schwartz & Dossey, 2010.
8-30 Horgan, 2003.

8-31 Tart, 1997.
8-32 Blackmore, 2004.
8-33 Mishlove, 1975, 1995.
10-1 Kelly, 1955.
10-2 Heider, 1944.
10-3 Emmons, 1999.
10-4 Rossano, 2010.
10-5 Fowler, 1981.
10-6 Ellis, 2011.
10-7 Cloninger, 2004.
10-8 Huxley's, 1944.
10-9 Hamer, 2004.
10-10 Nelson, 2011.
10-11 Newberg & D'Aquili, 2001.
10-12 Goodenough, 1998.
10-13 Spilka, Hood, Hunshberger, & Gorsuch; 2003.
10-14 Paloutzian & Park, 2005.
10-15 Nelson, 2009.
10-16 Ellison, 1983.
10-17 Rican & Janosova, 2010
10-18 Harrington, 2005;
10-19 Kashdan & Nezlek, 2012.
10-20 Emmons, 1999
10-21 Batson, 1993.
10-22 May, 1967.
10-23 Fromm, 1947.

10-24 Maslow, 1968.
10-25 Kluger, 2015.
10-26 Similarly to Kohlberg's (1984) sixth stage of development.
10-27 Freud, A, 1965.
10-28 Buhler, 1967.
10-29 Riegel's (1973) dialectic.
Erikson's (1964) integrity.
Loevenger's (1973) integration.
Kohlberg's (1984) ontological.
Fowler's (1981) universalizing.
10-30 Aronson, 1972.
10-31 Faber, 2004.
10-32 Kelly, 1955.
10-33 Adler, 1979.
10-34 Rotter, 1975.
10-35 Fromm, 1973.
10-36 Jung, 1938.
10-37 Allport, 1955.
10-38 Antonovsky, 1987.
10-39 Frankl, 1997.
10-40 Stapp, 2004.
10-41 Rossano, 2010.
10-42 Helminiak, 1998.
10-43 Wade, 2009.
10-44 Miller & Thoresen, 2003.
10-45 Gallup & Lindsay, 1999.
10-46 Durant, W & Durant, A; 1968.
11-1 The New English Bible, 1970.
11-2 Armstrong, 2006.
12-1 Campbell, 1988.
12-2 Cardena, Lynn, & Kripner; 2000.
12-3 Kurtz, 2007.
12-4 Dawkins, 2006.
12-5 Loftus, 1997.
12-6 Newberg & D'Aquili, 2001.
12-7 Strassman, 2000.
12-8 Powell, 2009.
12-9 Russell, 2008.
12-10 Eagleman, 2011.
12-11 Polkinghorne, 2007.
12-12 Goodenough, 1998.
12-13 Pert, 2006.
12-14 Collins, 2006.
12-15 Schwartz, 2006.
12-16 Braxton, 2007.
12-17 Dennett, 2006.
12-18 Dawkins, 2006.
12-19 Harris, 2004.
12-20 Stenger, 2003.
12-21 Festinger, 1957.
12-22 Taylor, 2007.

12-23 Bering, 2011.
12-24 Unwin, 2003.
12-25 Meyers, 2008, p 4.
12-26 Attridge, 2009, Ward, 2008.
13-1 Faber, 2004.
14-2 McCrae & Costa, 1999.
14-3 Goldberg, 1993.
14-4 Camus, 1960.
14-5 Teilhard de Chardin, 1965.
14-6 Seligman, 2002, 2011.
16-1 Cosby, 2008.
16-2 Cresswell, 2014.
16-3 Cresswell, 2014, 143.
16-4 Taylor, 2007.
16-5 Kay, Gaucher, McGregor, Nash, 2010.
16-6 Bauer, Schwab, McAdams, 2011.
16-7 Bai Lindsey, 1998.
16-8 Mayer, 2012.
16-9 Hofmann, 2011.
16-10 Cramer, 1990.

Climbing Higher

References

Adams, Nancy (2015). <u>A god that could be real: Spirituality, science, and the future of our planet</u>. Boston: Beacon.

Adler, A. (1979). <u>Superiority and social interest</u> (H. Ansbacher and R. Ansbacher Eds.) (3rd Ed.). New York: W.W. Norton.

Allport, G.W. (1955). <u>Becoming</u>. New York: Yale University Press.

Antonovsky, A. (1987). <u>Unraveling the mystery of health: How people manage stress and stay well</u>. San Francisco: Jossy-Bass.

Armstrong, K. (2006). <u>Mohammad: A prophet for our time</u>. New York: HarperCollins.

Aronson, E. (1972). <u>The social animal</u>. San Francisco: Freeman.

Attridge, H. (Ed.). (2009). <u>The Religion and science debate</u>. New Haven: Yale University Press.

Bai Lindsey, C. (1998). The tolerance of ambiguity. <u>Dissertation Abstracts International.</u> **Sec** B, 1901.

Barret, L.F., Niedenthal, P.M., & Winkielman, P. (Eds.) (2005). <u>Emotion and consciousness</u>. New York: Guilford Press.

Bass, D., Wells, F., & Ridgeway, R. (1986). <u>Seven summits</u>. New York: Warner Books.

Batson, D; Schoenrade, P.; & Ventis, W. (1993). <u>The religious and the individual: a social-psychological perspective</u>. New York: Oxford.

Battista, J. & Almond, R. (1973). The development of meaning in life. <u>Psychiatry, 36,</u> 409-427.

Baxton, D. (2007). Religious naturalism and the future of Christianity. <u>Zygon, 42(2),</u> 317-352.

Bauer, J.J.; Schwab, J.R.; & McAdams, D.P. (2011). Self-actualizing: where ego development finally feels good? <u>The Humanistic Psychologist. 39,</u> 121-136.

Baugh, J. (2014). Our unconscious mind. Scientific American. 310(1), 32-37.

Beauregard, M. &O'Leary, D. (2007). The spiritual brain. New York: Harper One.

Bem, D. & Honorton, C. (1994). Does psi exist? Replicable evidence for an anomalous process of information transfer. Psychological Bulletin, 115(1),4-18.

Bering, J. (2011). The belief instinct. New York: Norton.

Bernbaum, E. (1977). Sacred mountains of the world. Berkeley, CA: University of California Press.

Blackmore, S. (2004). Consciousness: An introduction. New York: Oxford.

Bowker, J. (2002). God: A brief history. New York: DK Publishing.

Buhler, C. (1967). Human life goals in the humanistic perspective. Journal of Humanistic Psychology, 7, 36.

Campbell, J. (1988). The power of myth. New York: Doubleday.

Camus, A. (1960). The myth of Sisyphus, and other essays. (J. O'brien, Trans.). New York: Vintage Books.

Cantor, N. (1990). From thought to behavior: "Having" and "doing" in the study of personality and cognition. American Psychologist. 45, 735-750.

Cardena, E.; Lynn, S.; & Kripner, S. (2000). Varieties of anomalous experience: Examining the scientific evidence. Washington, DC: American Psychological Association.

Chalmers, D. J. (1996). The conscious mind. New York: Oxford University Press.

Clayton, P. & Knapp, S. (2011). The predicament of belief. New York: Oxford.

Cloninger, R. (2004). Feeling good. New York: Oxford.

Collegiate Dictionary (11th Ed.). (2003). Springfield, MA: Merriam-Webster.

Collins, F. (2006). The language of God. New York: Free Press.

Cosby, D.A. (2008). <u>Living with Ambiguity</u>. Albany, NY: State University of NY Press.

Cramer, K.D. (1990). <u>Staying on Top When Your World Turns Upside Down</u>. New York: Viking.

Cresswell, J. (2014). Can religion and psychology get along? Toward a pragmatic cultural psychology of religion that includes mesning and experience. <u>Journal of Theoretical and Philosophical Psychology. 23(2)</u>, 133-145.

Crumbaugh, J.C. (1973). <u>Everything to gain</u>. Chicago: Nelson-Hall.

Davies, P. (2008). <u>The goldilocks enigma</u>. New York: Houghton Mifflin.

Dawkins, R. (2006). <u>The God delusion</u>. New York: Houghton Mifflin.

DeCharmes, R. (1968). <u>Personal causation</u>. New York: Academic Press.

Dennett, D. (2006). <u>Breaking the spell</u>. New York: Viking.

Dossey, L. (1996). <u>Prayer is good medicine</u>. New York: HarperCollins.

Durant, W. & Durant, A. (1968). <u>The lessons of history</u>. New York: Simon & Schuster.

Eagleman, D. (2011). <u>Incognito.</u> New York: Pantheon.

Ellis, G. (2011). Does the universe really exist? <u>Scientific American</u>. August, 38-43.

Ellison, C. W. (1983). Toward an integrative measure of health and well-being. <u>Journal of Psychology and Theology, 19</u>, 35-48.

Emmons, R.A. (1989). The personal striving approach to personality. In L. Pervin et al. (Eds.) <u>Goal concepts in personality and social psychology</u>. Hillsdale: Lawrence Erlbaum.

Emmons, R. (1999). <u>The psychology of ultimate concerns</u>. New York: Guilford.

Emmons, R. A. (2005). Emotion and religion. In R. Paloutzian & C. Park (Eds.) <u>Handbook of the psychology of religion and psychology</u>. New York: Guilford.

Erikson, E. (1964). <u>Insight and responsibility</u>. New York: Norton.

Eysenck, H. J. (1982). <u>Personality, genetics, and behavior</u>. New York: Springer-Verlag.

Faber, M. (2004). <u>The psychological roots of religious belief</u>. Amherst, NY: Prometheus.

Festinger, L. (1957). <u>A theory of cognitive dissonance</u>. Stanford, CA: Stanford University Press.

Fields, Jonathan. (2011). <u>Uncertainty: Turning fear and doubt into fuel for brilliance</u>. New York: Penguin.

Flanagan, O. (2009). <u>The really hard problem</u>. Cambridge, MA: MIT Press.

Fowler, J. (1981). <u>Stages of faith</u>. San Francisco: Harper.

Frankl, V.E. (1997). <u>Man's search for ultimate meaning</u>. New York: Plenum Press.

Freud, A. (1965). Normality and pathology in childhood: Assessments of development. In <u>Writings (Vol.6)</u>. New York: International Universities Press.

Friedman, M. & Rosenman, R.H. (1974). <u>Type A behavior and your heart</u>. New York: Knopf.

Fromm, E. (1947). <u>Man for himself</u>. Greenwich, CT: Fawcett.

Fromm, E. (1973). <u>The anatomy of human destructiveness</u>. New York: Holt, Rinehart, & Winston.

Gallop, G. & Lindsay, D. (1999). <u>Surveying the religious landscape: Trends in U.S. beliefs</u>. Harrisburg, PA: Morehouse.

Gazzaniga, M.S. (2008). <u>Human: The science behind what makes us unique</u>. New York: HarperCollins.

Gleiser, M. (2014). <u>The islands of knowledge</u>. New York: Basic Books.

Goldberg, L. (1993). The structure of phenotypic personality traits. <u>American Psychologist</u>, <u>48</u>, 26-34.

Goodenough, U. (1998). <u>The sacred depths of nature</u>. New York: Oxford University Press.

Gould, S. (2006). <u>The richness of life.</u> New York: Norton.

Guinness Word Records (1017). http://www.guinnessworldrecords.com/world-records/oldest-man-to-climb-mt-kilimanjaro.

Grassie, W. (2010). <u>The new sciences of religion</u>. New York: Palgrave Macmillan.

Haisch, B. (2010). <u>The purpose guided universe</u>. Franklin Lakes, NJ: New Page Books.

Hamblin, W.J. & Seely, D.R. (2007). <u>Soloman's temple: Myth and history</u>. London: Thames & Hudson.

Hamer, D. (2004). <u>The God gene</u>. New York: Doubleday.

Hameroff, S.R. & Penrose, R. (1996). Consciousness events as orchestrated space-time selections. <u>Journal of Consciousness Studies,3(1)</u>, 36-53.

Hameroff, S.R., Kaszniak, A.W, & Chalmers, D.J. (1999). <u>Toward a science of consciousness III</u>. Cambridge, MA: MIT Press.

Harrington, A. (2005). Reflections on a new research tradition. In C. Harper, Jr (Ed.), <u>Spiritual information</u> (p. 367-375). Philadelphia: Templeton Foundation Press.

Harris, S. (2004). <u>The end of faith: Religion, terror, and the future of religion</u>. New York: Norton.

Hebb, D. O. (1955). Drives and the CNS (conceptual nervous system). <u>Psychological Review</u>. <u>62</u>, 243-254.

Heider, F. (1944). Social perception and phenomenal causality. <u>Psychological Review</u>, <u>51</u>, 358-374.

Helminiak, D. (1998). <u>Religion and the human sciences</u>. Albany, NY: State University of New York.

Hemingway, E. (1927). <u>The snows of Kilimanjaro</u>. New York: Charles Scribner.

Hodge, D. (2007). A systematic review of the empirical literature on intercessory prayer. *Research on Social Work Practice*. *17(2)*, 174-187.

Hofmann, S.G. (2011). *An Introduction to modern CBT: Psychological solutions to mental health problems*. Chichester, UK: Wiley-Blackwell.

Holmes, J. (2015). *Nonsense: The power of not knowing*. New York: Crown.

Hood, R. (2005). Mystical, spiritual, and religious experiences. In R. Paloutzian & C. Park (Eds.) *Handbook of the psychology of religion and psychology*. New York: Guilford.

Horgan, John. (2003). *Rational mysticism.* New York: Houghton Mifflin.

Huxley, A. (1944). The perennial philosophical. New York: Harper & Row.

Ibarra, J.L. (1996). Estadisticas temporadas 95/6. *Servicio Medico Plaza de Mulas,* Argentina.

Jahn, R. & Dunne, B. (2011). *Consciousness and the source of reality*. Princeton, NJ: ICRL Press.

Jeans, James. (1933). *The new background of science*. New York: Macmillan.

Jung, C.G. (1938). *Psychology and religion*. London: Yale University Press.

Kauffman, S. (2008). *Reinventing the sacred*. New York: Basic Books.

Kaufman, G. (2006). *Jesus and Creativity*. Minneapolis: Fortress Press.

Kashdan, T. & Nezlek, J. (2012). Whether, when, and how is spirituality related to well-being? *Personality & Social Psychology Bulletin*. *38(11),* 1523-1535.

...ay, A., Gaucher, D., McGreger, I., & Nash, K. (2012). Relogious belief as compensatory control. Personality & Social Psychology Review. 14(1), 37-48.

...elly, G. (1955). The psychology of personal constructs. New York: Norton.

...och, C. (2004). The quest for consciousness. Englewood, CA: Roberts and Company.

...ohlberg, L. (1984). The psychology of moral development: The nature and validity of moral stages. New York: Addison Wesley.

...urtz, P. (2007). What is secular humanism? Amherst, NY: Prometheus Books.

...azarus, R.S. (1991). Emotion and adaption. Oxford, England: Oxford University Press.

...pton, B.H. (2005). The biology of belief. New York: Hay House.

...ttle, B.R. (1999). Personality and motivation: Personality action and the conative revolution. In L.A. Pervin & O.P. John (Eds.). Handbook of personality: Theory and research. New York: Guilford Press.

...uger, J. (2015). The pope makes peace between science and religion. http://time.com/4050465/pope-francis-us-visit-science-faith/, 9/25/2015.

...oevinger, J. (1973). Ego development. Psychoanalysis and Contemporary Science, 2, 77.

...oftus, E. (1997). Creating false memories. Scientific American, 277, 70-75.

...acfarlane, R. (2003). Mountains of the mind: History of a fascination. London: Granta Books.

...ackey, A. (1921). An Encyclopedia of Freemasonry. New York: Masonic History Company.

...aclaine, S. (1983). Out on a limb. New York: Bantum Books.

Markman, K., Prouix, T., & Lindberg, M. (Ed). (2013). The psychology of meaning. Washington DC: American Psychological Association..

Maslow, A. (1968). Toward a psychology of being. (2nd Ed.). New York: Harper & Row.

Maslow, A. (1971). The farther reaches of human nature. New York: Viking.

May, E.C.& Bhatt, S. (2014). Anomalous cognition: remote viewing research and theory. Jefferson, NC: McFarland.

May, R. (1967). Psychology and the human dilemma. New York: Norton.

Mayer, B. (2012). The Dynamics of Conflict: A Guide to Engagement and Intervention (2nd ed.). San Francisco: Jossey-Bass.

McClelland, D.C. (1961). The achieving society. New York: Free Press.

McCrae, R. & Costa, P. (1999). A five-factor theory of personality. In L. Pervin & O. John (Eds.) Handbook of personality: Theory and research (2d Ed.), New York: Guilford.

Menninger, W.C. (1957). Growing up emotionally. Chicago: Science Research Associates.

Mikuluk, A. (2015). All about awe. Association for Psychological Science Observer, 28, (4), 16-19.

Meyers, D. (2008). A friendly letter to skeptics and atheists. San Francisco: Jossey-Bass.

Miller, W. &Thoresen, C. (2003). Spirituality, religion, and health: An emerging research field. American Psychologist, 58, 24-35.

Mishlove, J. (1975). The roots of consciousness. New York: Random House.

Moody, R.A. (1975, 2001). Life after life: The investigation of a phenomenon – survival of bodily death. New York: HarperCollins.

Musolino, J. (2015). The soul fallacy. New York: Prometheus.

Nelson, J. (2009). Psychology, religion, and spirituality. New York: Springer.

Nelson, K. (2011). The spiritual doorway in the brain. New York: Dutton.

Newberg, A. & D'Aquili, E. (2001). Why god won't go away. New York: Ballantine Books.

Ornstein, R.E. (1977). The psychology of consciousness (2nd Ed). New York: Harcourt Brace Jovanovich.

Paloutzian, R. & Park, C. (Eds.) (2005). Handbook of the psychology of religion and spirituality. New York: Guilford.

Pert, C. (1997). The molecules of emotion: The science behind mind-body medicine. New York: Scribner.

Pert, C. (2006). Everything you need to know to feel Go(o)d. Carlesbad, CA: Hay House.

Pickover. C. (2001). The paradox of God and the science of omniscience. New York: Palgrave Macmillan.

Pihlstrome, S. (2013). Pragmatic pluralism and the problem of God. New York: Fordham University Press.

Polkinghorne, J. (2007). Science and religion: Bottom-up style, interface context. Zygon, 42(3), 573-576.

Popper, K.R. & Eccles, J.C. (1977). The self and its brain. Berlin: Springer.

Powell, D. (1009). The ESP enigma. New York: Walker.

Pribram, K.H. & Meade, S. (1999). The reality of conscious experience. In K. Shanor (Ed.) The emerging mind. Los Angeles: Renaissance Books.

Radin, D. (2006). Entangled minds. New York: Paraview Pocket Books.

Reigal, K. (1973). Dialectic operations: The final period of cognitive development. Human Development, 16, 346.

Rican, P. & Janosova, P. (2010). Spirituality as a basic aspect of personality: A cross-cultural verification of Piedmont's model. <u>International Journal for the Psychology of Religion, 20,</u> 2.

Pickover, C. (2001). <u>The Paradox of Rogers God</u>. NY: Palgrace Macmillan.

, C. (1961). <u>On becoming a person</u>. Boston: Houghton Mifflin.

Rossano, M. (2010). <u>Supernatural selection</u>. Oxford: Oxford University Press.

Rotter, J. (1975). Some problems and misconceptions related to the construct of internal versus external control of reinforcement. <u>Journal of Consulting and Clinical Psychology, 43,</u> 56-57.

Rue, L. (2006). Religion <u>is not about God</u>. New Brunswick, NJ: Rutgers University Press.

Russell, R. (2008). <u>Cosmology: From alpha to omega, the creative mutual interaction of theology and science</u>. Minneapolis: Fortress.

Ryle, G. (1949). <u>The concept of the mind</u>. London: Hutchinson.

Schachter, S, & Singer, J.E. (1962). Cognitive, social, and physiological determinants of emotional state. <u>Psychological Review, 69,</u> 379-399.

Schneider, K. (2004). <u>Rediscovering awe</u>. St Paul, MN: Paragon.

Schwartz, G. (2006). <u>The G. O. D. experiments</u>. New York: Atria.

Schwartz, G (2011). <u>The sacred promise</u>. New York: Atria.

Schwartz, S. & Dossey, L. (2010). Non-locality, intention, and observer effects in healing studies. <u>Explore, the Journal of Science and Healing. 6(5),</u> 295-307.

Seligman, M. (2002). <u>Authentic happiness</u>. New York: Free Press.

Seligman, M. (2011). <u>Flourish</u>. New York: Free Press.

Shaver, P. & Mikulincer, M. (Eds.) (2012). <u>Meaning, morality, and choice</u>. Washington DC: American Psychological Association.

Shermer. M. (2015). The moral arc: How science and reason lead humanity toward truth, justice, and freedom. New York: Henry Holt.

Silka, B; Hood, R.; Hunsberger, Stapp, H. (2004). Mind, matter, and quantum mechanics (2d Ed). Heidelberg: Springer-Verlag.

Steger, M., Frazier, P., Oishi, S., & Kaler, M. (2006). The Meaning in Life Questionnaire: Assessing the presence of and search for meaning in life. Journal of Counseling Psychology, 53, 80-93.

Stenger, V. (2003). Has science found God? Amherst, NY: Prometheus.

Stevenson, I. (1997). Where reincarnation and biology intersect. Westport, CT: Praeger.

Strassman,R. (2000). DMT: the spiritual molecule. Rochester, VT: Park Street Press.

Swaab. D. F. (2014). We are our brains: A neurobiography of the brain, from the womb to alzheimer's. New York: Spiegel & Grau.

Targ, R. (2004). Limitless mind. Novato, CA: New World Library.

Targ, R. (2012). The reality of ESP. Wheaton, IL: Quest.

Tart, C.T. (1992). Open mind discriminating mind: Reflections on human possibilities. New York: HarperCollins.

Tart, C.T. (1997). Body mind spirit. Charlottsville, VA: Hampton Roads Publishing.

Tart, C.T. (2009). The end of materialism. Oakland, CA: New Harbinger.

Taylor, M. (2007). After God. Chicago: University of Chicago Press.

Teilhard de Chardin, P. (1965). The phenomenon of man. (B. Wall, Trans.). New York: Harper & Row.

The new English bible (1970). Oxford: Oxford University Press.

Thomas, Dylan (1957). <u>Dylan Thomas collected poems.</u> New York: New Directions Books.

Thurman, R. & Wise, T. (1999). <u>Circling the sacred mountain</u>. New York: Bantum Books.

Unwin, S. (2003). <u>The probability of God</u>. New York: Crown Forum.

Vaillant, G. E. (2009). <u>Spiritual evolution</u>. New York: Broadway Books.

Wade, N. (2009). <u>The faith instinct</u>. New York: Penguin Press.

Walker, E.H. (2000). <u>The physics of consciousness</u>. Cambridge, MA: Perseus Books.

Ward, K. (2008). <u>The big questions in Science and religion</u>. West Conshohocken, PA: Templeton.

Waterman, A. (2013). <u>The best within us: positive psychology perspectives on eudaimonia</u>. Washington DC: American Psychological Association.

Wheeler, J.A. (1990). Informations, physics, quantum: the search for links. In: Zurek, W.H., (Ed.), <u>Complexity, entropy, and the physics of information</u>. Santa Fe Institute Studies in the Science of Complexity, vol. VIII. Reading, MA: Perseus Books.

Wheeler, R. & Haywood, J. (1995). Life goals and academic performance. Presented at the 103d <u>Annual Meeting of the American Psychological Association</u>, New York. <u>Higher Education Abstracts</u> 0833-31/GMT.

Wheeler, R.; Munz, D.; & Jain, A. (1990). Life goals and general well-being. <u>Psychological Reports, 66</u>, 307-312.

Wildman, W. (2017). <u>In our own image: anthromorphism, apophaticism, and ultimate reality.</u> Oxford, UK: Oxford University Press.

Wilson, E. O. (2006). <u>Creation</u>. New York: Norton.

Wong, P. (1998). <u>The Human Quest for Meaning</u>. Mahwah, NJ: Lawrence Erlbaum.

Zajonc, R.B. (1984). On the primacy of affect. <u>American Psychologist</u>. <u>39</u>, 117-123.

Zillman, D. (1983). Transfer of excitation in emotional behavior. In Cacioppo, J.T. & Petty, R.E. (Eds.), <u>Social psychophysiology: A sourcebook</u>. New York: Guilford Press.

Zuckerman, M. (1979). Sensation seeking and risk taking. In C.E. Izard (Ed.), <u>Emotions in personality and psychopathology</u>. New York: Plenum.

Climbing Higher

Appendix A
Sense of Purpose and Life-Esteem

Despite the recent interest in cognitive processes and self-concept as having a role in human health and well-being, relatively little tangible progress has resulted. For psychology in general, the proliferation of research findings continue to outstrip the cure rates of human psychological problems emphasized by Zax and Cowen in 1972. This may be because the basic cognitive foundations of human motivation are still being ignored even though the impacts of an individual's subjective feelings are now being given more credence. Self-esteem is the term applied to those portions of a person's self-concept that are evaluative feelings about self-worth and relationship with the world. It now seems appropriate to broaden self-concept and establish as a necessary adjunct the term "life-esteem" which is the individual's feelings about meaning, significance, purpose, and major goal in life. This has the potential of bringing purpose and meaning in life out of the ambiguous towers of philosophy and religion and of putting it into the arena of psychology where they can be objectively investigated with the scientific procedures of personality research, and applied to the cause of human health and well-being.

Sense of Purpose

The role of a person's sense of purpose has long been recognized as important to well-being and mental health, but only recently have psychologists considered this and it is still not systematically included in the study of personality or motivation. Carl Rogers (1961) felt it presumptuous to express opinion about the issue of purpose in life, however he showed significant patterns in the way troubled and maladjusted people view this subject. The need for more adequate meaning and purpose is being voiced by many sectors of society: popularity of psycho-religious movements such as Scientology, Arica, and Ekankar; publicity about parasitic elements of society such as alcoholics and drug addicts, thieves and muggers, and grafters and extortionists; and professional recognition of existential vacuum, philosophical neurosis, and spiritual discontent. Roger Sperry (1977) referred to the prevailing social neurosis of our times as a growing sense of valuelessness, apathy, hopelessness, and loss of purpose and higher meaning. Concerning such needs, Frank Severin (1973, p. 6) aptly stated, "If psychology does not address itself to the legitimate needs of people, some non-scientific or pseudo-scientific movement will. The fundamental human wants will not be denied; psychology must either concern itself with real-life problems or run the risk of losing its image as a relevant science." The importance to mental health practitioners of meaningless as a significant contemporary problem was summarized by Ruffin (1984), and Emmons (1986) demonstrated the importance to well-being of "personal striving" toward major goals.

Recent developments in cognitive psychology attest to the role of personal beliefs and attitudes as being important to these "fundamental human wants." In a review of this trend, Melvin Manis (1977) pointed out the situationally labile nature of self-concept and its relation to behavior as a major problem, but that "we should recognize that an effective analysis of the variables that control privately held beliefs would be no small accomplishment, even if these beliefs often proved ineffective as determinants of overt behavior" (p. 562). He also pointed out the importance of motivational variables that are given "scant consideration by many cognitive theorists."

There is rather general agreement that human behavior is motivated, and personality theorists "have customarily assigned a crucial role to the motivational process" (Hall and Lindzey, 1978, p. 5). However, there is considerable variation in concepts about the basis of motivation and the usefulness of dealing with underlying causes. The recent trend in theories of human motivation toward increasing complexity and importance for internal cognitive processes (Boles, 1974) renews interest in the basis of attitudes, beliefs, and values. Where a motivation base is provided in psychological theory, they range all the way from Freud's mechanistic concept of biological homeostasis to Jung's teleological concept of transcendent function. In between these extremes are theories that attribute basic motivation to drives or aspirations for such goals as adaption to contingencies of reinforcement (Skinner), release of interpersonal conflicts (Sullivan), integrity (Erikson), competence (White), achievement (McClelland), unity (Murray), propriate striving (Allport), congruency (Rogers), transcendence from animalism (Fromm), and actualization (Maslow).

Considerable research in psychology has emphasized the human need for meaning. The recently published book *The Human Quest for Meaning* (Wong & Fry, 1998) summarized recent research, some of which deals with meaning as a basic motivation to search for meaning and purpose in life that is related to well-being and health.

Even though these concepts of basic motivation relate to an individual's sense of purpose in life and indicate some of its characteristics, they do not provide the direct focus that is the scope of this paper. As used here, sense of purpose (sop) is defined as the view that an individual has of meaning, major goal, or purpose in life. Because the terms have different connotations but are frequently used interchangeably, meaning, significance, life-goal, and purpose are considered synonymous as a basic philosophy of life that is related to values, attitudes, beliefs, and commitments. The attainment of a goal is the purpose for one's behavior, and value is attached to that which is important according to attitudes and beliefs. Commitment, then, is the degree to which one is concerned with or involved with these items, and the subjective reasonableness of the purpose provides meaning and significance. SOP thus has the potential of being an integrating force that ties together goals, values, attitudes, beliefs, and behaviors into a coherently functioning person. It can be considered a primary motivation that provides force for efforts and drives, that makes contingencies of reinforcement effective, and that enables the buildup of secondary motives.

Life Goals Inventory

There are many theories about purpose in life based on theological conceptions involving divine plan, or on philosophical concepts involving speculation and ontological concerns; but those associated with empirical findings mainly grew out of psychotherapy and are largely confined to psychology and psychiatry.

A major attempt at organizing such concepts was that of the German born clinician, Charlotte Buhler. She categorized basic motivations into four life goals that she called basic tendencies (Buhler and Massarik, 1968). The first, need satisfaction, is action to reduce tension and obtain a homeostatic balance similar to that advocated by psychoanalysis. The second, self-limiting adaption, is adjustment and restraint necessary for efficient existence, and can be related to the behaviorist's attribution of reinforcement contingencies and conditioning as determinants of behavior. Third, upholding internal order is an attempt at integration, organization, coordination and unity that is similar to Murray's unity thema, Allport's proprium, Erickson's integrity, and Roger's congruency. The fourth, creative expansion, is the upsetting of homeostasis which enables advancement and change similar to the various aspects of self - actualization. The psychodynamic functioning of the id, ego, and super-ego form vectors with these four tendencies toward certain inherent ends and potential goals.

The overall result of this system is the "phenomenon of people wanting to live for something which then becomes for them, life's meaning" (p. 21). Buhler used the term "intentionality" to describe an essential characteristic of people to give their lives purpose that is something they choose to believe in or think they ought to believe in. She then applied the term "self-determination" for a life that is directed toward the fulfillment of such a purpose. This is fulfillment of meaning rather than of self or self-actualization, and represents a final goal that is defined and served by the four basic tendencies (Frankl, 1966). According to Buhler's theory and research, even newborn children demonstrate adaptive, coordinative, and creative tendencies in addition to those toward need satisfaction long before social and environmental factors force goals on them.

In an attempt to analyze goal orientations, Buhler developed the Life Goals Inventory (LGI). This is a self report questionnaire using 91 questions to measure the relative strength of eleven factors found to indicate orientation toward the four basic goals. Little application of this instrument has been reported in the United States, but according to Buhler, it is useful in psychotherapy and in investigating characteristics of healthy persons. She found (1965) that the LGI profiles of healthy people were relatively uniform without extreme scores, where neurotics and psychotics tended to exhibit jagged profile patterns with extreme and incompatible scores indicating stringent demands and limitations.

Purpose in Life

Viktor Frankl, the Viennese clinician, is more explicit in his concept of life goal and fulfillment, and he relates it directly to human well-being. He said that the pursuit of meaning is the essence of a person's "humanness." Anyone who represses it becomes vulnerable to "...the infernal pit of existential vacuum. If he devotes himself to this pursuit, life is filled not only with meaning, but also with the byproducts of a meaningful existence - and among these are happiness, security, peace of mind, mental stability, and such currently fashionable goals as self-actualization and peak experiences" (Fabry, 1968, p. 81). A strong meaning orientation is life prolonging, life preserving, and makes for both physical and mental health (Frankl, 1966). In Frankl's concept, existential vacuum is a human condition caused by a lack of meaning. When this combines with neurotic symptoms, a psychopathology results which he calls "noogenic neurosis," and the therapeutic system called "logotherapy" was developed by him based on this concept. Every human is unique in the nature of this meaning and its strength can vary according to situational factors and development. The role of psychotherapy is to assist the individual in realizing this meaning (Frankl, 1965).

James Crumbaugh (1973) applied Frankl's concepts in the United States calling his system "logoanalysis," and he developed the Purpose-In-Life test (PIL) to measure the degree to which an individual is free from the effects of existential vacuum. This is a twenty-item questionnaire with five items pertaining to ability to see life in a meaningful framework, nine dealing with sense of satisfaction, one item combining both factors, and five items about value orientations. The PIL has stimulated considerable research, the results of which have been diverse and in some cases conflicting. It has shown significant negative correlations with external locus of control (Phillips, 1980), depression, anxiety (Crumbaugh, 1968; Yarnell, 1971), and emotion-focused coping (Stevens, Pfast & Wessels, 1987); and positive correlations with subjective well-being (Zika & Chamberlain, 1987), time management (Bond & Feather, 1987), defensiveness (Crumbaugh, 1964), socioeconomic position (Crumbaugh, 1968), and trainee proficiency (Crumbaugh, Raphael, and Shrader, 1970).

In studying PIL score differences for various groups of people, Crumbaugh (1968) found a significant difference between "normals" and mental patients, and he found significant differences between ten groups consisting of various socioeconomic and mental health statuses. Successful business and professional personnel and church workers had conspicuously high scores, where alcoholics and neurotics had low scores. Garfield (1973) found significant differences in five subculture groups, but pointed out that interpretation of the test items may have contributed to the score differences. Using the Rokeach Value Survey, Crandall and Rasmussen (1975) found that low PIL scores were associated with high value placed on pleasure, comfort, and excitement, while high scores were associated with the value of salvation. Soderstrom and Wright (1977) found high correlation with a religious orientation motivated by an intrinsic personal faith and integrating high moral and spiritual commitment.

Many studies report no correlation between PIL scores and sex, IQ, or age; however, in a study of male prison inmates, Reker (1977) found a significant correlation with both IQ and age. In addition to demographic factors, Reker also investigated self- concept, locus of control, and personality as measured by the Edwards Personality Inventory and found significant PIL correlations with a coherent and favorable self-concept, internal locus of control, orientation toward planning and organizing, and general satisfaction with present life experiences. Two studies report age differences only between groups above and below about 20 years of age (Meier and Edwards, 1974; Yarnell, 1971). Using psychiatric outpatients, Pearson and Sheffield (1975) found that males had significantly higher PIL scores than females, but no difference for age. (This latter study also showed significant correlations of PIL scores with measures of idealism and anti-hedonism.) Martin and Martin (1977) clearly linked IQ as measured by the Otis-Lennon Mental Ability Test and grade point average with PIL scores for a group of high school juniors and seniors. (They also found a significant correlation for PIL scores with the Personal Orientation Inventory scales for time-competence and inner-directedness.)

Three studies conducted at the United States International University found high PIL scores to be related to high sense of meaning in work (Sargent, 1973), and low dogmatism and high self actualization (Ormand, 1973), and low sexual frustration (Sallee and Casciani, 1976). Social desirability has also been studied, and although Crumbaugh justifies insignificant confounding effect on PIL scores, and influence was found rising doubts about the role of social phenomena (Domino, 1972).

A complement for the PIL is the Seeking of Noetic Goals test (SONG) that Crumbaugh (1977) developed to measure the strength of motivation to find meaning in life. Reker & Cousins (1979) demonstrated its reliability and validity, and its relationship to the PIL. The SONG has shown a moderate negative correlation with the PIL and significantly differentiated between patient and non-patient groups. Another instrument that Crumbaugh (1971) feels is of supplementary value is the Future Time Perspective test (FTP) which measures the degree to which a person looks to the future for fulfillment of life goals. The FTP was reported to have high correlation with the PIL and with Rotter's locus of control scale.

Self-Actualization

Abraham Maslow popularized meaning in life as resulting from experiences that are worthwhile in themselves. In this conceptualization, meaningfulness is not derived from the pursuit and fulfillment of an ultimate purpose, but from experiences associated with the pursuit (Buhler and Massarik, 1968). Maslow added to the theory of human goal striving a hierarchical system of basic needs and goals where a higher need emerges as a lower one is satisfied. Over the basic needs is superimposed a complex set of "instinctoid" meta-needs with self-actualization being the highest (Maslow, 1968). It is possible to gratify basic needs and still suffer from meaninglessness, existential vacuum, anomie, etc. if there is not a commitment to the meta-needs (Maslow, 1966).

Everett Shostrom (1972) added to Maslow's theory the concept of four polarities: Strength-weakness and love-anger that can be used as indicants of an individual's degree of self-actualization. The refinements of courage, compassion, caring, and assertion serve as important orientation points from which one can perceive a relationship to the polarities, which come close to a concept of universal goals. This concept gives people something to which they can orient themselves, and "man must orient himself to something if he is to stay sane" (p. 34). The Personal Orientation Inventory (POI) was developed to measure these characteristics using a questionnaire of 150 pairs of two choice items that gives scores on twelve scales such as inner direction, self-regard, and self-acceptance. It demonstrated validity for distinguishing clinical and positive mental health groups, but differed with results from personality tests like the Edwards Personal Preference Schedule (EPPS) and Buhler's LGI (McKee, 1972). Tosi and Lindamood (1975) found significant correlations with some scales of the POI, EPPS, and MMPI, but did not consider the POI reliable for diagnosis. The attempt of the POI to measure self-actualization has been improved on by the Personal

Orientation Dimension (POD) (Shostrom, 1976). Jones and Crandall (1988) provided a summary of the shortcomings for five published scales about actualization, including the POI and POD, and proposed a 15-item index that discriminated between self-actualizing and non-self-actualizing people.

Life Regard

The development of meaning in life was investigated by Battista and Almond (1973) who felt that meaning has no true or ultimate nature, and emphasized the process of believing rather than the contents of belief. They defined meaning in life as an individual's belief in fulfilling his life as conceptualized in terms of some life-goal or framework. They called this "positive life regard" and developed the Life Regard Index (LRI) to measure it. The LRI is a questionnaire with 28 items rated on a five point scale resulting in three scores: framework which is the ability to see life within some perspective that produces for the individual purpose in life, life view, or set of life goals; fulfillment, which is the degree that the individual feels the framework has been fulfilled or is in the process of being fulfilled; and an overall score which is a sum of the two subscores. All three scores were found to produce normal distributions and have high intercorrelations. Concurrent validity was demonstrated with the POI and PIL, but Battista and Almond point out that further study of the interrelationships is needed about commonality of underlying concepts. Construct validity was shown by interview evaluation of high and low scorers. A specific investigation was made to determine that social desirability did not confound scores; however, as with studies of PIL scores, social desirability effects were shown indicating that the influence of social phenomena may not be clear. High life regard scorers were found to have a closer fit with the subcultures and social movements with which they were involved, and with their ideal self-concept. In studying self-esteem and childhood experiences, a significant difference was found between the high and low scorers. This resulted in the conclusion that development of positive life regard is a two-stage process. First, the individual must develop a positive self-image during late adolescence or early adult life. "The development of a positive life regard, which is the successful resolution of the second stage, is dependent upon the development of self-esteem in the first stage and commitment to fulfillment of life goals" (p. 418).

To measure the individual's feelings about position and rate of progress relative to a life goal, Battista and Almond (1973) designed the Life Orientation Index (LOI). The individual first ranks the importance of six major life orientations: interpersonal, service, understanding, obtaining, expressive, and ethical. Then the relative importance of the top three are rated and each is evaluated for its perceived proximity and progress toward attainment. Results correlated with LRI scores at $p < .01$. Validity was indicated by the significant differences between high and low life regard groups for their most important or their first two most important goals, but not for their third and lower ranked goals. This indicated that individuals were able meaningfully to distinguish between life goals options without a generalized halo effect of optimism, pessimism, or similar personality variable. LOI results also indicated that instead of a single encompassing belief, people with positive life regard were often committed to two or more belief systems, suggesting that in our complex society where many religions, values, occupations, and life styles compete, it may be that purpose in life is derived from an interaction of many sources.

Battista and Almond (1973) pointed out that self-report instruments such as theirs would be prejudiced against persons who have unconscious or non-conceptualized beliefs that serve as a framework for their experiencing of meaning in their lives. Such a subconscious component according to psychoanalysis theory could be expected to conflict with the conscious SOP and interfere not only with behavioral consistency, but also on realizing a healthy perception of purpose. This would be similar to libido fixation or personality "hang up." Arnold and Gasson (1954, p. 195) showed that "if there is a gap between the self-ideal as it actually is and the self-ideal as it ought to be, then there will be disturbance." It may be that those low in SOP have been more effectively trained by our current societal influences to subjugate any feeling of purpose that does not produce monetary reward or immediate pleasure. Toler (1974) found that alcoholics and drug addicts place more value on personal goals than societal goals indicating that turning inward away from socially recognized goals may be associated with psychosocial problems. History indicates that a greater sense of well-being exists when a person's society is oriented toward long-range idealistic goals and dynamic striving (Campbell, 1975). The passive and hedonistic orientation of our society today could well cause the individual's desire for idealistic efforts to be driven into the subconscious.

Life Goals Evaluation

Where the LOI measures the importance of interpersonal relation, service, understanding, expressing, and ethicalness as life goal orientations, Buhler's LGI measures functional orientations of adaption, balance, unity, and creativeness. A more specific set of life goals was used by Milton Hahn (1968) who developed the California Life Goals Evaluation Schedule (CLGES). This measures on a five point scale the relative strength of ten orientations

of life goals: social service, self-expression, interesting experiences, esteem, independence, security, leadership, fame, power, and profit. Mental patients who scored high on esteem, profit, fame, and power were found to leave the hospital sooner and remained out longer than those who scored low on those schedules. The CLGES was used by Mlott and Lira (1977) to investigate differences between mates in stable and unstable marriages for life goals, and it was found that dissimilarities in life goals of mates was associated with marriage stability.

Values

Even though a person's sense of values is different from a sense of meaning or purpose in life, there are similarities that have theoretical implications and indicate potential methods and directions for relevant research. Roger Sperry (1977, p. 237) emphasized the relationship of values to life goals and purpose in life, and stated that "Human values, in addition to their commonly recognized significance from a personal, religious or philosophical standpoint, can also be viewed objectively as universal determinants in all human decision making." Milton Rokeach (1973) defined terminal values as being beliefs concerning desirable end states of existence and referred to them as representing super goals that "do not seem to be periodic in nature; neither do they seem to satiate - we seem to be forever doomed to strive for these ultimate goals without ever quite reaching them"(p. 14). He considered self-conception as the base of a motivational hierarchy for behavior. Immediately above self-conception are terminal values, and then come instrumental values that are greater in number and represent desirable modes of conduct. Above these are attitudes and then beliefs. His concept of values attempts to integrate the social sciences and give expression to human needs by setting standards to guide actions, justifications, judgments, and comparisons with others; and to serve needs for adjustment, ego defense, and self-actualization. Values develop in a continual manner throughout life with culture, society, and personality being the major antecedents, and attitudes and behavior their major consequences.

The Rokeach Value Survey (RVS) measures the relative importance of eighteen terminal values such as salvation, inner harmony, and wisdom; and eighteen instrumental values such as honesty, helpfulness, and logicalness. Using this instrument, Rokeach (1973) conducted a series of experiments showing that in a single session of less than one hour duration in which an individual becomes aware of inconsistencies in values and self-concept, significant short and long term changes resulted in values and attitudes as well as behavior. These studies indicated that behavior and attitude change are more effective when they are based on value change, and that value change is unidirectional toward an increase in the importance of four values in particular: equality, freedom, beauty, and self-control. Rokeach pointed out that "Such changes can be initiated only by inducing an affective state of self dissatisfaction concerning contradictions with self-conceptions and are motivated by the desire at least to maintain and if possible, enhance conceptions of oneself as a moral and competent human being" (p. 328). Since self-conception as used here is similar to Battista's life-regard, Frankl's will-to-meaning, and Crumbaugh's purpose-in-life, this may be an efficient way of teaching, developing, or improving SOP. Changes thus made could have profound effects on values, attitudes, beliefs, and behavior.

Validity and limitations of the RVS has been summarized by Braitwaith and Law (1985), but it has demonstrated significant correlation between high PIL scores and religious values, and between low PIL scores and hedonistic values (Crandall and Rasmussen, 1975). It has been used in a number of studies about the role of values, such as that by Kristiansen (1985) that established value correlates with preventive health behavior. Life values correlates with personality characteristics were established using the Life Values Inventory that was based on the RVS (Mitchell, 1984). To overcome the rank-ordering shortcoming of the RVS, Homer and Kahle (1988) developed the List of Values questionnaire and used it to confirm the value-attitude-behavior hierarchy. Schwartz and Bilsky (1987) used the RVS to develop their universal structure of human values that consists of eight motivational domains: enjoyment, security, power, achievement, self-direction, prosocial, conformity, and maturity. These motivational domains form another structure to indicate the importance of considering the qualitative nature of a person's sense of meaning and purpose.

The study by Crandall and Rasmussen (1975) failed to show any correlation of the RVS with the Allport-Vernon-Lindsay Study of Values (AVLSV) that is another widely used instrument for evaluation of personal values. The AVLSV measures the relative prominence of six value orientations: theoretical, religious, aesthetic, economic, social, and political and has been useful in psychological counseling (Hogan, 1972). An example of research using the AVLSV is that of Hoge and Bender (1974) who investigated three groups of males who attended Dartmouth College between 1931 and 1969: students, young alumni, and older alumni. Little difference was found for the age groups, and change in any period was greater among students and young alumni than among older alumni. They concluded that value change was more a result of frustration and personal inadequacy in current experiences rather than life cycle development. They also concluded that emotionally immature men and those less intellectually gifted tended to have more individual value change. Another longitudinal study used the AVLSV to predict successfully occupation 25 years later (Huntley & Davis, 1983).

Social phenomena are recognized as important in values more clearly than in goals and purpose. Scheibe (1970) summarized investigation of development of values as being a socialization process. Social role modeling, imitation, and identification were shown to be essential for such development. An example of research about social factors is the study by Morris (1956) of students in six countries: India, China, Japan, Norway, Canada, and the

United States. Five factors emerged from a factor analysis of value orientations: 1) social restraint and self-control, 2) action in overcoming obstacles, 3) self sufficiency and self-awareness, 4) receptivity and sympathetic concern, and 5) sensuous enjoyment. For all groups 1 and 2 were ranked either first or second, and the remaining were in the order 4, 5, 3. He found that the importance placed on his value orientations varied with sex, somatotype, temperament, character, traditions, economic status, and size of community raised in.

Stress Moderators

The importance of one's SOP has surfaced in the recent research about factors that moderate the adverse effects of stress. Zika and Chamberlain (1987) studied the moderating effects on daily hassles of locus of control, assertiveness, and meaning in life (as measured by the PIL), and found that PIL score was the most consistent predictor of well-being. Although that study found limited moderating effects, a study by Wheeler and Frank (1988) of 22 potential stress moderators found that sense of purpose (as measured by a six item scale) was one of four significant moderators. In a study about substance use among adolescents, Newcomb and Harlow (1986) found that perceived loss of control and meaninglessness in life significantly moderated the effects of stress. However, the most powerful implications of SOP come from research about Suzanne Kobasa's construct of hardiness that consists of three components: control, challenge, and commitment. Commitment is similar to SOP and is usually measured by the Alienation From Self and Alienation From Work scales that indicate lack of involvement, fundamental sense of purpose, and meaningfulness (Kobasa, Maddi & Kahn, 1982). Using the composite hardiness score, Kobasa and her colleagues (1982) found significant main effects and moderator effects on health. Genellan and Blaney (1984) investigated the hardiness components and found that only commitment had significant main and moderator effects on depression.

On-Going and Long-Range Nature

Clinical experience and concern for societal well-being have provided the basis for major contributions about the importance and role of the individual's SOP. Rollo May (1953) stated that "the human being cannot live in a condition of emptiness for very long; if he is not growing toward something, he does not merely stagnate; the pent up potentialities turn into morbidity and despair, and eventually into destructive activities" (p. 24). According to Gordon Allport (1955) the possession of long-range goals distinguishes the human from the animal, "the adult from the child, and in many cases, the healthy personality from the sick" (p. 51). The relation between societal and individual SOP is reflected in Ruth Benedict's concept of synergy and elaborated on by Abraham Maslow (1968): in a high synergic society, virtue pays. Eric Fromm (1955, 1973) has been outspoken about the relationship between goals of the individual and those of society, and the impact of one on the other.

Many have stressed that the human sense of striving for meaning is an ongoing process rather than an end goal. For Carl Rogers (1961), the movement of a person toward being "that self which he most truly is" (p. 176) appears to be the highest value when one is free to move in any direction. Alfred Adler emphasized the importance of a long-range life goal and felt that it was idealistic, and for many people it was also unconceptualized (Ansbacher, 1956). Gordon Allport (1955) stated, "The most comprehensive units in personality are broad intentional dispositions, future pointed" (p. 92). Even Abraham Maslow recognized an ongoing dynamic process in his use of the term self-actualization, and he agreed with Frankl that our primary concern is "will to meaning" (Maslow, 1966). However, he pointed out that this may not be very different from what Buhler, Goldstein, Rogers, Jung, and others were referring to with terms such as values, purposes, ends, or philosophy of life.

External Focus

A number of psychotherapists have voiced the importance of externality and transcendence for SOP. Maslow (1971) felt that actualizing people were devoted to a goal outside of themselves, and provided for non-transcending actualizers and transcending actualizers in his "theory Z." Frankl (1966) emphasized the importance of two phenomena by which human existence is characterized. One is the capacity for self-detachment, and the other is the capacity for self-transcendence whereby healthy people point to something other than themselves individually. Erich Fromm advocated that in striving for meaning, "man must have a picture of the world to which he orients himself, a framework, and it does not matter whether this picture is correct or false. Man also must have an object of devotion that allows him to transcend over himself as just a feeding and loving machine. He must have a goal that extends beyond himself, and frees him from egocentricity" (Reif, 1975, p. 21). A somewhat similar component of getting outside of oneself is provided in therapeutic systems recently developed by such clinicians as Albert Ellis and William Glasser. An early idea similar to this was Alfred Adler's concept of "social interest" that was a universal drive healthy people had to contribute to society and to human well-being (Ansbacher, 1956).

Consistency

A fair degree of consistency has already been indicated for goal orientations, but little empirical support has been reported. Research about attribution theory has established as a consistent innate characteristic of people the need to find meaning and cause for their experiences (Taylor, 1983). Hogan, DeSoto, and Solano (1977, p. 258) predicted that "the most important consistencies in personality will be found in the goals people pursue rather than the means they use to achieve them," and suggested that it would be useful to define traits as consistent goals in life rather than consistent behavior across situations. This supports the contention that a person's self-concept may be less elusive or labile if it can be viewed from the person's sense of purpose orientation. It may even alleviate the problem summarized by Melvin Manis (1977) of predicting which situational or personal factors will be salient to an individual as determinants of behavior.

Life-Esteem

Information in the preceding review supports the concept of SOP as being important to human well-being, operationally definable, and capable of measurement. Two of the components have already been defined operationally by Battista and Almond (1973) as framework and fulfillment, where framework is the ability to see one's life in a perspective that provides meaning and purpose, and fulfillment is the degree that one feels that the process of fulfilling the framework is progressing properly. Together they comprise life-regard, which is similar to Crumbaugh's more general purpose-in-life.

A third component, which has not been proposed explicitly, but is implied in Buhler's theory of intentionality (1965), is commitment. Individuals may have a conceptualized framework, but if they do not feel that the topic is important and have little commitment to striving for what may be an elusive nebulous goal, the emptiness of Frankl's existential vacuum could become dominant. The measurement of commitment was reviewed by Locke, Latham, and Erez (1988), and was shown to have an important relationship with performance. Research about Suzanne Kobasa's construct of hardiness has found commitment to be important as a moderator of stress and related to depression (Genellen and Blaney, 1984). Commitment to a life goal may have more impact than commitment to shorter-range goals involved in day-to-day living.

A fourth component is quality. This is an extension of Frankl's "will-to-meaning" theory that considers the nature of one's goal to be unimportant. Clinical experience and research about personal goals and values indicates that for one's SOP to be most conducive to good well-being and health it should include a focus external to the individual with a long-range orientation toward what is generally accepted as higher type goals. These would be goals and values reflecting social interest and constructive contribution as opposed to those reflecting hedonism and egocentricity. A systematic study of the relationship of life goal orientations with general well-being has potential for establishing an empirical base for controversial or unstable social codes.

For people to be free from the adverse impacts of alienation, noogenic neurosis, philosophical discontent, and existential vacuum, they should have a conscious awareness of all four of the preceding components. These comprise what was defined as sense-of-purpose. However, there are indications that a person could have unconceptualized or subconscious elements, which might be called "subsense-of-purpose." If there are universal SOP characteristics, it could well be that for people having a seeming lack, a corresponding subconscious element would be in conflict with any conscious element inconsistent with it. Other versions of psychodynamic psychology posit more creative and constructive functions for the subconscious, but in either case, unconceptualized goals are difficult to act on and can further compound the dissatisfaction and adverse effects of an inadequate SOP. The conscious SOP together with effects of the subconscious make up the individual's operating esteem of personal life, and its relationship to other life and existence in general. This "life-esteem" seems to be an adjunct to self-esteem so that people are aware not only of what they think about themselves, but also are aware of what they think of their lives. Thus, the life-esteem construct becomes a philosophy of life based on an individual's sense of purpose. It interacts with self-esteem to form a basic cognitive motivation on which is built the higher order social and cognitive motivations and lesser goals. It develops naturally in conjunction with self-esteem, and can be changed through socio-cultural influences and therapeutic interventions.

Life Esteem Survey

The Life-Esteem Survey (LES) was developed to measure the relative importance of comprehensive set of 22 possible life goals selected by factor analysis and analysis of variance, and the four aspects of a person's sense of purpose: framework, perspective, commitment, and quality. It consists of two sections: the Sense of Purpose Survey that uses 30 five-step Likert-type items to produce scores for the Framework, Perspective, and Commitment components, and the Life Values Survey that produces a Quality score derived from the sum the values assigned to the 22 possible goals on a scale of 1 to 9 weighted as shown in Appendix B by the figures in parentheses. Reliability and construct validity were demonstrated, with coefficients alpha ranging from 78 to .61, and test-retest coefficients ranging from .81 to .79. The quality score had the lowest coefficient alpha of .61 (Wheeler, 1977). All four scales are constructed for direct comparison on a range between 1 to 5, and an overall index (LES) formed by averaging the component scores.

Appendix B is an abbreviated self-scoring version that was developed for use in workshops and presentations. This shows definitions of the 22 possible life goals, and the structure for the four component scores. Scaling for this version is different from the full Life Esteem Survey, however concurrent validity was acceptable. Items used to measure the three component scores were selected by item-total correlations and consequently provide only a quasi-operational definition of the component.

General Well-Being

The importance of Life-Esteem hinges on its relationship with health, well-being, longevity, and performance that constitute general well-being. At the time of this research, there was no adequate measure of general well-being, so a self-report General Well-being Questionnaire (GWBQ) was developed in conjunction with research and evaluation measures used in the St Louis University health promotion programs. It consists of 143 Likert-type items that produce scores for 30 components grouped into seven areas and an overall index. The manual (Wheeler, 1985) gives reliability and validity data. Appendix C is an abbreviated self-scoring version that shows the structure of components and areas with brief explanations.

In addition to showing change in health promotion program participants (Wheeler, 1981; Tindall, 1982), the GWBQ has been used in a number of studies investigating the impact of various components on general well-being of teachers (Zehner, 1980; Bensky and Wheeler, 1981; Portner, 1982), nurses (Borgerding, 1985), lawyers (Sweetman, Munz, and Wheeler, 1992), and cardiac patients (Nouri, Waterman, and Wheeler, 1995). A study about the relationship of well-being components and academic performance showed that growth environment, effectence, and medical condition significantly predicted final course grades for university students (Wheeler and Magaletta, 1997). A study of well-being structure revealed the top contributors to the general well-being index to be: happiness, coherence, and sense of purpose. In another study about structure, components were divided into three groups: stress precursors, adverse stress impacts, and possible stress buffers. Results concluded that four of 22 demonstrated significant buffering effects: competence, physical exercise, sense of purpose, and leisure activities (Wheeler and Frank, 1988).

Life Esteem Research Results

One study of the relationship of life goals with general well-being with the LES and GWBQ used university students that were divided into two groups: those scoring above the mean and those scoring below the mean for the general well-being index (Wheeler, Munz, and Jain, 1990). Three life-goal components were significantly different for the subgroups: framework, perspective, and commitment. The fourth component, quality of goals, was not significantly different. A tendency was shown for the value placed on more hedonistically oriented goals to differentiate the subgroups with the group on low well-being higher on the hedonistically oriented goals.

In Chapter 5, a study was mentioned that showed the different possible life goals scored highest for each of four groups (Wheeler, 1985). Belonging was rated highest for 304 teachers; understanding for 205 university arts & science students; individualization for 86 general working adults; and religion for 30 university theology students. The theology students scored significantly higher than other groups on all four components scores as well as the overall index (214.4). Arts & Science students were next highest (183.9), with general working adults and teachers lowest (176.6 and 175.8 respectively).

In a study of 194 university students, one half were

placed in a subgroup that had a final course grade above the median, and the other half were in the subgroup with final course grade below the median (Wheeler and Haywood, 1995). Framework and quality significantly differentiated between the groups, however perspective and commitment did not. Of the 22 possible life goals, rating of Justice, excitement, and freedom each discriminated between the two groups. Furthermore, analysis of the goals ratings showed that low performance group valued the hedonistically oriented goals significantly higher than the high performance group. Another study of 75 advanced psychology students using the course grade median split into high and low groups found significant difference only in the quality score with the high performance group scoring higher. Both groups rated understanding highest among the possible life goals, but the high group valued service equally and benevolence next, where the low group valued next belonging and achievement (Wheeler and Wyrick, 1999)

This summary of selected studies using the LES and GWBQ indicate the usefulness of life-esteem. It has enough stability to be considered a personality characteristic that can be measured in people. It discriminates between social groups and performance groups, and reveals the life goals system of an individual. Further study is needed to improve and validate the quality score of the LES, even though the current version produces systematic results.

References

Allport, G. (1955). <u>Becoming</u>. New Haven: Yale University Press.

Ansbacher, H. & Ansbacher, R. (1956). <u>The individual psychology of Alfred Adler</u>. New York: basic Books

Arnold, M. & Gasson, J. (1954). <u>The human person.</u> New York: Ronald Press.

Battista, J. & Almond, R. (1973). The development of meaning in life. <u>Psychiatry, 36,</u> 409.

Boles, R. (1974). Cognition & motivation: some historical trends. In B. Weiner, (Ed) <u>Cognitive views of motivation.</u> New York: Academic Press.

Bond, M. & Feather, N. (1988). Some correlates of structure and purpose in the use of time. <u>Journal of Personality & Social Psychology, 55(2)</u>, 321-329.

Buhler, C. (1965). Some empirical approaches to the study of life's basic tendencies. In F. Severin (Ed) <u>Humanistic viewpoints in psychology</u>. New York: McGraw-Hill.

Buhler, C. & Massarik, F. (1968). <u>The course of human life</u>. New York: Springer.

Campbell, C. (1975, February). Coming apart at the seams (interview with Robert Heilbroner). <u>Psychology Today,</u> 95-103.

Crandall, J. & Rasmussen, R. (1975). PIL as related to specific values. <u>Journal of Clinical Psychology, 31(3)</u>), 483.

Crumbaugh, J. & Maholick, L. (1964). An experimental study in existentialism:the psychometric approach to Frankl's concept of noogenic neurosis. <u>Journal of Clinical Psychology, 20(2),</u> 200-207.

Crumbaugh, J. Cross validation of purpose-in-life test

based on Frankl's concepts. Journal of Individual Psychology, 24, 74-81.

Crumbaugh, J., Raphael, M. & Shrader, R. (1970). Frankl's will to meaning in a religious order. Journal of Clinical Psychology, 26(2), 206-207.

Crumbaugh, J. (1973). Everything to gain. Chicago: Nelson-Hall.

Crumbaugh, J. (1977). The Seeking of Nooetic Goals test: a complementary scale to Purpose-in-Life test. Journal of Clinical Psychology, 33(3), 900-907.

Domino, G. (1972). In 0. Buros (Ed) Seventh Mental Measurements Yearbook. Highland Park, NJ: Gryphon Press, p. 131.

Emmons, R. (1986). Personel strivings: an approach to personality and subjective well-being. Journal of Personality & Social Psychology, 51(5), 1058-1068.

Fabry, J. (1968). The pursuit of meaning. Boston: Beacon Press.

Frankl, V. (1965). The doctor and the soul. New York: Knopf.

Frankl, V. (1966). Self transcendence as a human phenomena. Journal of Humanistic Psychology, 6, 97-106.

Fromm, E. (1955). The sane society. Greenwich, CT: Fawcett.

Fromm, E. (1973). The anatomy of human destructiveness. New York: Holt, Rinehart & Winston.

Ganellen, R. & Blaney, P. (1984). Hardiness and social support as moderators of the effects of life stress. Journal of Personality & Social Psychology, 47(1), 156-163.

Garfield, C. (1973). A psychometric and clinical

investigation of Frankl's concept of existential vacuum and of anomia. Psychiatry, 36, 396-408.

Hahn, M. (1968). The California Life Goals Evaluation Schedule. Los Angeles: West Psychology Service.

Hall, C. & Lindzey, G. (1978). Theories of personality. New York: John Wiley & Sons.

Hogan, R. (1972). In 0. Buros (Ed) Seventh mental measurements yearbook. Highland Park, NJ: Gryphon Press, p. 86.

Hogan, R., DeSoto, C. & Solano, C. (1977). Traits, tests, and personality research. American Psychologist. 30, 255-264.

Hoge, D. & Bender, 1. (1974). Factors influencing value change among college graduates in adult life. Journal of Personality & Social Psychology, 29(4), 572.

Homer, P. & Kahle, L. (1988). A structural equation test of the value-attitude-behavior hierarchy. Journal of Personality & Social Psychology, 54(4), 638-646.

Huntley, C. & Davis, F. (1983). Undergraduate Study of Values scores as predictors of occupation 25 years later. Journal of Personality & Social Psychology, 45(5), 1148-1155.

Jones, A. & Crandall, R. (1986). Validation of a short index of self-actualization. Journal of Personality & Social Psychology, 12(1), 63-73.

Kobasa, S., Maddi, 5. & Kahn, 5. (1982). Hardiness and health:a prospective study. Journal of Personality & Social Psychology, 42(1), 168-177.

Kristiansen, C. (1985). Value correlates and preventive health behavior. Journal of Personality & Social Psychology, 49(3), 748-758.

Locke, E., Latham, G. & Erez, M. (1988). The determinants

of goal commitments. Academy of Management Review, 13(1), 23-39.

Manis, M. (1977). Cognitive social psychology. Personality & Social Psychology Bulletin, 3, 550.

Maslow, A. (1966). Comments of Dr. Frankl's paper. Journal of Humanistic Psychology, 6, 107.

Maslow, A. (1968). Toward a psychology of being. Princeton: Norstrand.

Maslow, A. (1971). The farthest reaches of human nature. New York: Viking.

May, R. (1977). Man's search for himself. New York: Norton.

McKee, M. (1972). In 0. Buros (Ed) Seventh mental measurements yearbook. Highland Park, NJ: Gryphon Press, p. 151.

Meier, A. & Edwards, H. (1974). PIL test: age and sex differences. Journal of Clinical Psychology, 39(3), 384.

Mitchell, J. (1984). Personality correlates of life values. Journal of Research in Personality, 18, 1-14.

Mlott, 5. & Lira, F. (1977). Dogmatism, locus of control, and life goals in stable and unstable marraiges. Journal of Clinical Psychology, 33(1), 142.

Morris, C. (1956). Varieties of human values. Chicago: U of Chicago Press.

Newcomb, M. & Harlow, L. (1986). Life events and substance use among adolescents: mediating effects of perceived loss of control and meaninglessness in life. Journal of Personality & Social Psychology, 51(3), 564-577.

Ormand, H. (1973). Relationship of measurements of dogmatism, PIL and self-actualization. Dissertation Abstracts, 34(48), 1730.

Pearson, P. & Sheffield, B. (1975). PIL and social attitudes in psychiatric patients. Journal of Clinical Psychology, 31(2), 330-332.

Phillips, W. (1980). Purpose in life, depression and locus of control. Journal of Clinical Psychology, 36(3), 661-667.

Reif, A. (1975, April). Erich Fromm on human aggression. Human Behavior, 17. Reker, G. (1977). The Purpose-in-Life test in an inmate population. Journal of Clinical Psychology, 33(3), 688-693.

Reker, G. & Cousins, J. (1979). Factor structure construct validity and reliability of the Seeking of Noetic Goals (SONG) and Purpose in Life (PIL) tests. Journal of Clinical Psychology, 35(1), 85-91.

Rogers, C. (1961). On becoming a person. Boston: Houghton-Mifflin.

Rokeach, M. (1973). The nature of human values. New York: Free Press.

Ruffin, J. (1984). The anxiety of meaninglessness. Journal of Counseling and Development, 63, 40-42.

Sallee, D. & Casciana, J. (1976). Relationship between sex drive and sex frustration and PIL. Journal of Clinical Psychology, 32(2), 273.

Sargent, G. (1973). Motivation and meaning: Frankl's logotherapy in the work situation. Dissertation Abstracts, 34(48), 1785.

Scheibe, K. (1970). Beliefs and values. New York: Holt, Rinehart & Winston.

Schwartz, 5. & Bilsky, W. (1987). Toward a universal psychological structure of human values. Journal of Personality & Social Psychology, 53(3), 550-562

Severin, F. (1973), Discovering man in psychology: a humanistic approach. New York: McGraw-Hill.

Shostrom, E. (1972). Freedom to be. Englewood Cliffs, NJ: Prentice Hall.

Shostrom, E. (1976). Actualizing therapy. San Diego: Edits.

Soderstrom, D. & Wright, E. (1977). Religious orientation and meaning in life. Journal of Clinical Psychology, 33(1), 65-68.

Sperry, R. (1977). Bridging science and values. American Psychologist, 32(4), 237.

Stevens, M., Pfost., K. & Wessels, A. (1987). The relationship of purpose in life to coping strategies and time since death of a significant other. Journal of Counseling & Development, 65(8), 424-426.

Taylor, S. (1983). Adjusting to threatening events. American Psychologist, 38, 1161-1173.

Toler, C. (1974). The personal values of alcoholics and addicts. Newsletter for Research in Mental Health & Behavioral Sciences, 16(3), 17.

Tosi, D. & Lindamood, C. (1975). The measurement of self-actualization: a critical review of the Personal Orientation Inventory. Journal of Personality Assessment, 39, 215.

Wheeler, R. (1985). Life Esteem: quantitative and qualitative differences. Presented at the 93rd Annual Meeting of the American Psychological Association, Los Angeles, 1985. (ERIC Document No. ED 262 322).

Wheeler, R. & Frank, M. (1988). Identification of stress buffers. Behavioral Medicine, 14(2), 78-89.

Wheeler, R. & Haywood, J. (1995). Life goal orientation and academic performance. Presented at the 103rd Annual Meeting of the American Psychological Association, New York, 1995. (Higher Education Abstracts 0833-31/GMT).

Wheeler, R.;Munz, D.; & Jain, A. (1990). Life goals and general well-being. <u>Psychological Reports, 66,</u> 307-312.

Wheeler, R. & Wyrick, M. (1999). Life-goals, performance, & academic major in University students. Presented at the 107th Annual Meeting of the American Psychological Association, Boston, 1999. (<u>Higher Education Abstracts 0024-35/GMT</u>).

Wong, P. & Fry, P. (1998). <u>The human quest for meaning</u>. Mahwah, NJ: Erlbaum.

Yarnell, T. (1971). PIL test: further correlates. <u>Journal of Individual Psychology, 27,</u> 76.

Zax, M. & Cowan, E. (1972). <u>Abnormal psychology, changing concepts</u>. New York: Holt, Rinehart and Winston.

Zika, 5. & Chamberlain, K. (1987). Relation of hassles and personality to subjective well-being. <u>Journal of Personality & Social Psychology, 53(1)</u>, 155-162.

Climbing Higher

Answering Big Questions

Appendix B

SENSE OF PURPOSE SURVEY

The following statements concern ways of looking at ones life with respect to a major long range goal or set of goals. On the scale to the right of each statement, circle the number that indicates the degree to which it applies to you as follows:

	1	2	3	4	5
	Strongly Disagree	Largely Disagree	Neutral	Largely Agree	Strongly Agree

1. Life has no particular meaning or central purpose for me. 1 2 3 4 5 *
2. I have a view or framework that allows me to understand why I'm alive. 1 2 3 4 5
3. There is a philosophy that gives my life significance. 1 2 3 4 5
4. I don't know what I really want to do in my life. 1 2 3 4 5 *

Framework ☐

5. Other people seem to feel better about their lives than I do. 1 2 3 4 5 *
6. I really feel good about my life. 1 2 3 4 5
7. I think I am living fully. 1 2 3 4 5
8. I don't seem to able to make much progress. 1 2 3 4 5 *

Perspective ☐

9. I am usually conscious of the relationship between my life goals and the activities I pursue. 1 2 3 4 5
10. I don't normally consider a purpose or goal in my life when making decisions. 1 2 3 4 5 *
11. Even though there may be a purpose in my life, I don't 1 2 3 4 5 *
12. I feel a strong commitment to a major life goal or set of goals. 1 2 3 4 5

Commitment ☐

For each of the three sets of statements above, add the numbers you circled <u>after</u> reversing the scale for those marked *. (i.e., If you circled 4 for statement 1, give yourself 2 points.) Place this sum in the box for each of the three factors. The sum for each factor gives the following indication of its strength for you:

High	16 - 20
Medium	11 - 16
Low	5 - 10

Climbing Higher

Life Esteem Survey

LIFE VALUES SURVEY

Twenty-two possible life goals are listed below. Read through their definitions thinking about how they might pertain to you as a major goal or purpose in living. Even though they may not fit perfectly or you think you don't have a major goal or set of goals, select the five that seem most important to you. Place a check by the item number for each of the five goals you select.

___ 1 PRODUCTION: To make things or contribute by producing goods. (3)
___ 2 FREEDOM: To be able to do what I want regardless of consequences. (2)
___ 3 UNDERSTANDING: To acquire wisdom and knowledge. (4)
___ 4 EQUALITY: To develop fair & impartial treatment for everyone. (3)
___ 5 EXCITEMENT: To have thrilling & stimulating activity. (0)
___ 6 SERVICE: To benefit, help or improve people or nature. (4)
___ 7 PLEASURE: To do things that are pleasurable. (1)
___ 8 HARMONY: To produce order, peace & balance in the world. (4)
___ 9 EXPRESSION: To communicate ideas & things I feel are important. (3)
___ 10 SUPERIORITY: To be recognized as having more or being better than others. (0)
___ 11 ECONOMIC: To obtain wealth, possessions & material goods. (2)
___ 12 BENEVOLENCE: To give love, affection & companionship to others. (4)
___ 13 BEAUTY: To be able to percieve & enjoy beauty. (1)
___ 14 TRANSCENDENCE: To fill requirements for salvation, union, & atonement. (3)
___ 15 RELIGION: To live in accordance with belief in a supreme being. (4)
___ 16 AESTHITICS: To contribute and stimulate beauty. (3)
___ 17 BELONGING: To have love, affection, & companionship from another. (1)
___ 18 EXISTENCE: To continue my life efficiently, making the most of situations. (1)
___ 19 JUSTICE: To be treated with fairness, honesty, & equality. (1)
___ 20 ACHIEVEMENT: To produce results providing a sense of accomplishment. (3)
___ 21 INDIVIDUALIZATION: To find and develop my own potential. (3)
___ 22 PROCREATION: To perpetuate certain ideas or physical characteristics. (3)

Quality ☐

For each item you selected, add together the numbers in parentheses to the right of those items. This score indicates the quality of your life values as compared with the three sense of purpose factors.

Appendix C
General Well-Being Questionnaire

GENERAL WELL-BEING SELF EVALUATION

This questionnaire provides an indication of your status pertaining to 32 factors that have been shown to contribute to general well-being and overall healthfulness. Follow the instructions at the beginning of each section. Complete all sections before reading the scoring instructions. The last page is a summary sheet to aid in interpreting scores.

Scoring

After completing Sections A, B, C, D, & E score sections A, B, & C as follows: add together the two numbers you have circled for each factor after reversing the scale for those items marked *. For example, in the Control Locus factor, if you circled 4 for item 1 and 5 for item 2, you would add 2 and 5 for an overall score of 7. Place this total score in the space by the factor title.

For sections D & E, add the number of points shown in parentheses above the frequency number you circled. For example, under the factor for Physical Complaints - Emotional, if you circled 1-2 for item 57 and 3-5 for item 58, your score for that factor would be 4+3=7.

Place the total score for each factor in the appropriate blank space on the summary sheet to aid in interpreting the scores.

Interpretation

The resulting scores provide a relative indication on a scale on 1 to 10 your state of well-being for each factor. A score above 6 means that factor provides special strength for you. A score below 6 means that you may benefit from looking at ways of improving you life style pertaining to that factor. These scores do not assess illness and should not replace medical examination or treatment.

Climbing Higher

A. Circle the number that best describes the extent to which you agree or disagree with these statements: 1- <u>S</u>trong <u>D</u>isagree; 2-Largely <u>D</u>isagree; 3- <u>N</u>ot <u>S</u>ure; 4-Largely Disagree; 5-<u>S</u>trongly <u>A</u>gree.

Control Locus   <u>S</u> <u>D</u> <u>N</u> <u>A</u> <u>S</u>
1 Without the right breaks, it is difficult to get ahead.   1 2 3 4 5 *
2 I have a lot of influence over the things that happen to me.   1 2 3 4 5

Health Control Locus
3 It is better for me to avoid thinking about my health.   1 2 3 4 5 *
4 I can avoid illness if I try.   1 2 3 4 5

Health Attitude
5 Having a good insurance policy keeps one from worrying about   1 2 3 4 5 *
   taking care of one's health.
6 There is a special advantage in having a private physician who   1 2 3 4 5
   knows you.

Permeability
7 Issues get confused when people look at both sides.   1 2 3 4 5 *
8 Even in today's world it is easy to be creative or come up with   1 2 3 4 5
   new ideas that are useful.

Achievement Drive
9 It is important for me to be the best in most things I do.   1 2 3 4 5 *
10 I don't get annoyed when I have to wait for something, and am   1 2 3 4 5
   usually pretty patent.

Time Perspective
11 Today is more important than yesterday or tommorrow.   1 2 3 4 5
12 I still feel resentment about some things that have happened to   1 2 3 4 5 *

Life Goal Framework
13 For me, life lacks meaning or a central purpose.   1 2 3 4 5 *
14 I think that I am living fully.   1 2 3 4 5

Spiritual Attitude
15 A person's soul or spirit stops at death.   1 2 3 4 5 *
16 Spiritual or non-physical forces influence my life.   1 2 3 4 5

Ethics
17 The reason I am nice to others I so that they will be nice to me.   1 2 3 4 5 *
18 It is important to actively help other people or society.   1 2 3 4 5

Answering Big Questions

B Circle the number the number that represents the relative value of that item to you: 1-Very Low value; 2-Moderately Low value; 3- Neutral value; 4-Moderately High value; 5-Very High value.

Life Values	VL	ML	N	MH	VH	
19 Exansion: To develop, grow, or have accomplishments.	1	2	3	4	5	
20 Economic: To have money, superiority or freedom.	1	2	3	4	5	*

C Circle the number the number that represents how these statements describe your general style of life: 1-Never; 2-Rarely; 3- Sometimes; 4-Often; 5-Usually.

Environment	N	R	S	O	U	
21 My working conditions are well organized & orderly.	1	2	3	4	5	
22 Where I live is uncomfortable and noisy.	1	2	3	4	5	*
Social Situation						
23 People seem to understand me pretty well.	1	2	3	4	5	
24 I am lonely.	1	2	3	4	5	*
Occupatonal Situation						
25 There is a lot of stress in my work.	1	2	3	4	5	*
26 My present job is a big source of satisfaction to me.	1	2	3	4	5	
Financial Situation						
27 Problems with having or managing money bother me.	1	2	3	4	5	*
28 I have enough money for the standard of living I want.	1	2	3	4	5	
Growth Environment						
29 Teaching or learning is an important activity for me.	1	2	3	4	5	
30 I am involved with a civic or social organization.	1	2	3	4	5	
Physical Activity						
31 Each day I participate in some physical exercise.	1	2	3	4	5	
32 Each day I take a walk or spend some time outdoors.	1	2	3	4	5	
Coping Activity						
33 I take tranquilizers or sleeping pills.	1	2	3	4	5	*
34 When I have problems, I try to work them out right away.	1	2	3	4	5	

Climbing Higher

Religious Activity

35 On a daily basis I have some form of meditation, prayer, or reflection.   1 2 3 4 5
36 Religious activities are an important part of my life.   1 2 3 4 5

Eating

37 Each day I have a coke or a soft drink.   1 2 3 4 5 *
38 Each day I eat a good breakfast.   1 2 3 4 5

Habits

39 I use drugs for purposes other than medical treatment.   1 2 3 4 5 *
40 Each day I smoke the equivalent of one pack or more of   1 2 3 4 5

Sleep

41 My sleep is interrupted.   1 2 3 4 5 *
42 I get seve to eight hours of sleep at night.   1 2 3 4 5

Health Practices

43 Even though I probably should go to a doctor I don't in order to save money, time, or effort.   1 2 3 4 5 *
44 I have a dental checkup at least once a year.   1 2 3 4 5

Leisure Activities

45 Daily I spend some time at a recreatioal activity.   1 2 3 4 5
46 Lesiure or recreational activities are a wast of my time.   1 2 3 4 5 *

Composure

47 I feel rested.   1 2 3 4 5
48 I feel worthless.   1 2 3 4 5 *

Happiness

49 I am downhearted and blue.   1 2 3 4 5 *
50 Life is enjoyable for me.   1 2 3 4 5

Coherence

51 I am uncomfortable in my surroundings.   1 2 3 4 5 *
52 I fit in well with the people around me.   1 2 3 4 5

Effectence

53 My work is inefficient.   1 2 3 4 5 *
54 I accomplish things that are important to me.   1 2 3 4 5

Body Esteem

55 I think my appearance is unattractive.   1 2 3 4 5 *
56 I feel physically strong and capable.   1 2 3 4 5

Answering Big Questions

D   Circle the number the number that indicates the number of times during the <u>past month</u> you have:

Physical Complaints-Emotional	(5)	(4)	(3)	(2)	(1)
57 My working conditions are well organized &	0	1-2	3-5	6-8	9+ *
58 Where I live is uncomfortable and noisy.	0	1-2	3-5	6-8	9+ *
Phsysical Complaints-Medical					
59 Had a cold or other illness.	0	1-2	3-5	6-8	9+ *
60 Had nausea or upset stomach.	0	1-2	3-5	6-8	9+ *

E   Circle the number the number that indicates the number of times each of these events have occurred to you in the <u>past twelve months</u>:

Physical Complaints-Emotional	(5)	(4)	(3)	(2)	(1)
61 Marriage, divorce, or sex problem.	0	1	2	3	4+ *
62 Major change in work activities, responsibility, or time schedule.	0	1	2	3	4+ *
Phsysical Complaints-Medical					
63 Taking on a sizeable debt or had money problems.	0	1	2	4	4+ *
64 Major illness, accident, or injury.	0	1	2	3	4+ *

Climbing Higher

GENERAL WELL-BEING PROFILE

Attitudes & Dispositions
—   CONTROL LOCUS (How much control do I have over things?)
—   HEALTH CONTROL LOCUS (How much control do I have on my health?)
—   HEALTH ATTITUDE (Do I have beneficial ideas about health?)
—   PERMEABILITY (Am I mentally flexible?)
—   ACHIEVEMENT DRIVE (Am I "easy going" enough?)
—   TIME PERSPECTIVE (Do I enjoy the "here & now?")

Beliefs & Values
—   LIFE GOAL FRAMEWORK (How meaningful does my life seem to me?)
—   SPIRITUAL ATTITUDE (Do I have a provision for the unknown?)
—   ETHICS (Do I think about morals, standards, & ethics?)
—   LIFE VALUES (Do I have constructive personal values?)

Environmental Situation
—   ENVIRONMENT (How comfortable are my physical surroundings?)
—   SOCIAL SITUATION (Do I have a social support network?)
—   OCCUPATIONAL SITUATION (How are my working conditions?)
—   FINANCIAL SITUATION (Am I free of financial worries?)
—   GROWTH ENVIRONMENT (Do I continue to grow?)

Behaviors & Habits
—   PHYSICAL ACTIVITY (Do I have healthful exercise?)
—   COPING ACTIVITY (How do I react to problems?)
—   RELIGIOUS ACTIVITY (Do I take time for "deeper things of life?")
—   EATING (Are my eating habits nutritious?)
—   HABITS (Am I free of smoking, drinking, or drug habits?)
—   SLEEP (Are my sleep patterns healthful?)
—   HEALTH PRACTICES (How well do I take care of my body?)
—   LEISURE ACTIVITIES (Do I benefit from leisure time?)

Feelings
—   COMPOSURE (How contented and relaxed am I?)
—   HAPPINESS (Do I feel happy and enjoy life?)
—   COHERENCE (Do I have a feeling of fitting in with things?)
—   EFFECTENCE (Do I feel efficient and competent?)
—   BODY ESTEEM (Am I happy with my body?)

Physical Complaints
—   EMOTIONAL (is my body free of neurological type problems?)
—   MEDICAL (Is my body free of disease problems?)

Recent Events
—   RELATIONAL (Do I have energy reserve for interpersonel relations)
—   PERSONAL (Do I still have energy reserve for personal affairs?)

Appendix D
The Relative Effects of Stressors on Mountain Climbers

High altitude mountaineering has always been a challenge for persons living in a low altitude environment, because of acute mountain sickness (AMS) which can strike quickly and not only degrades performance but can cause death. The recent increase of aircraft and space operations and the growing popularity of mountain climbing have stimulated interest in the effects on humans of exposure to high altitudes. Considerable research has been reported about the relationships to AMS symptoms of performance, personality, and mood (Paul & Fraser. 1994; Shukitt-Hale, Banderet, & Liebmen, 1991; Magni, Rupolo, Simini, De Leo, & Rampazzo, 1985). However, most of these studies looked only at altitude as an independent variable and used a limited class of dependent variables. The purpose of the present study was to determine the relative effects of the physical stress from exertion and cold temperature, the psychological effect from danger and anticipation, as well as the stress from low air pressure.

In recent years, the world's highest mountains have become populated with mountain climbers responding to the challenge of this vigorous sport. Unfortunately, many are not adequately prepared or knowledgeable about the risks, and incur serious injury or death. During the Spring 1996 climbing season 200 climbers attempted Mount Everest and nine lost their lives (Thukten Sharpa, personal communication, July 25, 1966). During the 1995-6 season, 1,956 attempted to climb Mount Aconcagua (tallest outside the Himalayan range) and three died (Ibarra, 1966). Mount

Aconcagua has become particularly popular for climbers due to its accessibility and nontechnical requirements. Situated about 100km northwest of Mendoza, Argentina, a base camp at 4,230m can be reach after 2 days of hiking (with mule assistance) from the village of Puente del Inca (2720m). Under ideal conditions, the summit at 6,962m is normally reached with 5 days of nontechnical climbing from the base camp. Even at the warmest period of the summer, though, the upper part of the mountain is subject to frequent snow storms with winds up to 100km/hr and temperatures as low as -40°C, so that normally a summit attempt is a significant challenge both physically and psychologically for even experienced climbers. Out of those that attempted this summit in the 1995-6 season, 395 required medical attention and 27 were evacuated (Ibarra, 1996).

Method

Participants

Data for this study were obtained from seven males and one female who attempted a summit climb of Mount Aconcagua in January of 1996. Ages ranged from 27 to 67 with a mean of 37.5. Three experienced mountaineers led the group from Mendoza, Argentina. Two males from Buenos Aires, two from St Louis, and one from San Francisco had limited mountain climbing experience.

Measures

Spanish and English versions of the Profile of Moods States questionnaire (McNair, Loor, & Droppleman, 1992) were used to assess the psychological impacts. To assess performance a Wocher grip meter was used. This is an elliptical shaped device made of stainless steel that fits into the palm of the hand. A calibrated scale measures the strength of a squeeze in kilograms of pressure.

Procedure.

The first set of measures were taken after two days at the base camp (4,230m) when climbers were rested, relaxed, and reasonably acclimated to that altitude. The second set of measures was taken after establishing a temporary camp at 5200m. At this point two climbers had turned back - one because of heart irregularities and one because of exhaustion. Threatening weather produced a snowstorm that confined the group to tents for two nights, with temperatures down to -20°C and winds of about 60km/hr. After the storm subsided, the group climbed with all equipment to the second temporary camp at 5,950m. After camp was established, hot supper, and rest, the six remaining participants completed the third set of measures. The next day all six of the climbers reached the vicinity of the summit and returned to the second temporary camp. Because of heavy snow, threatening weather, and shortage of daylight, only four got all the way to the summit, but the other two considered their climb successful. As participants returned and rested for about two hours, they completed the fourth set of measures.

Results

Consideration of the actual conditions during the climb indicated that the best indication of altitude stress effect was a comparison of the first and third set of measures taken at base camp and camp 2 respectively. The best indication of physical stress effects was a comparison of first and second measures taken at base camp and at camp 1 after the most strenuous exertion. And the best indication of the psychological stress effect was a comparison of the third and fourth measures when danger was highest and after danger and anticipation had subsided.

A Wilcoxon test (SPSSx, 1988) indicated that for altitude stress, the following measures were statistically significant: strength performance, tension, fatigue, and vigor. These results are summarized in Table 1. Also in Table 1 are the results of a repeated measures analysis of variance used to obtain greater sensitivity about the relative strength of the significant effects. The greatest effect was on the mood of fatigue.

For physical stress; strength, fatigue, and vigor were significant with the greatest effect on strength. Results are in Table 2.

For Psychological stress; strength, fatigue, vigor, and tension were significant with the greatest effect on vigor. Results are in Table 3.

To determine if there were any major differences between the six who finished the climb and the two who did not, a Mann-Whitney U test was made on the first set of measures taken at base camp. The non-finishers were significantly higher on tension and depression, and when the female was omitted from the analysis, vigor and strength were also significant. These results are summarized in Table 4. Since statistically significant differences existed between finishers and non-finishers, univariate analyses of variance were made to determine if there were significant differences between the six finishers using all four sets of scores. They were different for depression ($\underline{F}$=4.16, $\underline{df}$=5, $\underline{p}$=.01), Anger ($\underline{F}$=3.67, $\underline{df}$=5, $\underline{p}$=.02), and strength ($\underline{F}$=25.45, $\underline{df}$=5, $\underline{p}$=.00).

A repeated measures analysis of variance was made to determine if the measures changed significantly over time. These results are in Table 5. Over the four sets of measures, tension, vigor, fatigue, and strength were significantly different. The mean scores showed a consistent pattern in an adverse direction for the first three measures (except for strength that improved slightly at time 3); however, the scores of the fourth measure after the summit attempt recovered closely to the first (baseline) measure scores.

Conclusions

These results indicate that high altitude mountain climbers display a differential effect on mood and performance for physical stress, psychological stress, and altitude. For physical stress due to exertion and cold temperature, the greatest effect was on strength. For psychological stress due mainly to anticipation of danger and of reaching the summit, the greatest effect was on the mood of vigor. For altitude, the greatest effect was on the mood of fatigue.

Feelings of depression, anger, and confusion were not significantly related to changes in any of the stressors, nor did they significantly change over the course of the climb.

Mood and performance deteriorated over the course of the climb in a curvilinear manner. Deterioration increased until the final summit attempt. After the summit attempt while exertion, frigid temperature, and altitude were still high, all scores reverted close to the baseline measure. This indicated that mood and strength are more a function of anticipation and risk exposure than of exertion, environment, or altitude.

It is useful for individuals participating in high altitude climbing to recognize that mood and strength will change over the course of a climb, and that:

1. Strength and vigor will decrease while fatigue and tension will increase due to exertion, cold, risk, and anticipation independent of altitude.
2. Effects of stress will vary with individual climbers, particularly for strength and the moods of depression and anger.

3. Delays during a climb can be useful by facilitating acclimatization to altitude.
4. Degree of success in a climb may be predicted by measures of strength, vigor, tension, and depression.

Further multivariate research is needed about the relative effects of different types of stress on mountaineers; however, the results of the present study provide information that has the potential of reducing untoward events associated with the growing popularity of high altitude mountain climbing. Broad assumptions and overlapping data were justified by use of conservative analyses, and because of the scarcity and difficulty in collecting data during a high altitude climb.

References

Bonbon, Michael; Noel-Gerund, Marie-Christine & Theorem, Pierre (1995). Psychological changes during altitude hypoxia. Aviation, Space, & Environmental Medicine. 66(4), 330-335.

Ibarra, Jorge L. (1996). Estadisticas temporadas 95/6. Servicio Medico Plaza de Mulas, Argentina.

Jason, Gregor W.; Pajurkoava, Eva M.; & Lee, Robert G. (1989). High-altitude mountaineering and brain function: neuropsychological testing of members of a Mount Everest expedition. Aviation, Space, & Environmental Medicine. 60, 170-173.

Kramer, Arthur F.; Coyne, John T.; & Strayer, David L. (1993). Cognitive function at high altitude. Human Factors. 35(2), 329-344.

Magni, G.; Rupolo, G.; Simini, D.; Leo, D.; & Rampazzo, M. (1985). Aspects of the psychology and personality of high altitude mountain climbers. International Journal of Sports Psychology. 16, 12-19.

McNair, D. M.; Lorr, M.; & Droppleman, L. F. (1981). Manual for the Profile of Moods States. San Diego, CA: EDITS.

Paul, M. A. & Fraser, W. D. (1994). Performance during mild acute hypoxia. Aviation, Space, & Environmental Medicine. 65(10), 891-899.

Shukitt-Hale, Barbara; Banderet, Louis E.; & Lieberman, Harris R. (1991). Relationships between symptoms, moods, performance, and acute mountain sickness at 4,700 meters. Aviation, Space, & Environmental Medicine. 62, 865-869.

Shukitt-Hale, Barbara; Rauch, Terry M.; & Foutch, Richard (1990). Altitude symptomatology and mood states during a climb to 3,630 meters. Aviation, Space, & Environmental Medicine. 61, 225-228.

SSX User's Guide, 3d Edition (1988). Chicago: SPSS. Inc.

Table 1 **Effects of Altitude Stress**

Impact	Mean 1	Mean 3	Wilcoxon z	ANOVA p	F
Tension	5.67	10.67	1.99*	.05	6.05
Depression	.50	6.67	1.75	.08	2.09
Anger	1.50	4.00	.8	.40	1.12
Fatigue	3.50	19.33	2.20*	.03	24.51*
Vigor	22.67	8.50	-2.20*	.03	18.90*
Confusion	2.17	6.17	1.36	.17	2.14
Strength	144.67	123.00	-2.20*	.03	10.27*

* $p<.05$ N=6   df=1,5

Table 2 **Effects of Physical Stress**

Impact	Mean 1	Mean 2	Wilcoxon z	ANOVA p	F
Tension	5.67	10.17	1.36	.17	2.60
Depression	.50	5.00	1.83	.07	1.82
Anger	1.50	3.17	1.15	.25	1.62
Fatigue	3.50	13.17	2.20*	.03	6.75*
Vigor	22.67	12.17	-2.20*	.03	6.34*
Confusion	2.17	4.50	1.15	.25	1.61
Strength	144.67	115.83	-2.20*	.03	36.10*

* $p<.05$ N=6   DF=1,5

Table 3 <u>Effects of Psychological Stress</u>

Impact	Mean		Wilcoxon		ANOVA
	4	3	$\underline{z}$	$\underline{p}$	$\underline{F}$
Tension	5.17	10.67	2.20*	.03	16.96*
Depression	1.67	6.67	1.83	.07	2.95
Anger	2.00	4.00	1.21	.22	1.40
Fatigue	6.33	19.33	2.20*	.03	31.30*
Vigor	18.17	8.50	-2.20*	.03	36.25*
Confusion	3.33	6.17	1.36	.17	1.96
Strength	139.83	123.00	-2.20*	.03	8.43*

* $\underline{p}$<.05   N=6   df=1,5

Table 4 Differences Between Finishers and Non-finishers

	Mean			Mann-Whitney			
	NF	F	F	z	p	z	p
N	2	6	5	6	6	5	5
Tension	16.50	5.67	4.80	-2.01*	.04	-1.95*	.05
Depression	12.00	.50	.40	-2.10*	.04	-2.03*	.04
Anger	1.50	1.50	1.60	-.17	.86	-.20	.84
Fatigue	6.00	3.50	3.40	-.17	.86	-.20	.85
Vigor	13.50	22.67	24.20	-1.67	.10	24.20*	.05
Confusion	7.50	2.17	2.20	-1.86	.06	-1.76	.08
Strength	97.50	144.67	158.60	-1.33	.18	1.94*	.05

* $p<.05$ F=Finisher   NF=Non-finisher   N=number

Table 5 <u>Differences Between Time</u>

	Mean				F	p
	1	2	3	4		
Tension	5.67	10.17	0.67	5.174	.87*	.02
Depression	.50	5.00	6.67	1.67	2.21	.13
Anger	1.50	3.17	4.00	2.00	1.13	.37
Fatigue	3.50	13.17	19.33	6.33	13.34*	.00
Vigor	22.67	12.17	8.50	18.17	10.05*	.00
Confusion	2.17	4.50	6.17	3.33	1.73	.20
Strength	144.67	115.80	123.00	139.80	13.87*	.00

* $p<.05$ N=6   df=3

Climbing Higher

Appendix E
Plaza de Mulas
By J. C. Corvalan

During my childhood growing up in Mendoza, Argentina, I dreamed many times about climbing Mount Aconcagua. With a summit at 22,841 feet, Aconcagua is the tallest mountain in the Western Hemisphere, and looms up in the sky about 80 miles north of Mendoza. After living in the United States for about 30 years, the time had come. I had been under observation for variations in my heart's rhythm, but the cardiologist said I could do it as long as my pulse was regular. So, there I was at the Plaza de Mulas base camp in a mountain climbing party with some of my friends.

Now, though, not all was good. The two day climb from the trail head at Puente del Inca was strenuous going from an elevation of 8,400 feet to 13,879 feet, but aside from the normal breathing problems associated with such an ascent, a bit of weakness and muscle soreness, and a sense of apprehension and wonder about the snow covered peak above, I was feeling fair on arrival at Plaza. We then spent several days waiting for good weather and acclimating before making the first climb carrying provisions to a temporary campsite at a ridgeline saddle called Nido de Condores. That was tough. Fortunately, we had planned to return to Plaza for the night before the second climb to Nido. At that time, my heart had started an irregular beat, and during the night, my pulse got up to 120 beats per minute, so I was relieved when our guide said that the weather was threatening again and that we would wait for the next climb to Nido. My health continued to deteriorate and, when the time came for the second climb to start my pulse was irregular and I was coughing up pink sputum. These were symptoms that could develop into pulmonary edema. The base camp doctor said that the only treatment was immediate return to lower altitude, so our guide arranged for me to leave the next morning for the descent to Puente del Inca on a mule with "los arrieros." Arrieros are sort of "gaucho" cowboys who live in the local area, ride horses, and use mule trains to bring supplies and climber's equipment to the base camp. That is as far as mules can go - thus the name, "Plaza de Mulas."

It was cold, snowing, and dark that next night when I had to stay in the unfinished hotel, a new building which because of funding problems, had no running water, no electricity, no upstairs bathrooms, and no heating, There was a common bathroom in the basement, all very dark and cold. I went to bed, and thought about my friends who by now could have reached Nido de Condores. The room was cold, the water frozen and I had a terrible night coughing, wheezing, with palpitations, asking myself why I was there. I could hardly wait for the morning. I missed my friends, who by now were way up on the mountain.

When day came, I got ready and went looking for the "arrieros." There they were, with their mules, unloading and getting ready to go down to Puente del Inca. It took us two days hiking from Puente del Inca to reach the base camp in Plaza de Mulas. Now, with luck in few hours I will be down. They assigned a mule to me, but it did not have a saddle, since they were set to carry loads rather than people. After I insisted, they rigged a makeshift saddle covered with a blanket. It was not very comfortable, but it provided a reasonable sense of security and was better than walking. It was getting late, and the light snow flurries were changing into heavy down bursts. Wind was picking up and we had to get started. Initially the mules walked slowly to the trail that would take us down, and we began descending during, what by now, had become a blizzard.

The Wall and the River

The trail was the same one we had come up on, and the first part of the descent was on what was called the "Subida Brava," meaning hard climb. This section, that is about 1,000 feet vertically, was exhausting when we climbed. It was also rather dangerous because the trail was on a ledge cut out of a rock wall in ancient times by water flowing from the Horcones Superior glacier. On one side was the rock wall, and on the other side was a steep drop off to a branch of Horcones River below. With the best of weather, there is the big risk in coming down the abrupt descent, but in a snowstorm, the risk seemed monstrous. I had no choice but to trust my mule. I could not see a thing, not even the trail, just the neck of my mule. The snow was blowing horizontally, and whirling around me. Everything was white. I could hear at times the sound of water, the river tumbling down there somewhere. The lack of visibility and the sounds of wind and water mixed with the noise the mule's hoofs when hitting the trail's rocks (I hoped) were giving confusing clues to my sense of orientation, so with difficulty I hung on tightly to my mule. My body went up and down, forwards and backwards and, thankfully not much to either side. It was like a wild plane ride, but slow, as if it would never end.

Finally, after a long, long ride down, the river sounded closer and we merged into the riverbed. The Horcones River was there, and now the mules were splashing in the water. Wind and snow constantly changed directions, but I did not care much because if I fell now, it would only be from the mule to the rocks or water rather than down a precipice. The arrieros now got all the mules together and started down following the river, which we would cross a few times.

El Galope

Now we were following the river, descending to a place called Confluencia at 10,500 feet, where two branches of the Horcones Rivers meet. Gradually the arrieros increased their speed, changing from walking to galloping. My mule had trouble galloping, probably because of the improvised saddle, which I did not think could endure these movements, and then started trotting. That was torture, because I could not synchronize my bounces with those of the mule. As I could hardly hang on, I yelled for the arrieros to slow down, which they did; but after few minutes, they would start again galloping. It became so painful I finally yelled for them to stop. After several of my agonizing yells, they did stop, and I explained to them the physics and the mechanics of the need to continue at a lower speed. They were not very friendly. They said that they were in a hurry, because it was "viernes" (Friday) and they did not want to miss the fun awaiting them in town. I insisted that because I had no real operative saddle it was difficult to follow their speed. They agreed and slowed down. It was getting colder, the wind continued, but not the snow. We could see the river as well as the trail and the rocks.

At one point, the arrieros stopped, talked among themselves looking at me menacingly, but then started moving forward again. When the snow started again, I became worried, thinking that they might be plotting against me. They continued acting suspicious. The riverbed now was very wide, with many small streams rather than the river. I thought that if they decided to get rid of me, this was the place - no one would be able to find my body in years. After this blizzard there would be many more, and it would be a long time before my body would be discovered. I called them and asked them to keep a regular speed in order to be sure we arrive at the Puente del Inca Base on time, because there were people from Mendoza waiting for me there, and if I did not return on time, they would send a patrol, implying that they would be held responsible for my return. They listened, looked at each other and we continued at a more steady speed.

Rocks and Mules

It was cold and windy with snow blowing everywhere including in my face. The riverbed now was wide with many small streams. We had been riding for a few hours when we stopped near some big rocks. As I started to dismount, my mule decided to move, and I fell on the ground with one foot tangled in the stirrup, my head just barely missing a rock. The mule moved slowly, then stopped and looked at me with what seemed to be a grin while I was struggling to avoid hitting stones with my head. The arrieros were near, but just looked, remained silent, and made no attempt to help me. After a while, I was able to free my foot and get hold of the mule reigns. I got to a big rock nearby, and was able remount by jumping down on to my mule - not very elegant, but it was effective. By now the arrieros were on their way, not a word was said about the incident.

Confluencia

Once I was back on the mule, we continued our "trotting" to Confluencia where the two rivers meet coming from the Superior and Inferior Horcones Glaciers. At this point, the arrieros became friendlier. They suggested, then recommended, and finally insisted that I relax and let my mule that knows the way take me the rest of the way back. They said that they had to go faster since this was Friday and they had to get into town. They were sure that it was the best solution. I objected because it was getting dark and we were not yet close to Confluencia. I was not going to let a mule decide if I was going to survive. They finally agreed, and we continued without problems until we reached Confluencia.

After crossing the river, we were now on the last leg of the trip to the 8,400-foot elevation trailhead at Puente del Inca. I remembered this part of the trail because I had hiked it before with my nephews going to the base of the South Wall of Aconcagua. I felt somewhat secure now. The snow and the wind were down, the temperature was up, and I felt better; so, I told the arrieros to go on. The mule also seemed to feel better (probably recognizing the last leg of the journey) and tried to go faster. As we approached Laguna Horcones that I knew was close to the trailhead, I decided to dismount and proceed on foot. Now I was on my own, walking and enjoying the mountains. I could see and hear the river that we had been following. The lake was beautifully clear, and I crossed the river again for the last time.

Puente del Inca and Mendoza

From the lake, the trail ascended. I was feeling pretty good now, so climbing on foot was not unpleasant. Besides, the mule had gone on ahead of me. The sky was clear, the air crisp, and even though I was exhausted and sore, a great feeling of joy came over me when the flag on the roof of the ranger hut at the entrance of the park came into view. What a relief, because it was really getting dark now. To my surprise there was a pickup truck there waiting to take me to the arrieros's shop. My two duffle bags had survived the trip on the mule's backs and were there waiting for me. The driver then took me to the military post in Puente del Inca where we had left our summer clothing. A driver from Mendoza sent by my friend Nicolas was supposed to be waiting there for me.

A car was leaving from the military post as we arrived. I had the feeling that was the one sent for me, so I stopped it and asked if he was looking for me. He answered yes, and informed me he was told at the post that they did not know me, that I had never been there, and that they could not help him. So much for my rescue plan! The bag I had left was finally found, and I was ready to go to Mendoza.

It was good to get in the car and start shedding layers of clothes. I had gone from sub-freezing blizzard winter to hot humid summer in the course of one day, and it was with a great sense of relief that I relaxed in a comfortable car gliding smoothly down the highway. We stopped in the small village of Uspallata for a well-deserved beer and pizza, and then continued to the International Hotel in Mendoza. How pleasant to be at such a nice, hospitable, clean place. After soaking in a warm shower, I lay down in the soft bed with a cold beer, turned the TV on, and reveled in the comfortable feeling that my heart was calm, regular, and strong. The TV was showing "The Little Prince" based on the inspiring book by Saint Exupery about another difficult experience. I sympathized with that story, but now the grueling experiences were over, and my eyes closed in a restful sleep

Appendix F
Five Factor Evaluation

Each graph below represents a dimension of personality characterized by the term at each end of the graph. The terms describe extremes for that dimension. Most people fall in between. Between the two ends on the graph, circle the number that you think shows the way you are typically, that is, in general.

```
       private  1----2----3----4----5----6----7  public
         quiet  1----2----3----4----5----6----7  talkative
      reserved  1----2----3----4----5----6----7  friendly
                Sociability Total_____

          Firm  1----2----3----4----5----6----7  tender
      critical  1----2----3----4----5----6----7  pleasant
     assertive  1----2----3----4----5----6----7  accepting
                Agreeableness Total_____

    easy going  1----2----3----4----5----6----7  hard driving
process seeking  1----2----3----4----5----6----7  goal seeking
   uncommitted  1----2----3----4----5----6----7  committed
                Conscientiousness Total_____

         Tight  1----2----3----4----5----6----7  loose
  conservative  1----2----3----4----5----6----7  tolerant
     practical  1----2----3----4----5----6----7  imaginative
                Openness Total_____

      flexible  1----2----3----4----5----6----7  firm
     emotional  1----2----3----4----5----6----7  unemotional
       anxious  1----2----3----4----5----6----7  calm
                Stability Total_____
                          Overall Total_____
```

Interpretation

Total up the numbers circled for each factor, and sum the five totals to give an overall total. The scores give only a rough indication of your characteristics, and should not be thought of as indicating good or bad as long as factor scores are between 6 and 18. Extreme scores may be a source of stress.

For individual factors, most people score between 12 and 18. Greater spiritual development is related to a higher score for each characteristic. If you scored below 12, you might want to decide if that is really the way you want to be, or you might consider ways that would cause your score to be higher. A score greater than 18 may indicate that factor is over bearing and limiting flexibility. Even though these factors are partially determined by genetic based temperament, they can change for different situations and experiences. And, they can be changed by you if you so desire.

If your overall score is less than 60, look at the low scoring factors to see if you want to change. A score greater than 90 might indicate rigidity that could interfere with overall spiritual development.

About the Author

Robert Wheeler developed a keen interest in the view people have about meaning and purpose in their lives during 20 years of military experience working with people of various cultures as an infantryman, aviator, engineer, advisor, and research & development coordinator. His last assignment before retiring was Chief of the Foreign Technology Office at the U.S. Army Aviation Systems Command. For another 20 years, he filled positions at St Louis University to include Director of Health Promotion Research and adjunct Associate Professor of Psychology. His major work was research about personality characteristics that contribute to health, well-being, and performance. He also developed measuring instruments and performed analyses for health promotion programs from a didactic viewpoint to assist participants, from an evaluation viewpoint to determine effectiveness, and from a research viewpoint to increase knowledge of health enhancement and quality of life improvement. Now retired, his current work is with spirituality as a personality characteristic, and its role in human nature and health. In 2014 he set a new Guinness World Book Record as the oldest man to climb Mount Kilimanjaro in Africa.

Climbing Higher

Index

A

Abraham 120, 130
Aconcagua, Mount 26, 27, 28, 31, 32, 35, 37, 46, 49, 157,
actualization 20
Adam 129, 134,
Adams, Nancy 107
  A God That Could Be Real, 107
Agassiz Peak 95, 96, 97, 98,
Agnosticism 118, 174, 175, 178
Adler, Alfred 243, 245,
Allport, Gordon 20, 113, 227, 229, 241, 243, 244
altered states of consciousness (ASC) 84,
Andes Mountains 30, 70, 71, 72
Ambiguity 103, 194, 195, 196, 197, 198
Amoeba 19,
Anasazi 100
animism 2, 54, 55, 75, 103, 118, 120, 122,
  early form of religion 2
  extensions of 120
  supernatural explanations of 75, 103
anthropic principle 81
anthropomorphism 54, 121
Argentina 26, 27, 31, 49, 157
Astronomers 105
Atheism 110, 118, 142, 151, 175, 178
attribution theory 106, 245
Attridge, Harold 149
  Religion & Science Debate, the 149

awe 49-50, 52-54, 68, 70, 75-76, 88, 101-103, 107, 112, 123, 133, 145, 151, 190, 196, 203
   brain activity 52, 78, 81, 106, 112, 126, 145
   definition of 50
   in Lamaism 57, 67, 70
   as a powerful emotion 53
   of sacred mountains 55, 68, 88, 101-102, 127, 128
   source of 49, 103, 113-114, 120, 123, 140, 180, 194
   in triggering ontological imperative
xiii, xiv, xvi, 48, 55, 77, 87, 103, 106, 118, 125, 138, 154, 154, 156, 166, 167, 168, 177-179, 198, 202, 203

B

Babylonia 129
Bass, Wells, and Ridgeway xii
   Seven Summits xii
beliefs
   animistic 67,
   esoteric 134
   religious 77, 139
   as social enterprises 118
   in the supernatural 70. 127
Berkeley, George 78
Bering, Jesse 153
Bernbaum, Edwin xii, 55
   Sacred Mountains of the World xii, 55
biophilia 94
Blackmore, Susan 85
   Consciousness: An Introduction 85
Blanca Peak 88, 89, 91, 92, 93, 157
Bon mysticism 57, 58
Bottom-up approach xi, 143, 151, 152
Boudhanath 59

Boudha Stupa 59, 60
Brain based 57
brain processes 52
Buddhism 2, 57, 58, 65, 67
  Tibetan 57, 58,

C

Calientes, Aguas 73
Campbell, Joseph 139
Cardena, Lynn, Kripner 141
  Varieties of Anomalous Experience 140, 141
Cardiovascular 10, 11
Caucasoid 1
Chaco Canyon 100
Chalmers, David 78, 79
Chimpu Mount 58, 63, 65
Christian 108, 120, 129, 131,139, 176, 195
chorten 63, 64, 65
Church of the Holy Sepulcher 135
Cloninger, Robert 106
Coconino 95, 98
dissonance 153, 196
imperative xiii, xiv, xvi, 48, 55, 77, 87, 103, 106, 118, 125, 138, 154, 154, 156, 166, 167, 168, 177-179, 198, 202, 203
labeling 51
Coleridge 204
Collins, Francis 82, 151
Como Lake 90, 91, 93, 94,
complexity 107, 112, 152, 171, 174
conciliation 167, 170, 175
confabulation 144

consciousness 40, 58, 76, 77-88, 102, 107, 111, 121, 140, 141, 147, 195, 201, 203
   altered states of 84
   definition of 76
   Eastern 58
   level of 77
   studies on 78, 80,
   theories of 79 81
   views of 78
Copenhagen Interpretation 120, 121
Cosby, David 194
cosmic mountain 55
cosmologist 81
Creator 108, 136, 144
Crumbaugh, James 21, 231
Cultural Revolution 68
Curandero ceremony 72

D

Dalai Lama 59, 61, 68
D'Aquili, Eugene 52
David (king) 129
Davies, Paul 81
  Goldilocks Enigma, the 81
Dawkins, Richard 142, 143, 151
debate 154
deity 48, 77, 82, 84, 87, 104, 107, 112, 121-123, 139, 141-143, 146-147, 151-154, 175, 179-180, 196
Demilitarized Zone 3
Dennett, Daniel 79, 139, 143, 151
Descartes, Rene 77
Dome of the Rock 128, 131, 133, 136

Dmt 145
Drigung Mountain 68
Drigung Valley 68
dualism 78, 81, 85, 125

E

Eccles, John 78
Ecumenical humanism 176-177
Einstein 116
Ellingwood 91-93
elusiveness paradox 150, 174
emergent interactionism 78-86
emergent properties 83
emotions x-xi, 24, 47, 49, 50-53, 87, 103, 113, 145, 173, 197
  evolution theory of 50
entangled 80, 83
epiphenomenalism 78
Erikson, Erik 201
Eudaimonia 24, 112
excitation level 10
existential dilemma 114
extraversion 171-172
Eysenck, Hans 12

F

Faber, M. D. 119
faith viii, xiii, 63, 104, 110-111, 113, 117-118, 121, 135-136, 138-139, 142, 146, 148-152, 170, 176-177, 180-181, 195
  in religion 110, 118
Festinger, Leon 196

fictional finalism 20
Fields, Jonathan 197
   Uncertainty: Turning Fear & Doubt into Fuel for Brilliance 197
fight-or-flight response 50
first cause 80, 144
five factor spirituality 171
Flanagan, Owen 112
   Really Hard Problem, The 112
flourishing 24, 70, 112, 203
Foss 204
Foundation Stone 129-130, 133, 136
Fowler, James 117
Frankl, Viktor 20, 22, 230
   Mans's Search For Ultimate Meaning 22
Freedom's Frontier 3
Freemasonry 108-109, 118
Fromm, Erich 114, 244
frozen carcass v, xiii, 193
Fuji Mount 1-4, 10, 156-157, 165
  aerial view of 3
  history of
  summit 4-5, 157
Fuji shuffle 160
Fujiyoshida 4, 8

G

general well-being ix, 23-24
Gleiser, Marcelo 147
   Islands of Knowledge, the 147
Global Consciousness Project 83
Goals viii, 19-23

Goodenough, Ursula 151
goraiko 2, 157
Gould, Stephen 148-149
great dilemma 149-150, 170
great mysterious caregiver 119, 168
Great Observer 81, 146
great paradox 149-150, 165, 170, 174, 182, 194-195
Guinness xiii, 291
Guru Rinpoche 57

H

Haisch, Bernard 80
Hamer, Dean 106
Hameroff, Stuart 79
hard problem 79, 81, 112
Harris, Sam 139, 143, 151
Hedonism 232, 247
Heipori, Mount 57-58, 63, 65-66
Hemingway v, 182, 193
   Snows of Kilimanjaro, the v, xiii, 193
Herod (king) 130-131
heterophenomenology 79
Hinduism 67
Holmes, Jamie 196
Hopi 88, 95-96
Horcones 27, 31, 37, 283-284
Horgan, John 150
   Rational Mysticism 150
Hot bath 8, 157-158, 164
Hotel Refugio Plaza de Mulas 32
Huayna Picchu 70, 74
human dilemma 114

human nature vii, 76, 119, 136, 141, 149, 168, 170, 201
Humphreys 88, 94-100
  Peak 88, 94-100
  Trail 98
hypothermia 5-6, 43
hypoxia 275

I

Idealism 78, 81, 85-86, 120, 145, 232
immunology 47
India 1, 15, 57, 66, 88, 91, 241
Infinity 7, 92-93, 105
Institute of Noetic Sciences 58
institutional religion xi, 121-123, 142-143, 150, 178
intercessory prayer 83
Intipunku, the Sun Gate 72, 74
Isaac 129
Ishmael 129
Islamic 139
Israel 127-128, 131-132

J

Jeans, James vi
  New Background of Science, The vi
Jeffrey Mishlove's *Roots of Consciousness* 85
Jerusalem 128-132, 134, 136
Jews 129
Jokhan 61
Judaism 107
Jung, Carl 20

K

katsina 95-96
kata 60-61
Kathmandu 58-60
Kauffman, Stuart 106
  Reinventing the Sacred 106
Kaufman, Gordon 108
  Jesus and Creativity 108
Kelly, George 169
Kilimanjaro, Mount v, xiii, 182-186, 188, 192-193, 291
King Herod's Temple 130-131
King Solomon's Temple 108, 129
kiva 95-97, 100
Koch, Christof 81
Kolberg, Lawrence 117
Koran 146
Korea 1, 3, 12, 41
Kurtz, Paul 142

L

Lamaism 57, 67, 70
life commitments 20
life-esteem 225, 245, 247-249, 251
life-goal 228, 235, 250
Life Esteem Survey 22-23,
Life Regard Index 21-22
life space 105
Lipton, Bruce 82

locus of control 54
Loftus, Elizabeth 144
Logoanalysis 231
Logotherapy 21
Longfellow 204

M

Macfarlane, Robert 55
  Mountains of the Mind 55
Machu Picchu 70-71, 73-74
  ancient ruins 71, 74
  summit of 70, 74
macrocosm 105
mandala 65
Maslow, Abraham *20, 49*
May, Rollo 114,
meaning vii-xiv, 20-24
mediumship 82, 146,
memes 139
Menninger, William 20
Menninger Clinic 20
mentalism vii, 86
metaphysical ix, xiii, 78, 82, 86-87, 118
  beliefs xiii, 118
  realm xiii
microcosm 105, 145
militant atheism 110, 142, 178
Military Assistance Advisory Group 199
Mind 76-86
misattribution 54
Mislove, Jeffry 85
  Roots of Consciousness 85

Mohammad 130
monism 78
Moody, Raymond 82
Moriah, Mount 127-136
Mount of Olives 128
multiverse theory 81
Mumba 68
Muslim 129-133, 135
Musolino, Julien 82
   Soul Fallacy, the 82
mysticism ix, 2, 49, 53, 55, 57-58, 62, 70, 75, 101-102, 110, 118-119, 150, 167
Myers, David 153
   A Friendly Letter to Skeptics & Atheists 153
myths 112, 127, 139

N

Nagarkot 59
Naze, Mount 199
Navajo 88-90, 94
Near-death experiences 82, 86, 140
Needs xii, 19-25, 55, 76, 84, 114-117, 152-154, 168-178
   heirarchy of 20
   metaneeds 114
   spiritual 124
Nepal 58-59, 67, 75
neuroscience 51-52, 81, 84, 112, 123
neurotheology 151
Newberg, Andrew 52, 106
Nitsaa, Dibe 90
Nognosticism 174-175
Nonoverlaping magisteria 148-149

noogenic neurosis 21

O

Ollantaytambo 73
ontogenetic 105, 113
ontological x-xiii, 48, 55, 77, 87, 103, 106, 111, 115, 118, 125, 138, 154, 156, 166-168, 177-179, 198, 202-203
   engineering 111, 115
   imperative x-xi, xiii, 48, 55, 77, 87, 103, 106, 118, 125, 138, 154, 156, 166-168, 177-179, 198, 202-203
   research 111, 115
Osley Gampa 59-60
oxygen 39, 53-54, 106, 162, 185, 193

P

Padmasambhava 57-58
paganism 118
Panchen Lama 68
panpsychism 77
pantheism 118, 178
paradox 124, 138, 148-150, 156, 165-167, 170, 174-175, 180, 182, 184, 194-195, 198
paranormal 84, 141
Pascal 124, 153
Pashapati Park 59
perennial philosophy 106
personality vi, x, 10, 106, 110-111, 171-172
  type A 10, 12
  type B 12, 32
  type T 10
personal projects 19

personal strivings 20
Pert, Candace 82, 151
philosophy vii, x, xii, 77-78, 81, 86, 106, 111-112, 119-120, 145, 157, 176, 179, 201,
   Eastern 78, 86
   of idealism 81, 120, 145
   of life vii, 179,
   ontological x, xii
phylogenetic 104, 113
physicalism 79, 81
Pickover, Clifford 124, 149, 195
   The Paradox of God 124, 195
pluralism 85, 178-179
Popper, Karl 78
Positive psychology 24
Potala Palace 61
Pragmatic pluralism 178-179
prayer 60, 64, 83, 121, 130, 132, 142, 144-145
preachers 122
probability 123, 200
Pribram, Karl 81
priests 122
propriate striving 20,
psi 83, 141
psychic phenomena 140-141
psychology vi, vii, x, 19, 24, 81, 84, 104, 110, 119, 123, 140-141, 143, 153, 156, 183-184, 196, 198, 201,
Psychology, Religion, and Spirituality 110
psychometric 110
Pueblo 89, 100
Puente del Inca army camp 30
Purpose in Life questionnaire 21-22

Q

qualia 79
quantum mechanics 79-81, 86, 145-146
quantum mind 80
quasi-material 79
quasi-religious 118

R

Radin, Dean 83
  Entangled Minds 83
reactivity 10, 12
reincarnation 68, 82, 86, 112, 120, 140
Reinecke 205
Religion 21-24, 77-82, 103-113, 118-125
religious naturalism 107, 151, 178
religious sentiment 113, 119
Rinpoche Myngur 59-61
Rogers, Carl 105
Rosicrucian 118, 125
Rotter, Julian 54
Rue, Loyal 113
  Religion is not About God 113

S

sacred mountains xii, 55, 88, 101-102
Sacsayhuaman 72
Samye 57-58, 62-63, 65-67
Schwartz, Gary 82, 151
self-transcendence 106
Seligman, Martin 24, 177

Flourishing 24,
Shamans 122, 145
Shaver, Phillip 21,
  Meaning, Mortality, & Choice 22
Shintoism 2
Sierra Blanca Peak (Sisnaajini) 89
Sisyphus 174
sky burial 64, 68-69
sociobiologist 49
Solomon (king) 108, 129
soul 68, 76-77, 82-83, 85-86, 125, 203
Spilka, Hood, Hunsberger, and Gorsuch
  Psychology of Religion 110
spiritual intelligence 111
spirituality xi, 58, 105, 107-108, 110-123, 125, 140-141, 149, 169, 171-173
  aspects of 110-111
  definition of 105
  dimensions of 114-116
  measure of 110
  see also religion
  striving process of 113
Stevenson, Ian 82
string theory 81
Stenger, Victor 139, 151
stupa 59-60, 63
supermind 81, 87, 146
supernatural ix, xi, 47-48, 50, 56, 70, 75, 83-84, 86-88, 101-103, 105-108, 112, 115, 118, 120-121, 123-124, 127, 138-142, 149, 151, 153, 167, 169, 174, 195-196
  deity 141-142, 151, 196
  explanations xi, 50, 56, 75, 101-103, 123,

forces 48, 87, 101, 103, 107, 118, 120, 123-124, 127, 142, 151, 195
  form of mentalism 86
  phenomena 70
  realm 88, 112, 115, 140
supernature 122
Swaab, D. F. 111
  We Are Our Brains 111

T

Taiwan 199
Tart, Charles 141
  End of Materialism, The 141
Taum Sauk Mountain 12, 13
Taylor, Mark 153, 195
  After God 195
Temple Mount 130
terrorism 138-139, 147
Tewa 89
theocracy 59, 61, 68, 100
theology vii, 23, 108, 151, 175
Thomas, Dylan 7
Thurman and Wise xii
  Circling the Sacred Mountain xii
Tibet 57-59, 61-62, 64-68, 75
Top-down approach 77, 151-152
Torah 146
Totemism 118
transcendent function 20, 119
transnoetic 120
Trisong Detsen 57
Tsoodzil 90

U

U6 Beaver 199-200
ultimate concerns 103-104, 111-112, 118-119, 121, 127, 136-137, 173
ultimate reality xi, xiii, 1, 55, 85, 102-104, 107, 109, 111, 140, 143, 147-150, 154, 167, 174-175, 201
uncertainty 22, 103, 121, 147, 170, 175, 181-182, 184, 193-197, 201
United States 15, 21, 30, 46, 88-89, 94, 120, 123-125, 170, 192
  culture 120
  sacred mountains of 88-89
Uhuru Peak 189-190
University of Arizona 79
Unwin, Stephen 123
  Probability of God, the 123
Urubamba River 70
Urubamba Valley 73
Ute 89
Utse 66

V

Vacillation 113
Vaillant, George 113
  Spiritual Evolution 113
Vietnam 13
volcanic 96, 159, 164, 182
volcano 1, 95, 98, 162, 190

W

Wadsworth 204
Wailing Wall 131-133, 135-136
Walker, Evan 80
Waterman, Alan 24
  Best Within Us, the 24
Wheeler, John 80
Whitney, Mount 15-17
Wildman, Wesley 104
Wilson, E.O. 170

Y

Yamanakako 164
Yarlung River 62-63
Yerkes-Dodson law 9
Yoshida 157

Z

Zeus 174
Zuckerman, Marvin 9
Zygon 140

www.ingramcontent.com/pod-product-compliance
Lightning Source LLC
Chambersburg PA
CBHW021354290426
44108CB00010B/230